HEWLETT PACKARD CORP.
ROSEVILLE RESEARCH LIBRARY
8000 FOOTHILLS BLVD.
ROSEVILLE, CA 95747
(916) 785-5548

QA
76.64
D46
1994

**ROSEVILLE RESEARCH LIBRARY
HEWLETT PACKARD COMPANY
8000 FOOTHILLS BLVD. MS R5S9
ROSEVILLE, CA 95747
(916) 785-5548**

DEMCO

OBJECT ENGINEERING
The Fourth Dimension

OBJECT ENGINEERING

The Fourth Dimension

PHILIPPE DESFRAY

Addison-Wesley Publishing Company

Wokingham, England • Reading, Massachusetts • Menlo Park, California
New York • Don Mills, Ontario • Amsterdam • Bonn • Sydney • Singapore
Tokyo • Madrid • San Juan • Milan • Paris • Mexico City • Seoul • Taipei

MASSON

Paris • Milan • Barcelona

1994

© 1994, Masson éditeur, 120 boulevard Saint-Germain, 75006 Paris, France.

All rights reserved. No part of this publication may be reproduced, stored in a retrieval system, or transmitted in any form or by any means, electronic, mechanical, photocopying, recording or otherwise, without prior written permission of the publisher.

The programs in this book have been included for their instructional value. They have been tested with care but are not guaranteed for any particular purpose. The publisher does not offer any warranties or representations nor does it accept any liabilities with respect to the programs.

Cover designed by Arthur op den Brouw, Reading,
and printed by Société des Nouvelles Éditions Liégeoises, Liège.

CRC prepared by the author.

Printed and bound by Société des Nouvelles Éditions Liégeoises, Liège.

First printed 1994.

ISBN : 0-201-42288-3

British Library Cataloguing-in-Publication Data
A catalogue record for this book is available from the British Library.

Library of Congress Cataloguing-in-Publication Data is available.

Preface

This book is the result of five years of intensive research and practical experience, during which the **class relation** approach evolved and was enhanced to take into account comments made both by theoreticians and experts practising in this field. It follows on from a first book published in France in 1992, more than 70% of which has now been rewritten. It maintains the initial model approach, but also includes significant extensions: it pulls together all the requirements covered by the various models, integrates new modelling features, proposes and backs up additional model properties and finally defines an innovative modelling paradigm called *hypergenericity*.

I would like to thank all those who have helped me develop the class relation model through their advice and valuable comments. I would especially like to thank the Softeam staff whose work has contributed significantly to the success of this method. This book would never have come to fruition without the conviction and determination of Marc Clavereau and François Salaün. The class relation methodology has greatly benefited from the work conducted by Marc Clavereau on software development phase formalization and the class determination technique. The dynamic model has been fine tuned with the assistance of the MASI laboratory, and particularly Hafeda Bachatène and Pascal Estraillier. Unit test formalization is the result of work by Laurent Fourmy, who implemented and then automated unit testing on large-scale projects. Finally, Philippe Boutet has significantly improved the quality of this book by reviewing it with a very critical but friendly eye and by making constructive comments on the class relation model.

This book was translated from French by Alison Bourdel, Director of ART, a company specializing in technical communication, and was reviewed by Livleen Singh, Editor-in-Chief of the *C++ Journal*.

Contents

Preface	v
1 Introduction	**1**
1.1 Keeping tight control on objects	1
1.2 Essence of a model	1
1.3 Class relation model background	4
1.4 Contents	6
2 Object model	**9**
2.1 Conceptual approach	9
2.2 Object-oriented programming	18
3 Basic notions of the class relation model	**29**
3.1 Class relation model overview	29
3.2 Key class relation premises	36
4 Structure model basic notions	**41**
4.1 Class and inheritance concepts	41
4.2 Class members	45
4.3 Correspondence between attributes, methods, relations and classes	57
4.4 Inter-class dependency	61
4.5 Application invariants	64
4.6 Visibility	65
4.7 Decomposition by inheritance	73
4.8 Objects	76
5 Operating model	**81**
5.1 Introduction	81
5.2 Pre- and post-conditions	82
5.3 Specifying the object lifecycle: control automaton	87
5.4 Exception programming: pre- and post-condition extension	96
6 Dynamic model	**99**
6.1 Overview	99
6.2 Representing the processing sequence (object flow)	100
6.3 Processing scenarios	108
6.4 Trigger automata	111
6.5 Events	112
7 Structuring	**119**
7.1 Concepts	119
7.2 Software structuring	121
7.3 Schemas	127
7.4 Structuring domains	135
7.5 System modelling	141

8 Modelling rules — 145
- 8.1 Handling instances — 145
- 8.2 Normal form laws — 151
- 8.3 Correct and valid modelling — 154
- 8.4 Design rules — 158
- 8.5 General modelling approach — 164

9 Methodology: software development phases — 167
- 9.1 Software lifecycle basics — 167
- 9.2 Lifecycle definition — 173
- 9.3 User-oriented approach: iterative analysis and design technique — 178

10 Analysis — 183
- 10.1 Purpose — 183
- 10.2 Preliminary analysis — 184
- 10.3 Detailed analysis — 186
- 10.4 Example: elevator system — 193

11 Design — 203
- 11.1 Preliminary design — 203
- 11.2 Case study: databases — 213
- 11.3 Case study: multi-tasking applications — 221
- 11.4 Using genericity — 224
- 11.5 Preparing integration — 226
- 11.6 Class relation design approach (review) — 231
- 11.7 Example: designing the elevator application — 232

12 Carrying through a model: hypergenericity — 239
- 12.1 Introduction — 239
- 12.2 Implementation directives — 243
- 12.3 The H language — 244
- 12.4 Temporary or persistent hypergenericity — 253
- 12.5 Examples using hypergenericity — 254
- 12.6 Structuring hypergenericity rules — 270
- 12.7 Hypergenericity methodology — 272
- 12.8 Impact of hypergenericity on the lifecycle — 273

13 Development — 275
- 13.1 Detailed design — 275
- 13.2 Coding — 277
- 13.3 Unit tests — 288

14 Comparing models (OMT) — 293
- 14.1 Overview — 293
- 14.2 Need to upgrade existing models — 294
- 14.3 Class relation/OMT comparison — 296
- 14.4 Conclusion — 306

Appendix I Class relation model syntax **309**
   I.1 Backus–Naur form   309
   I.2 Syntax review   309

Appendix II Class relation graphic model review **313**
   II.1 Structure model   313
   II.2 Operating model   315
   II.3 Dynamic model   316

Appendix III   Glossary **319**

Appendix IV   References and bibliography **325**

Index **327**

1 Introduction

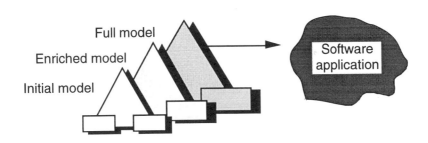

1.1 Keeping tight control on objects

Keeping tight control on large-scale software development projects is a constant challenge for software engineers today. In particular, they aim to improve development techniques, tools and languages in order to increase productivity and reduce development times. Consequently, object-oriented languages have generated great interest and expectations. Unfortunately, their evident technological contribution is not in itself enough to meet these objectives. Like all other development techniques, they must be used in conjunction with the appropriate models and methodologies.

The purpose of this book is to provide theoretical tools for software engineering projects using object-oriented programming. The contents of this book are based on:

- **Models** used to describe a problem and then to specify requirements or define a solution.
- **Methods** specifying model usage rules.
- **Methodology** used to implement the models throughout the application development life-cycle.

After reviewing the object model and object-oriented languages, this book discusses a new generation of methods which not only extend and enhance already existing modelling techniques, but also specify and automate the transformation of a model into an actual software product.

1.2 Essence of a model

Before analyzing the strong points of a particular model, the reader must first understand the need for such models and what might be expected from them in an ideal world.

1.2.1 Idea development and structuring

One of the most evolved human faculties is the ability to develop an idea, by defining the problems and suggesting the best way of overcoming them. This process cannot be achieved directly through simple mental thought triggered by intuition, a spark of imagination or even by lateral thinking. A written medium is the minimal requirement when describing facts, formalizing intuitions and structuring intellectual thought, as it removes all spoken language ambiguities and enables ideas to be recorded, shared and submitted for criticism.

Writing is in itself insufficient when specifying and describing ideas. Therefore, different professions use different notations to communicate ideas. For example, an architect uses a plan to describe a building, a fashion designer uses drawings rather than words, and so on.

In computing, ideas and theoretical models must first be expressed and then these, in turn, must address the requirements of the required program, with all its inherent non-material and theoretical aspects. In short, a model is the way in which the image of the computer system to be developed is projected from a person's understanding of the problem. The model is the only reliable way in which the team of engineers who are to design a system can share and reconcile their understanding of the problem. A model is simultaneously a support for individual mental thought, a means of communication and a series of guidelines for the development of the new computer system.

1.2.2 Reasoning and simulation support

A model is the abstract representation of an element (a problem, phenomenon or idea), which enables that element to be explained, understood, built upon or implemented. For example, a *town plan* (model) is required if someone is to find their way easily around an unknown town. Another example is the *molecular models* used by chemists to explain chemical reactions. By basing reasoning on a model, the behavior of a real application can be imagined and thus simulated. The chemist can, for example, simulate the process triggered when different chemical products are mixed together.

Model simulation is used to forecast how the represented element will work and conduct validation tests and checks, without the technical and economic consequences inherent in full-scale development or the risks of real-life experimentation.

1.2.3 Consistency and constraint control

Any technical or scientific field has constraints imposed on it. For example, an architect would not be expected to design a roof for a house with no walls. Chemical formulae cannot be used to represent all types of molecule. The model must be accompanied by consistency controls for verification purposes.

Essence of a model 3

1.2.4 Development guidelines

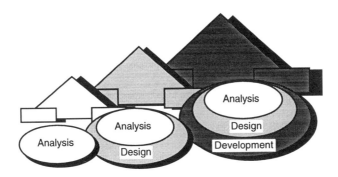

Figure 1.1 Enhancement of a model through to final implementation.

A programming model must provide more than just guidelines and support for mental thought; it must also enable an idea to be transformed as efficiently as possible into a result. If a problem is expressed explicitly, its transformation into a program is greatly simplified and much of the conversion process can be automated: in some applications developed with the class relation method (see section 1.2.6), up to 90% of the final program coding can be generated automatically from the modelling.

The reader will appreciate that this process is not as straightforward as it may seem at first sight. It is made up of several mandatory phases, during which ideas must be expressed as precisely as possible until it becomes clear how they will be implemented. A stepwise refinement process is applied to the same model until the final solution is reached. *Modelling*, during which a problem is described in model form, is gradually decomposed from phase to phase by bringing in additional information (Figure 1.1).

1.2.5 Means of communication

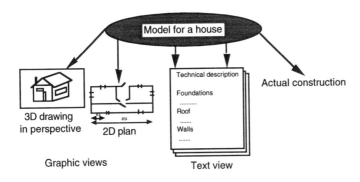

Figure 1.2 Various model views or representations for a house.

4 Introduction

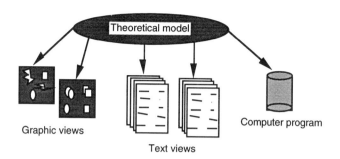

Figure 1.3 Various views of the same theoretical model.

A model must also be a *means of communication* between different people: these can be members of the same field (computer engineers) or people with different requirements or functional roles (users). These users may be concerned with such issues as quality, project or configuration management, or costs. For example, an architect uses the same technical plan to draw perspectives or models for non-technical people and for the construction company who sets up work descriptions, schedules, and so on (Figure 1.2).

A model must provide a full description of the thoughts expressed to enable different *views* or *representations* to be extracted, depending on the user category concerned (Figure 1.3).

The machine that executes the final instructions (the computer) is a special case for which step-by-step representations or summarized views of the application are not provided; this is because a full non-ambiguous description is required in terms of data, data formats and execution orders.

1.2.6 Suitability for the object model

The object model provides an excellent opportunity to implement such an approach, provided that the appropriate representation models are available. Computer models developed today are converging towards this approach. Its principles are described in this book using a formal representation called the **class relation** model.

1.3 Class relation model background

1.3.1 Origins

The object model was applied at a very early stage by database specialists, who extended the *entity–relationship* model (Chen, 1976) by inheritance and formalized its theoretical properties. To meet software development requirements when using object-oriented languages, the class relation model evolved in 1987; it was based on the *extended entity–relationship* model. It reuses the theoretical foundations and some of its terminology, and adapts it to object-oriented programming. This model was then implemented and consolidated through to 1989 and since then, several papers have been published on this subject (Desfray, 1989a; 1989b).

1.3.2 Industrialization

The Softeam company was founded in 1989. Its two main aims were to provide users with an object-oriented development method and to research model feature extensions. Its goals are to cover all modelling requirements and automate code generation by building software engineering tools, help client companies to apply this method and develop specific training programs.

Since 1989, the class relation method has been applied to many large-scale projects and after its initial success in France, received international recognition (Desfray, 1989a; 1989b; 1993).

An international trend for object-oriented methods is emerging (Chapter 14). The class relation method is part of this process. Its current success, and because its principles help define object-oriented development and it makes use of several important, original concepts, led to the publication of the original book in France in 1992.

1.3.3 Evolution since 1992

The research conducted by Softeam, in collaboration with several laboratories and enhanced by the practical experience of its employees, has enabled the model to be consolidated and new extensions to be added. In 1992, the discovery of *hypergenericity* (Desfray, 1993) enabled this approach to be reinforced still further and the class relation methodology to be enriched.

As compared with the previous book, this new work specifies existing concepts in greater detail and adds new ones which enhance features of the original class relation model:

- *Scenarios* (Chapter 6): These diagrams represent procedures whereby several classes can cooperate. They are used as examples and also enable major system functions to be validated and demonstrated.

- *Dynamic model* (Chapter 6): This model was introduced in the first version of the approach, but has been significantly extended in this updated edition. It takes full advantage of the consolidation work conducted with the MASI laboratory.

- *Structuring* (Chapter 7): The *domain* notion is discussed and the complementarity between domains and schemas is highlighted.

- *Flow diagrams* (Chapter 7): The role of flow diagrams is essential as they provide an overall view of an architecture. The use of domains enforces a structuring approach compatible with the object model.

- *Elementary classes* (Chapter 8): This notion improves on the normal form laws, and some class definition and management rules.

- *Methodology* (Chapters 9, 10, 11 and 13): The class determination technique is discussed in detail, based on the work conducted by Marc Clavereau, who systemized the modelling approach. Moreover, the lifecycle is defined in order to take into account a greater variety of applications. The upward phases (tests, integration, validation) are then described and reinforced by specific models.

- *Hypergenericity* (Chapter 12): This new concept provides a fully-fledged language enabling modelling to be carried through to the final stages and

6 Introduction

implementation rules to be defined. It is used to automate any repetitive model implementation work. It provides the means effectively to apply a reiterative fine-tuning principle to the same model from analysis through to final coding.

This book has been written to formalize these major evolution processes.

1.4 Contents

1.4.1 Fundamentals

The fundamental concepts of the object model are reviewed in Chapter 2. This concept-oriented approach gives a better understanding of the principles of the fundamental model and presents new mechanisms to:

- Structure concepts,
- Determine and justify new concepts.

1.4.2 Class relation model

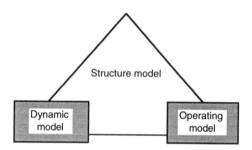

Figure 1.4 The three components of the class relation model.

Chapter 3 contains an overview of the class relation model and describes each of its sub-models (Figure 1.4). Briefly, they are:

- **Structure model**: This model describes the application concepts (Chapter 4). The *class*, *relation*, *inheritance*, *attribute*, *method*, *invariant* and *visibility* concepts are defined.

- **Operating model**: This model describes how these concepts are used (Chapter 5). The *control automaton*, *pre*–and *post–condition* notions are discussed.

- **Dynamic model**: This model contains both the reactive model and a functional model; it is used to represent how the application works (Chapter 6). At this stage, the *trigger automaton*, *object flow*, *event* and *scenario* concepts are presented.

Chapter 7 explains how to *structure* large-scale development projects. It is based on the *schema* and *domain* concepts. A structure diagram (*schema views* and *domain views*) and *flow diagrams* are used to give a summarized view of the system structure, how the system works, and its architecture.

1.4.3 Method

The method (model usage rules) is presented in Chapter 8. The following rules are described:

- Modelling consistency,
- Modelling validity,
- Software design.

1.4.4 Methodology

The methodology (model application during each lifecycle phase) is presented in Chapter 9. The techniques used to determine and justify class definitions and to ensure model reusability are described. Finally, each phase is covered in detail:

- *Analysis* in Chapter 10, that is both the preliminary analysis required when computerizing a system and the actual analysis phase. *Qualification* is also presented.
- *Design and integration* in Chapter 11.
- *Development* in Chapter 13, in which *coding* techniques and *unit testing* are described.

1.4.5 Hypergenericity

Hypergenericity, a new development paradigm, is presented in Chapter 12. It is used to carry through the information defined in one model, rules being applied to this information in order to execute transformations and deductions automatically. More specifically, it enables model implementation principles to be described for specific requirements and is applied during the design phases. Fine-tuning of the same model during analysis, design and then implementation is now possible with the *H* language. This language is used to define fine-tuning principles and to automate them (fine-tuning invocation rules). Many examples are provided to give the reader an idea of its scope.

1.4.6 Model Comparison

Chapter 14 briefly presents a few object models, and then makes a detailed comparison between the object modelling technique (OMT) model and the class relation model. Although the strong and weak points are highlighted, the main purpose of this chapter is to set up a clear correspondence between the concepts presented in each model.

1.4.7 Appendices

The appendices in this book contain:

- A glossary for all terminology used,

8   Introduction

- A summary of graphic notations,
- A summary of the class relation syntax,
- An index.

Figure 1.5 shows diagrammatically how this book is structured.

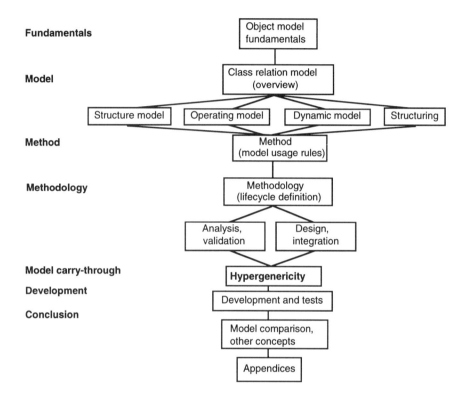

Figure 1.5 Structure of this book.

2 Object model

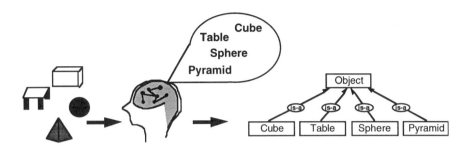

2.1 Conceptual approach

2.1.1 Fundamentals

The main problem inherent in information processing does not lie in the computer's calculation or information storage capacities, but in the aptitude of programs to organize and retrieve this information. (Papert and Goldstein)

Although a computer can calculate more efficiently than a human, it is unable to understand or handle unexpected situations; nor is it capable of reasoning about vague or imprecise situations. In more general terms, the computer cannot organize its knowledge in the same way as a human does.
    Ideally we would like computers to be able to organize knowledge as humans do, so that the complex nature of software could be dealt with more easily. To achieve this end, research programs have applied the resources of:

- *Psychology*, the study of the mind, to explain human behaviour and reasoning from an external point of view.
- *Epistemology*, the theory of knowledge that attempts to determine the ways in which notions and reasoning specific to each science have evolved over the years.
- *Ethnology*, the science that observes humans in all known societies and determines invariants.
- *Neurology*, the study of the nervous system in which human brain mechanisms are observed from an internal point of view. This research has led to the study of neural networks, the purpose of which is to define machine architectures based on neuron structures.
- *Cognitive psychology*, the purpose of which is to understand the learning and reasoning mechanisms used by humans. Experimentation and machine-based simulation have been used in this field.
- *Pedagogics*, the science and principles of teaching, so that knowledge can be transmitted to humans in the most efficient way possible.

Through these studies, it has been clearly established that the main element used by man when organizing knowledge, regardless of culture or race, is the **concept**. A concept is a means of representing human knowledge.

2.1.2 How concepts develop

The following example considers newborn babies, on which researchers such as Jean Piaget conducted long-term studies. A newborn baby suddenly finds itself in a foreign environment about which it knows nothing. It stores objects which it perceives via its five senses (sight, hearing, smell, taste and touch) without having any initial references with which to associate this information. For each object perceived, it stores the information acquired by each of its senses: *thing X: (sight, hearing, smell, taste, touch)*. It is already classifying this information. The newborn baby has a growing capacity to recognize things in its environment, the first no doubt being its mother.

The child therefore knows how to store information and retrieve it. This implies that the child is able to compare objects with existing stored information. For example, in order to determine that object X perceived by its senses corresponds to its mother, the child must first compare it with the information stored on its mother.

Specific criteria enable it to recognize elements. The child is able to distinguish between not just individual items, but also *categories* of items. For example, any element with a form similar to a teat will remind it of its bottle, even though it is not the bottle usually used by the child.

The child can thereby classify perceived objects. It groups them together by category, associating each one with the criteria that enable it to determine that a thing belongs to one category rather than to another (the perceived object belongs to the bottle category).

Finally, the child knows how to name object categories. The members of its family, who have already organized their own knowledge in a similar way, transmit predefined categories by using examples and by giving them a name (*dog*, *table*, *bottle*, and so on). Moreover, the child spontaneously develops concepts designated by a common name and learns about others from other people.

2.1.3 What characterizes a concept

What is a *dorse*? At this stage, the reader will have no knowledge about a *dorse*, as it is a figment of the author's imagination.

Definition: a dorse is a very rare species of mammal.

Much information has already been gained on a *dorse*, as it has *hair*, *eyes*, and so on, and some of its aptitudes (*eat*, *breathe*, for example) are known. If the reader is now told that *the dorse is a dog*, this new concept becomes even more precise: the *dorse* has four legs, barks, and so on.

Definition: the dorse is a large brown-coloured dog, with a long tail and short hair. It has a mane.

Before this last piece of information was given, the *dorse* had only been defined by indicating in which category it belonged (*mammal*, *dog*). The final description gives its specific properties. It links the *dorse* to other concepts (*tail*, *hair*, *mane*).

Figure 2.1 Example of a dorse.

In a very few words, a new element has been added to the reader's realm of understanding. A lot of information is now available on a dorse, although it has never been seen. The reader is capable of visualizing it (Figure 2.1), although it has only been described in abstract terms. A new concept linked with already known concepts has been added to the knowledge model.

In the above example, the concept of a dorse has been defined in three different ways (Figure 2.2):

- It belongs to known object categories; this method corresponds to the use of the *is a* link, or more specifically the *is a type of* link (*dorse* is a type of *dog*, which is a type of *mammal*). This specific link will later be called **inheritance**, and is expressed by the *is_a* notation,

- *Properties* have been defined (size, colour) and *links* between this concept and other known concepts have been established (*tail, mane, hair*),

- The characteristics that distinguish members of this concept have been established (*its tail is long, its hair is short*).

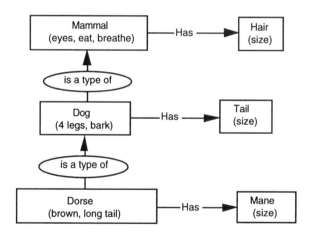

Figure 2.2 Describing a dorse using *is-a* type of links and properties.

New concepts can be described in other ways as well; *examples* can be used. An example provides typical representations of the concept, and calls on comparisons to determine whether an element is part of this concept or not. A series of examples and counter-examples for a concept enables the invariant and characteristic properties to be determined. Automatic learning programs have been developed, in which elements are classified, similar properties are distinguished and the resulting elements are grouped into categories. These programs deduce concepts from examples and counter-examples alone (but they have only a very limited understanding).

It is very likely that the newborn baby, who probably does not have any *innate* concepts with which it can associate its discoveries, initially uses only the example and counter-example technique. On the other hand, adults who understand many concepts can acquire new ones more efficiently by connecting them with ones they already know.

Knowledge about a concept is transmitted both by describing specific properties, using the *is a type of* link, and by example. Similarly, in teaching students about the *derivative* notion, a mathematics teacher will indicate that it is a *function* and that, as a result, all the properties of a function are true for a *derivative*; the teacher then goes on to specify the characteristic properties of a *derivative* and provides examples and counter-examples. Here, it can be seen that teachers use more or less intuitively concept description mechanisms when transmitting knowledge.

Concepts are not always defined very precisely. This is particularly the case for concepts designating most common objects. For example, there is no necessary and sufficient condition characterizing a *table*. Some objects are thus considered to be either *tables* or *chairs* by different humans. A *table* is recognized because of its possible uses and also because it resembles a *typical representation* that humans have of this notion.

The notion of typical representation or image will from now on be called a **concept prototype**. For concepts corresponding to physical objects, humans have typical images (*table*, *dog*, *man*, and so on). They recognize that an object belongs to a concept by comparing this object with the concept prototype. It has been proved that the time required by a human to recognize an item (where *recognize* means classifying this element among known concepts) depends on the degree of resemblance between the element and the concept prototype.

In scientific fields, particularly in mathematics, concepts tend to be defined in terms of necessary and sufficient conditions. For example, there is no confusion between a *triangle* and a *square*.

2.1.4 Concepts as real world models

Concepts are artefacts

Has a *mammal* ever been seen? In fact, nobody has ever seen a *mammal*. We have actually only seen the neighbour's dog, a bear in the zoo, and so on, but never a *mammal*. A *mammal* does not exist as such. A *mammal*, apparently a very concrete thing for which human imagination can create images, is in fact only an artefact set up by humans. These humans in fact reacted as if they were zoologists, by classifying all animal species and grouping them together by similarities. Thus they determined that a subset of animals possessing similar characteristics had to be created and called *mammal*.

Continuing along this line of reasoning, it can be seen that notions, such as *dog*, *tail*, *table*, are all man-made artefacts which have no real existence. In this manner, humans use concepts to build up a model of the outside world, as required for their own information handling requirements.

Humans are subjective in their understanding. The real-world model used by humans is:

- *Limited*: only the knowledge of this human is represented in a finite number of concepts.
- *Changing*: each new piece of information, each new viewpoint about that knowledge, causes the model to change.
- *Arbitrary*: humans create concepts based on the importance that they attach to each piece of information and the classifications they use.
- *Specific* to each human: all humans build up their own models using experiences, interests, their current state of mind, senses and required information.

A concept is defined in a context: its domain

Concepts are context-dependent: a *car sales* person, a *car driver* and a *car mechanic* each consider the same thing from different points of view – a *potential sale*, a *vehicle* and a *mechanical device* respectively. The *car* is in fact all these things at the same time, but, depending on the interest of each individual, generally only one aspect of the concept is taken into account. In the same way, some people may consider that a *car* is linked to one or more people via an *insurance policy*. An insurance company, however, will consider the *insurance* notion to be a fully-fledged concept, to be divided into sub-categories, such as *third-party insurance*.

People define and handle these concepts in their own specific context. This context notion is called a **domain** in this book.

Humans do not handle all their knowledge on the same level: when people talk about their children, negotiate a contract with customers or study mathematics at evening school, they concentrate on different domains and only handle part of their understanding, as seen from a specific angle.

Definition: *a domain is a way of structuring concepts.*

2.1.5 Concepts as means of communication

Concept sharing

Concepts are categories based on some form of logic and an arbitrary choice among all possible groups. Two mechanisms are apparently essential when defining new concepts:

- Definition guided by requirements,
- Majority choice.

Why did man feel the need to create the *mammal* concept? One simple interpretation is that the need arose when discussing animals. In practice, the repetition of a phrase such as *a vertebrate animal with teats, skin generally covered with hair, a four-chamber heart and a relatively highly developed brain* necessarily stimulates people to create a concept. The repetitive use of an idea or notion, for which it is possible to provide a description or definition, generally leads to the development of a concept. A name is then chosen and associated with the definition and any related concepts.

When several individuals develop concepts separately, these concepts will vary; each individual brings their subjective view of the concept. When individuals talk together about these concepts, they adapt them so that they can easily be understood by others and, conversely, they accept the concepts about which they hear and merge them with their own. This generates a concept sharing and consolidation phenomenon, enabling concepts to be shared by the greatest number of people, and this is what is called *majority choice*.

This phenomenon is not specific to individuals, as different human groups (races, specialists, and so on) also create and share notions specific to their viewpoint. For example, an extremely abstract concept like *democracy*, for which we have no set definition in terms of necessary and sufficient conditions, is obviously interpreted in different ways from country to country.

Consistent concept grouping

The *domain* notion is essential when structuring knowledge within a society. Domains are institutionalized, made consistent and represented by the corresponding specialists. They can be scientific fields (*physics*, *theory of sets*) or professional areas (*car mechanics*, *company management*, *trade*). In each of these domains, a limited set of concepts is selected and defined, and consistent interrelations are set. Dialogue between specialists in that field is greatly simplified as these people discourse on a limited part of reality from the same viewpoint.

Language

The basic communication medium for concepts is language, whether written or spoken. In this book, it will be referred to as *natural language* as compared with computer languages, which are more restrictive by nature. The mechanisms inherent in the conceptual model underpin the natural language structure, as it uses:

- Common names to designate concepts (a *dog*, a *book*),
- Proper names to designate objects (my dog *Snoopy*),
- Adjectives which qualify the objects with which they are associated (*Snoopy* is small),
- Verbs which express the actions taken by concept representatives (*Snoopy barks*),
- Prepositions and invariable particles which connect two words together using a dependency notion. They are used to navigate through the relations defined between concepts (*the tail of Snoopy wags*).

This representation is, of course, over-simplified. Chomsky dedicated much of his work to the study of linguistic structures, his aim being to determine rules and invariants, and, particularly to isolate innate linguistic faculties. He attempted to define an elementary universal syntax for any spoken language. A debate between Chomsky and Piaget on innate human faculties has occured in 1978.

All concepts are not necessarily expressed in human language. Only the most formalized or carefully structured concepts reach this stage. There is no doubt a period of time that must elapse before an idea or intuition matures into a concept. It is when a set of people feels the need to communicate that a concept is formalized and generalized, and a new word is added to the language.

2.1.6 Real world versus abstract world

Abstract concepts

New concepts can be defined in two ways: either they are required to understand the *real world* and are then created from examples and generalizations, or they are created in a totally abstract way and result from reasoning and logic. In this book, a distinction will be made between abstract concepts, based on an isolated logical analysis, and concrete concepts which represent the real world.

In this way, a man-made domain, such as a science, leads to the creation of a set of abstract concepts, with precise definitions and a clear representation using one model per concept. Each representative of these abstract concepts is created from its model (a *triangle*, a *set*, and so on), and is always defined within that model.

Real-world objects exist before concepts

All humans define and organize their concepts with the aim of modelling their actual environment. They attempt to use an internal model to represent the elements they cannot control. Unlike real-world objects that exist before any modelling is used to determine their existence, abstract objects are taken from a predetermined model. When we meet such objects, we try to place them in our conceptual model or adapt this model to them.

Understanding the real world

If, for example, we meet an unknown object from another universe, we will try to determine what it is and, to classify it. If there is only one such object, we will call it *the unidentified object* or *the object discovered on Friday 13th*. If several people discover more than one object of a similar nature, a concept will then be set up to designate this new category.

Let us now imagine that we are watching a film in which every object is completely new to us; every object is different from every other object and changes form constantly. We then have no model enabling us to *understand* this film and so watch it with a fixed stare, as if hypnotized by the unending falling of snowflakes.

Definition: *to* understand *reality, a conceptual model must be built and each element in this reality defined or situated with respect to it.*

Concepts are related to each person

Strictly speaking, each object in the real world is not defined or taken from one particular concept in an absolute way: a *piece of wood* could be considered to be a *toothpick* by some people, a *chair leg* by a furniture-maker, or a *gun* or a *horse* in a child's imagination. Each individual applies a personal model to real-world objects, and communicates with other humans using only those parts common to both models.

Communication ambiguity stems from one entity which designates a concept by name, while the other entity visualizes a similar but different object.

2.1.7 Conceptual model validity

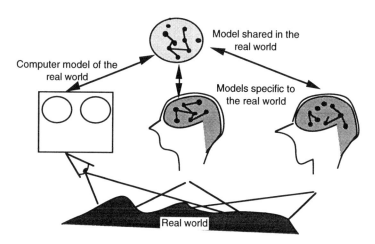

Figure 2.3 Program models must communicate with the conceptual model.

Human reasoning and the structure of societies are founded on a theoretical, concept-based model of reality.

Definition: *a concept is an approximative model of reality, as seen from a given viewpoint.*

In computing, the capacity of computers to represent the real world in the same way as humans is the ultimate goal, as the people developing and implementing computer programs cannot handle models that surpass their faculties.

The validity of the conceptual model can thus be questioned, but the objective assigned to this model is of the highest order in the programming field (see Figure 2.3).

2.1.8 Extracting and justifying the right concepts

A conceptual model may be correct but absurd

A conceptual model is used to define a class relation model representing concepts, their links and their properties. The model is founded on modelling rules and properties which help the achievement of consistent modelling.

It is, however, possible to set up an absurd model which defines useless concepts, even though it may still be consistent. For example, in the 19th century there was a would-be science called *phrenology*, the purpose of which was to determine human faculties by studying the bumps on the skull. Phrenologists built up a theory by defining specific concepts and corresponding rules, until the lack of scientific proof led to its disappearance. It can thus be said that phrenology was a consistent but absurd model. The key problem in modelling is the ability to determine the right concepts to be modelled.

Rule: *models are a means of representation, but do not give any fundamental help in determining the concepts and guaranteeing their validity.*

Justifying a concept definition

Rule: *a concept definition is only justified by the fact that it is actually used.*
We will now try to determine the concepts represented in Figure 2.4.

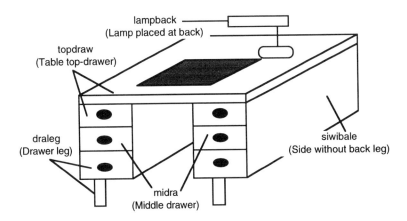

Figure 2.4 Non-justified concepts.

A human logically sees a *drawer*, a *desk*, a *set of drawers*, and so on. The concepts in this diagram (*midra*, *siwibale*) then come as a surprise. They are however *apparently* no less justified than those used more commonly. If we try to determine the best conceptual model for this diagram, our final conclusion will no doubt be that the *desk, drawer* model is better suited than the *midra, siwibale, draleg* model, even though we would find it difficult to give a clear-cut reason for this choice. Some might argue that the *desk, drawer* model yields a more elegant, clear decomposition, as a leg and a drawer are separate entities.

There are in fact no formal definitions or rules enabling the best model to be selected. The only basis on which a choice is made is whether these concepts are used in the everyday world. In the desk example, *users* of the desk concept (furniture store, user, manufacturer) have thus determined that it is more practical to use the *desk* and *drawer* notions, because they correspond to a sales unit, a manufacturing unit or an interchangeable unit and are therefore a better decomposition.

Only *use* enables a concept definition to be justified. This very simple principle provides the concept creation and selection mechanism, based only on our need to handle information.

When a new problem is to be modelled, the following approach must be applied:

- Use of tried and tested notions. If this problem is to be handled by other people, they will know the suitable concepts. For example, if accounting problems are to be handled, notions from the corresponding domain (*balance sheet, invoice*) are no doubt appropriate,

- Definition of the *users* of these notions. A *user* is any active agent who is outside the domain delimiting the selected concepts and who must handle them (*accountant, auditor, company director*),
- Justification of the new concept definitions in terms of the *users*' need to handle this information.

It is this fundamental approach which guides the class relation methodology when setting up a model.

2.2 Object-oriented programming

2.2.1 Overview

The model

Object-oriented languages result from a series of separate research projects. There is now a great variety of object-oriented languages, each representing a specific dialect of the object model. The most frequently referenced language, which served as the basis and inspiration for other object-oriented languages, is the *Simula* language (1967).

Two basic approaches were used to develop current object-oriented languages:

- Representation of knowledge in artificial intelligence, which led to the development of other object-oriented languages, such as *flavors*, *objvlisp* and more particularly *smalltalk* which is the typical example of an object-oriented language.
- Research on programming languages, first with *Simula*, then with *Ada* and *Modula2* to implement abstract types, and finally with languages such as *Eiffel* and *C++*.

Most object-oriented languages respect the simplified model illustrated in Figure 2.5, and it will be used as a basis for the rest of this book.

Previous languages and models made a distinction between data and processing. Data models (such as entity-relationship) and processing models (like data flows) were thus defined individually and the two parts put together later in the process.

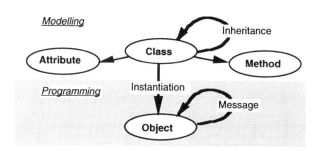

Figure 2.5 Simplified object model.

In this case, however, the object model merges data and processing together in the same notion: the *class*. The class is the cornerstone of the model, from which new classes can be defined and the operational elements of the program (*objects*) created.

Object-oriented program development is therefore divided into two parts:

- *Class* definition, using *inheritance*, *attributes* and *methods*. This part corresponds to program modelling. Inheritance is a link defined between two classes. Other inter-class links, called use links, appear at this level (the nature of these links is specified in the class relation model). They are not defined in the object model.

- *Object* implementation, using *instantiation* and *message* transmission mechanisms, to specify the various actions to be taken by the system. This part corresponds to programming.

Objects and classes

A **class** is a model defining a family of objects with similar properties. It describes these properties in terms of attributes and methods. A class encapsulates its data and processing definitions with methods and attributes. For each method defined, a class has a method implementation which is masked from its users. One object is distinguished from another by its name and the values of the class attributes.

An object is created by class instantiation. Class instantiation creates an element which complies with the model represented by its class. An object is considered to be an independent operational element, with properties and behaviour defined for the class.

As seen in section 2.1.6, computer objects have one important specificity as compared with real-world objects: they are all created from a pre-existing model, the class. This process is called **instantiation**. On the other hand, real-world objects exist before any model has been set up to define them. The concepts are set up later to model the existing elements, using a classification mechanism. Computer programs are therefore only a simulation, a mere copy of the real world, which results from the development process illustrated in Figure 2.6.

Two transformation stages are therefore required before a program can be written:

- Firstly, the concepts must be defined for the real world,

- Secondly, the human representation must be transformed into a computer model.

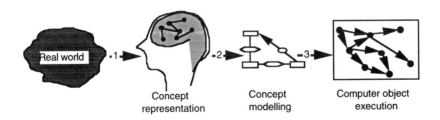

Figure 2.6 Transformations from the real world to a computer representation.

Method, attribute and message

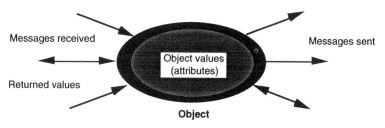

Figure 2.7 The object receives messages, handles its specific values and transmits messages.

Objects are the operational elements in a program. Each object reacts to stimuli when it receives messages from and transmits messages to other objects (Figure 2.7). The main part of object-oriented programming is therefore the instantiation of objects and the transmission of messages to these objects. **Messages** are the basic control structure in object-oriented languages.

Methods are used at class level to define the various messages that can be processed by each class. A *method* defines the required information (**parameters**) for each message and the processing performed by the objects when such a message is received. A message sent to an object is therefore associated with a given method, for which the parameter values are passed.

Objects have specific values (**attributes**) and are responsible for handling their attribute values which can modify their methods. Up to this point, attributes and methods have been applied to individual objects of a class. Attributes and methods can also be defined for a class, in which case they are shared by all class instances. For example, when the value of a class attribute is modified, this modification also takes effect for each instance of that class.

A typical example of a class method is `create()` used to create class instances. For example, the instruction `my_dog := Dog create()` creates a new representative of the `Dog` class by instantiation, referred to as `my_dog`.

Inheritance

Inheritance is used to define new classes from already existing classes. A derived class is a specific case of the class (base class) from which it inherits. Its specific aspects are defined by:

- Adding attributes,
- Adding methods,
- Redefining methods.

Some object-oriented languages have more extensive inheritance-related features. In the example Figure 2.8, inheritance can be used to specify the `graphic_form` class further and to create the `square` and `circle` derived classes.

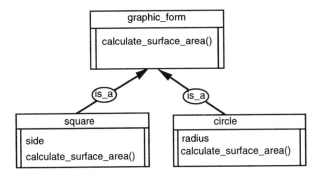

Figure 2.8 Inheritance diagram for *graphic_form*.

The graphic_form class has a calculate_surface_area() method, which returns the value 0. It returns 0 because there is not enough information at this level of abstraction to calculate the surface area Only detailed sub-classes are able to implement the corresponding processing (in this case, the abstract method notion is used). The square class has the side attribute and redefines the calculate_surface_area() method to return the value side * side. The circle class has the radius attribute and redefines the calculate_surface_area() method to return the value radius * radius * π.

One of the specific aspects of inheritance is that any instance in class c2 inheriting from class c1 can be considered to be an instance of class c1 (Figure 2.9).

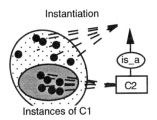

Figure 2.9 The instances of *c1* are equal to the sum of its own instances and those of its derived classes.

If an application processes an instance of the graphic_form class, it can also process any instance of its derived classes, such as circle. During that particular processing, the circle is handled as if it were a graphic_form, that is using the properties of a graphic_form. This is because it is not specified whether it is a generic graphic_form, a square, a circle or an instance of any other class derived from graphic_form and, as a result, the specific properties of each special case are not known.

In the same way, when we meet a *man* in the street, we do not know beforehand whether he is a *doctor, teacher, engineer, factory worker, secretary, senator* or *author*. More often than not, when handling an object, it is not known to which end class it belongs. Our vision of the object stops at a parent class, which provides sufficient information for it to be handled.

For example, a bus is defined to transport passengers, who must be able to get_into_the_vehicle() and get_out_of_the_vehicle(); these methods must be valid for any type of *person*, regardless of their profession. If a farmer gets into the bus, only the passenger properties are of interest when defining how the bus works.

When an object receives a message, it uses its own specific characteristics to process the message. This object can be considered to be an instance of one of its base classes (which will be called *processing classes*) by the message transmitter, but will react according to its end class definition. If the current_object calculate_surface_area() message is sent to the representative of the graphic_form class called current_object, then the calculated value will be 0, side x side, or radius x radius x π, depending on the actual nature of current_object (graphic_form, square, circle) (Figure 2.10).

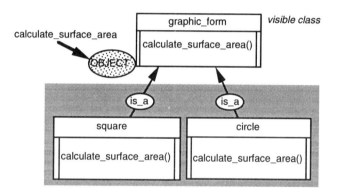

Figure 2.10 The message is interpreted by the object in terms of its end class.

This property of object-oriented languages is called **polymorphism**. When an object receives a message, the corresponding method is retrieved dynamically: if the object class does not have this method, the base class is accessed, and so on. This mechanism is implemented in different ways depending on the language and has significant impact on their efficiency.

In most object-oriented languages, there is a class called *object* from which all classes are derived. Thus, this class is the root for any inheritance diagram. It defines the initial operators required by all classes:

- The create() class method used to create a new instance,

- The delete() method used to delete an instance.

This class is not defined explicitly in some languages, particularly C++, but the above operators exist for any class in this language; it can therefore be accepted that the *object* class is defined implicitly.

Advantages of the object model

Over and above the advantages inherent in encapsulation, which will be discussed in greater detail in section 4.6, here are some of the advantages provided by inheritance, as compared with traditional programming methods.

Reusability, factorization

The object model is a code factorization model. In traditional programming languages, the main factorization device used is a *sub-program* definition. This approach enables a sub-program to be defined empirically. It resides in the fact that two programs may be similar and thus grouped together. If the inheritance notion is used, program concepts can be classified and, if similarities exist, the corresponding concepts can be factorized into a base class. For example, the *doctor, farmer, teacher* and *senator* notions can be factorized into a more general notion of *person*.

The advantages of factorization are two-fold: firstly, the definitions created at the base class level are implicitly reused by derived classes (for example, the get_into_vehicle() method does not need to be recoded individually for *doctor*, *farmer*), and secondly, an application uses these notions on an appropriate level of generalization. For example, *bus* limits visibility to the *person* class, as more specific profession-related concepts are of no interest in this case. In traditional programming languages, processing must be defined at *bus* level to enable a *doctor* or a *secretary* to get into the bus.

Removing control structures

The fact that each instance adapts the way it reacts to the messages it receives enables the application control structure to be considerably streamlined. For example, to calculate the total surface area for all graphic forms, object-oriented programming requires the following type of processing:
```
FOR any instance of current_form of graphic_form
    total_surface_area := total_surface_area +
                        current_form calculate_surface_area()
```
whereas traditional programming languages would require the following type of routine:
```
FOR each item handled
  DEPENDING ON item type
  - IF square : total_surface_area :=
         total_surface_area +
              calculate_square_surface_area (square_item)
  - IF circle : total_surface_area :=
         total_surface_area +
              calculate_circle_surface_area (circle_item)
  ...
```
As a result, the inheritance diagram determines special cases which can then be processed on a more general level, without type-specific instructions such as IF square or DEPENDING ON square, circle.

Extensibility

An application can be extended by adding to the inheritance diagram for class c. New classes inheriting from c can be created in order to define new special cases without changing either the processing in c or the routines using c. For example,

24 Object model

the birth of a new category of *man – computer engineers* – has no impact on the *man* class definition, nor on that of the *bus* class, which uses only the *man* class; the object-oriented surface area calculation program is not affected by the appearance of a new `graphic_form` – the `triangle` - whereas in traditional programs, the processing, and more particularly the control routines, would have to be modified to allow the `triangle` case to be handled correctly.

Conclusion: *on a more general level, use of an object-oriented language considerably simplifies programming.*

For example, we do not know if it would have been possible, given the complexity, to develop some applications with a traditional programming language.

The main difficulty met by novice object-oriented programmers lies in the way they reason: they must no longer think in terms of functional processing sequences.

2.2.2 Example: graphic software programming

The following example is based on object-oriented programming, its purpose being to clarify the principles used by these languages. To do so, an object-oriented pseudo-language will be used when appropriate. It is based on a structured freeform text (using the words FOR, IF, DEPENDING ON, WHILE) and applies the following format to express the transmission of messages: `object message (parameters)`; for example, `my_book read(page_15)`. If an instance sends a message to itself, the notation is simplified: `message(parameters)`. The assignment method (:=), which should be written `target_object = (assigned_object)`, will be written in the following manner for ease of use: `target_object := assigned_object`. Study the example to find the classes and their relationships.

A software product must handle an interactive graphic picture in a multi-windowing environment. The picture is made up of graphic_objects, each of which reacts in a different way when selected by the mouse. When the user clicks on a window, the picture receives a message (sent by a multi-windowing system such as X_windows or MS-Windows) with the selection point coordinates as its parameters. The picture must handle the appearance and disappearance of graphic elements, must be printable and must transmit user selections to the appropriate objects.

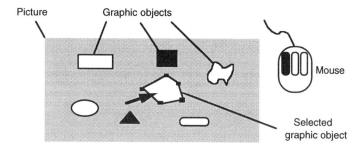

Figure 2.11 Selection of a graphic object on the picture.

Two object classes are thus defined: the `picture` and the `graphic_object`. The actions (methods) taken on the `picture` are:

- `process_selection(position : coordinates)`
- `print ()`

The `graphic_objects` have the following methods:

- `process_selection ()`, where the object must react in a specific way to the selection,
- `contain_position (position : coordinates)`, which must return a boolean value indicating whether the object contains the position passed as a parameter.

When the user clicks on the `picture`, this object is informed of the selection by a `process_selection()` message. The following processing is then invoked:

```
FOR each current_object in the graphic_object class
    IF current_object contain_position(position)
        current_object process_selection()
    ENDIF
```

The example can then be further specified as follows (see Figure 2.12).

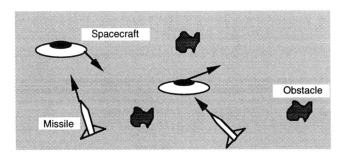

Figure 2.12 Spacecraft, missiles and obstacles.

The following `graphic_objects` exist:

- `Spacecraft`: Mobile `graphic_objects` created periodically by the `picture`, which cross the screen from one side to the other, avoiding the `graphic_objects` on their path.
- `Obstacles`: Fixed `graphic_objects` located on the `picture` and created when the application is run. When a `mobile_object` collides with one of them or when they are selected, they change forms.
- `Missiles`: `Mobile_objects` created randomly, which move towards the nearest `spacecraft` in order to collide with it.
- `Mobile_objects`: `Spacecrafts` or `missiles`. They move and are able to change paths when selected.

These new classes all inherit from the `graphic_object` class and additional aspects are specified:

- Their particular forms are described,
- Given methods, such as `process_selection()`, are redefined,
- The properties specific to some classes, such as `move()`, are added.

26 Object model

This system then operates in the following manner: the picture has a method called process_cyclically(), which is invoked on a cyclic basis. This method then acts as a sequencer for mobile_objects:

```
IF time interval elapsed
    spacecraft create()
    missile create()
FOR each current_object in mobile_objects
    current_object move()
END FOR
```

From an external point of view, the impression will be given that individual representatives of the mobile_object class move in parallel.

Moreover, the mobile_objects must process the position of other graphic_objects before reacting. The spacecraft must avoid obstacles, whereas the missile must aim at spacecraft. The following methods are thus defined:

- presence (required_path: path), to return to a boolean value indicating whether the current object is on the required path,
- determine_position (), to return the position of the current object.

An application schema of the type illustrated in Figure 2.13 is thus obtained. In this example, the processing performed by the move methods in the spacecraft and missile classes has been described.

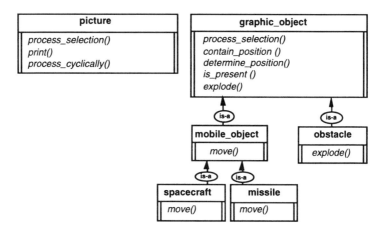

Figure 2.13 Graphic application classes.

```
move() method for the spacecraft class:
    WHILE current_path is incorrect
        FOR each current_obstacle in obstacle class
            IF current_object is_present (current_path)
                correct current_path
    END WHILE
    move along path
move() method for the missile class:
    best_distance := maximum_value
    FOR each current_spacecraft in spacecraft class
```

```
        IF (current_spacecraft determine_position() -
                 determine_position() < best_distance)
             update best_distance
             target_spacecraft := current_spacecraft
        ENDIF
    END FOR
    move towards current_spacecraft
    IF target_spacecraft determine_position() =
determine_position()
         target_spacecraft explode()
         explode()
    ENDIF
```
Of course, program coding is far from being complete, but the principle is clear. More importantly, some notions, such as `coordinate` and `path`, must be better defined in terms of classes.

3 Basic notions of the class relation model

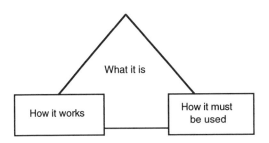

3.1 Class relation model overview

3.1.1 Three model components

Overview

Before describing the class relation model in detail, the basic structure will be defined. Section 3.1.2 gives a general overview of the model using a modelling example.

The class relation model is implemented in three major stages:

- Outline the problem concepts
- Explain how they are used
- Explain how they work

For implementation purposes, this model contains three model categories (Figure 3.1):

- The *structure model* (describes the problem concepts): This is the basic model used to define application *concepts* in terms of *classes* and the **relations** between them. It also provides class structuring mechanisms to group together a number of classes into intermediate structuring elements.

- The *operating model* (how the concepts are used): Once the classes have been defined, this model describes the services provided by each class by specifying their *usage mode*.

- The *dynamic model* (describes how the concepts work): Once the software has been fully specified, this model is used to describe the processing order or system dynamics.

Basic notions of the class relation model

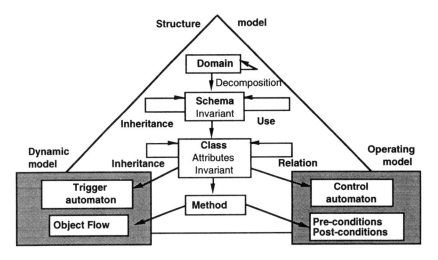

Figure 3.1 The three class relation models.

Class relation diagrams

Table 3.1 summarizes the diagrams associated with the concepts of the three models.

Table 3.1 Types of diagrams associated with each model concept.

Diagram/model concept	Domain	Schema	Class	Method	Automato
Structure model					
Domain diagrams	✓				
Flow diagrams	✓				
External schema diagrams		✓			
Internal schema diagrams		✓			
Detailed class diagrams			✓		
Operating model					
Control automaton diagrams					✓
Dynamic model					
Scenario diagrams	✓	✓			
Trigger automaton diagrams					✓
Object flow diagrams				✓	
Validation scenarios diagrams	✓	✓		✓	

The class relation model is used to develop the diagrams indicated above and presents the basic modelling items. Most model notions, such as inheritance, relations and element visibility, can be represented in these diagrams.

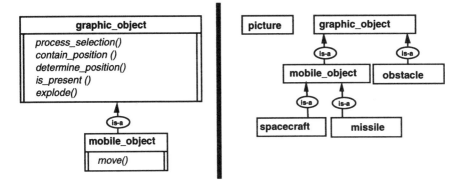

Figure 3.2 Two different views of the same model (internal schema diagram).

If a *schema* is taken as an example of a class relation model element, each of the diagram types allowed can be represented in different **views** to cover all or part of the model (see Figure 3.2).

Syntax view

All elements illustrated in Figure 3.2 can also be represented in *syntax form* to highlight the following items:

- Class or schema *invariants*,
- Method *pre-* and *post-conditions*,
- *Text descriptions* for attributes, relations, methods, automata, classes, schemas or domains,
- *Directives* specifying the individual properties of each element or the way it is implemented in a given environment,
- *Coding information* in the appropriate programming language, the purpose being to add further low-level information and to carry a model through to the coding phase,
- *Unit test* descriptions for each class.

Structure model

Fundamentals

The structure model uses the *class, method, attribute* and *inheritance* concepts in the object model (section 2.2.1). In addition, the fundamental concept of *relations* is used to express conceptual links between classes. A strict set-based approach is applied to the class notion in order to provide a formal definition of the *class* **invariant** concept which describes the properties that class *instances* must have at all times. This first part of the structure model is described in Chapter 4. The structure model also provides a series of mechanisms to adapt class *visibility* and properties.

Basic notions of the class relation model

Structuring

The structure model is also used to structure classes into **schemas** and *domains*. A *domain* can contain either schemas or other domains. A *schema* groups together *classes* and determines class visibility (exported or not). The modeled software is itself the root for the domain view (**Project** domain). Domains and schemas can have inter-dependency links. This part of the structure model is described in Chapter 7, Section 7.20.

Class relation diagrams

The following class relation diagrams are used to represent the Structure model.

Domain views

Using the *Project* domain as a starting point, since it represents the application root, the other domain views then enable each of the application components to be situated approximately (domains, schemas or classes):

- *Internal* or *external view*: A domain view represents the contents of a domain, that is, the domains, schemas and classes it contains, together with their dependency links. It models all or part of the domain items. Depending on its position in relation to a given domain, it represents either the dependencies between that domain and other domains or schemas (*external domain view*), or its actual contents (*internal domain view*). It is frequently used to describe the general makeup of the software project, facilitate project management or set up the integration plan,

- *Flow diagram*: a flow diagram is used to highlight the data exchanged between various domains. This type of view is useful when representing a system or describing an architecture.

Schema views

Schemas are represented in domain views and in two other specific views:

- *External schema view*: this diagram is a special case of the domain view, in that it illustrates the schema's external dependencies. It is useful during the design and integration phases,

- *Internal schema view*: this diagram defines the fundamental class relation model and represents all inter-class links within the schema. It defines the notions that make up the schema, their properties, external accessibility and interrelations.

Class views

Classes are defined in internal schema or domain views:

- *Detailed class view*: this diagram gives a detailed representation of all class properties and indicates all data (classes, events, and so on) which can be accessed by a class. It is also used to highlight a given concept by showing its full description.

Operating model

The operating model defines class usage modes and object lifecycles. Frequently, it is not possible to send messages to an object in any random order: rather, a specific protocol must be respected. This protocol is specified in a class-level **control automaton** and thus defines the object lifecycle. Each class can have one or more views to represent these control automata.

The way in which each *method* is used is described in *pre-conditions* (conditions that must exist before a method is invoked) and *post-conditions* (conditions that must exist once it has been executed). Post-conditions specify the services provided by a method but do not stipulate the processing order. Chapter 5 explains that these two concepts are closely coupled with the *invariant* concept.

Dynamic model

The dynamic model is used to specify how certain classes behave and the order in which their processes are implemented.

Process ordering

Object flow diagrams define how methods react within each class. They describe the process ordering and the data exchanged between methods.

A **scenario** is used to represent significant examples of inter-instance processing cooperation. It highlights the key processes in the system.

Behaviour

A **trigger automaton** is used to describe how objects react when specific states exist, predefined conditions are met or a particular **event** occurs. A class can have several trigger automata, each of which is systematically associated with a control automaton to which it must conform.

An *event* corresponds to the occurrence of a signal at a specific moment in time. Event transmitters and receivers are generally not aware of each other and an event frequently represents the reception of data from an external system. This means of communication provides low coupling between system components and dialog can be either synchronous or asynchronous.

3.1.2 Modelling example

Figure 3.3 represents the *domain* for a hotel and illustrates the associated input and output *flows*. For example, the `hotel` receives customer `payments` in input and issues `customer_invoices` as output.

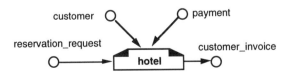

Figure 3.3 Flow diagram for a hotel.

34   Basic notions of the class relation model

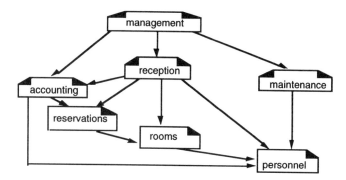

Figure 3.4 Domain view for the `hotel` domain.

The *domain view* in Figure 3.4 is used to define the various services provided by a hotel. The `rooms` and `personnel` services are not decomposed into sub-levels and therefore can be represented as *schemas*.

A *flow diagram*, shown in Figure 3.5, is used to express the data exchanged between each service. For example, `reception` transmits a `payment_note` to the `accounting` service. Several different views can thus be set up to present only part of the data flows between each view.

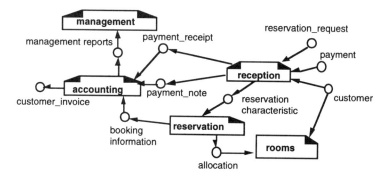

Figure 3.5 Internal flow diagram for the hotel domain.

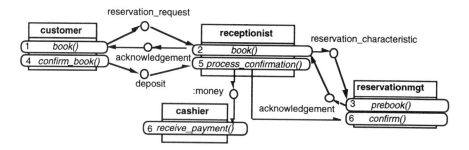

Figure 3.6 Reservation scenario.

Class relation model overview 35

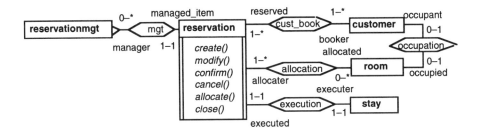

Figure 3.7 Internal schema view.

Many repetitive procedures exist when running a hotel, such as booking a room, as defined by the *scenario* in Figure 3.6.

In this scenario, a customer must contact reception, which in turn contacts the reservation service who accepts or rejects the booking. It then asks the customer to confirm the reservation by paying a deposit, at which stage the booking is confirmed. This *scenario* handles several instances in several services and is described in the general hotel domain level.

Each of these notions is defined with the associated links. As a result, the *internal schema view*, illustrated in Figure 3.7, represents the reservation notion (*class*) and associated concepts. Here it defines the *methods* and *relations* for the reservation class.

In this model a reservation may concern a group of customers. The *methods*, that is, the services provided by the reservation class (modify(), confirm(), and so on), are represented.

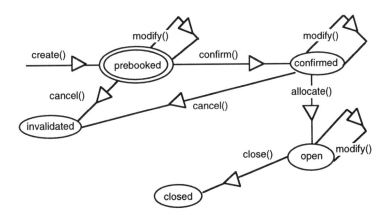

Figure 3.8 Control automaton for the *reservation* class.

If the order in which reservation services can be activated is to be defined, a *control automaton* must be used, as shown in Figure 3.8. This control automaton also defines the valid states of the reservation class and the reservation instance lifecycle.

The control automaton in Figure 3.8 stipulates that a reservation can only be modified (modify() method) if it is either in the prebooked, confirmed or open states.

The most detailed level is the object flow model which describes how the various services are provided.

In the object flow model shown in Figure 3.9, a reservation is allocated when the customer arrives at the hotel. First, the booking is checked, a *stay* is then created to handle invoicing procedures and finally the customer is assigned a room.

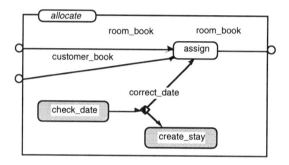

Figure 3.9 Object flow model for the allocate() method in the *reservation* class.

3.2 Key class relation premises

The principles and objectives that guided the building of this model were described in Chapter 1. The theoretical foundations for the class relation *approach are the theory of sets and the conceptual model (reviewed in section 2.1).*

3.2.1 Basic computer models

The chen *entity-relationship* model (Chen, 1976) was the initial source of the class relation model as far as data modelling is concerned. The *abstract machine* model (Par, 1979; Robinson, 1979; Booch, 1986) was used to define a basic encapsulation control system during software design. The processing model was based on the *finite state automaton* and *data flow* models. The *petri network* model enabled these models to be fine-tuned and specified still further. The work by Harel (1987, 1988) on automata was also a valuable source of information.

Moreover, when researching a more comprehensive model formalization method based on mathematical expressions, valuable contributions to the *invariant, pre-* and *post-conditions* concepts were obtained from the work of Hoare (1985). The ideas expressed by Meyer (1988), who implemented both these notions and the object model in the Eiffel language, have been applied here as well.

A series of research papers published on this subject are referenced in the Appendix.

Premise: *the class relation model development strategy was based on the need to merge existing models into one object model, lay down the associated consistency rules, add features unavailable in existing models and take into account the operational results of the first implementation projects.*

3.2.2 Defining a modelling language

Formal modelling

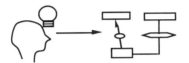

Figure 3.10 Expression of an idea in model form.

A formal class relation representation is not specific to one programming language. It includes different problem description techniques (directives, coding sections, *hypergenericity*) to express how the model is implemented in the development environment (programming language, hardware environment, libraries, and so on). This representation (Figure 3.10) cannot, however, be compared with a programming language, the purpose of which is to describe how a program works using a sequence of machine-based instructions.

Graphic and syntax views

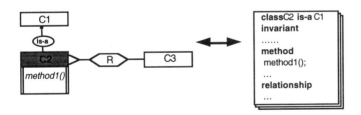

Figure 3.11 The class relation model uses a dual representation.

The class relation model can be expressed both graphically and syntactically (Figure 3.11). A graphic view represents ideas in a more general way and communicates them quickly, whereas a syntax view provides additional information that is difficult to express in graphic form alone.

The syntax view is also used to add code (programming language) or documentary information (text description) to specific modelling areas. All the code or development documentation can thus be generated automatically from a class relation source. It is used to apply several formal representations to the same class at the same time (for example, programming languages, test description, and so on).

38 Basic notions of the class relation model

Model fine-tuning mechanism

Figure 3.12 The same model is fine-tuned by iteration using automatic or manual processes.

The class relation method is used to model a problem during the analysis and/or design phases. It provides mechanisms to carry the same model through from analysis to coding (Figure 3.12). *Hypergenericity* (Figure 3.13) is a mechanism whereby systematic specification rules are defined for a model, using the *H* language. Finally, unit testing and validation are performed by adding new information to the original model.

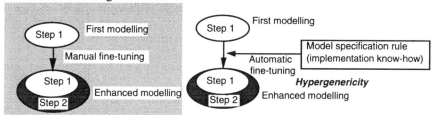

Figure 3.13 Successive fine-tuning on the same model.

3.2.3 Basic premises

Different class views

Definition: *an object class is a computer representation of a concept, a series of possible instances and a coding module.*

The same entity (class, concept, set, module) can be viewed from different positions. Each of these viewpoints is of specific interest depending on the development phases:

- When starting to define the classes (software analysis), the conceptual viewpoint is essential,

- During the design phase, the class structuring concept is applied,

- The set-based viewpoint is used to check modelling validity, modelling rules and the respect of constraints within coding,

- The code module notion is used only during the implementation phase.

Classes define the concepts handled within an application. They are the starting point when building the operational elements (objects) used to execute processing.

Selecting the relevant modelling items: stability criterion

A computer application implements a limited number of concepts, and only the *key notions* in an application are represented by classes.

Generally speaking, when a system is modelled, the corresponding problem is decomposed down to a predetermined level of detail. This level is defined by the application information handling requirements. One of the criteria used to select the elements to be modeled is *stability*.

Definition: *an element is said to be stable within an application when its definition remains unchanged throughout a given period of time.*

The purpose of the class relation model is to define the invariants applicable to its stable application elements. It provides the application framework or the rules to be respected at all times during processing.

Class stability

A *class* is a *stable element* in an application. This means that a concept defined by a class exists from the moment the application is started up and its structure remains unchanged throughout application processing. The set of possible instances in a class is therefore an application invariant.

The class stability premise also means that an instance belongs to the same class throughout its lifetime. For example, if the `married_woman` and `single_woman` classes were defined for a given application, the instantiation of object X in the `single_woman` class means that X can never change classes and become a `married_woman`. In this model, no woman can get married or divorced. On the other hand, if a woman should be able to get married or divorced, the `single_woman` and `married_woman` classes are invalid as they are not stable categories within the application and only the woman class should be defined with the marital status as an attribute of the woman class.

The stability rule, as applied to the modelled classes, is essential if the model is to highlight predetermined elements and application invariants.

Object stability

An *object* is said to be stable when it is inactive, that is, it is not processing any messages. It will be seen later that system invariant rules are applied exclusively to stable objects. The modelled *states* correspond to stable states that are significant for a given object.

Inter-object link stability

An inter-object link is said to be stable when it exists between two stable objects. In the model, this link can be represented by a *relation* between the classes to which these objects belong.

Classes = model, objects = implementation

In object-oriented programming, application classes define the framework within which instances can be created and executed. Objects are created and exchange messages in compliance with their model. They are the operational elements of an application for which they perform processing. Objects and messages are programming concepts and are implemented by programming languages, whereas classes are part of the analysis and design phases, and are described in the class relation model.

The class relation method does however enable objects and messages to be described within *scenarios* and *object flow* diagrams.

4 Structure model: basic notions

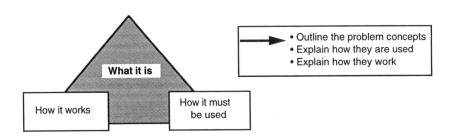

4.1 Class and inheritance concepts

4.1.1 Class concept

Modeling viewpoint

Class = concept handled by the application

When modelling an application, certain basic concepts are highlighted. These concepts are represented by classes, which can correspond to concrete elements in the real world (a *table*, a *toy*), specific concepts in given domains (a *file*, a *football game*, a *salary*) or more abstract concepts such as *space*, *triangle*, *vector* or *class*. These result from classifying the various elements to be handled by the application.

Selecting sets of pertinent objects

Definition: *in analysis terms, a class corresponds to the set of possible instances. This set is described by class characteristics (methods, attributes, relations, invariants, and so on) from the understanding point of view.*

Any set of elements that can be characterized within an application is a potential class. The skill of designers lies in their ability to determine the most pertinent sets for the application. For example, if the *red cars*, *dirty cars*, *old cars* and *small cars* subsets were determined for the *car* category, it is unlikely that they would correspond to a *key concept*. However, the square and the circle subsets of the `graphic_form` class are likely to become classes.

The class relation model provides various criteria to help you decide on class pertinency (see section 2.1 for the definition of pertinent concepts, section 4.3 for the correspondence between relations, classes and attributes and chapter 8 for modelling rules). One of these criteria is *set stability* with respect to the application, that is, whether the current elements are always members of that set.

Careful characterization of object sets

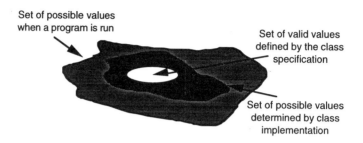

Figure 4.1 Possible valid values within an application.

In the case of a payroll program, salary is a *key concept* for the application and therefore becomes a class in the model. The salary handled by a computer program may correspond to the most general cases met (that of an employee in a given category, and so on) or to more specific cases (that of a part-time employee, and so on), but it is unlikely that highly specialized cases will be taken into account by the program. If an employee is on a part-time mission abroad and is paid partially in local currency and the rest in the currency of his or her country of residence, this case is probably not taken into account by the program, as it does not belong to the set of possible instances for the `salary` class. This particular case is not, therefore, covered by the `salary` class specification for this program.

The application model in terms of classes is used to define the set of cases handled by the application and all program features. The union of all classes defining an application gives the set of values that it must handle.

Each of the possible instances in a class has a value which can change within certain limits stipulated by the class specification. The various characteristics of the class relation model are used to give a more precise definition of this range and guarantee that the values taken into account for each instance in a program can never be out of range (Figure 4.1). The quality of the class relation model is closely correlated with the precision of the sets defined.

Programming viewpoint

Definition: *in coding terms, a class represents the set of actual representatives.*

If a snapshot of a program is taken at a given moment in time, each class has a finite number of instances. Later in this book (chapters 8 and 14), it will be shown that this set can be managed via the class itself.

The `create()` and `delete()` methods are used to handle the class by adding or deleting one of its instances.

The 'object' class

In many programming languages there is an *object* class which represents all the possible instances in an application. By definition, all classes inherit from this class and so it is the root of the class inheritance diagram.

Class and inheritance concepts

In the class relation method, it is implicitly understood that all classes inherit from the object class. The class properties inherited by all classes are:

- Construction,
- Destruction.

Class representation

A `salary` class is defined using a graphic view and a formal syntax representation, as shown in Figure 4.2.

```
class salary ...
--syntax description for "salary"
```

```
┌─────────┐
│ salary  │
└─────────┘
```

Figure 4.2 Graphic view of the *salary* class.

4.1.2 Inheritance

Inheritance between two classes is used to specify that one class, called the derived class, is a special case of another class, called the base class. For example, the `part-time salary` class is a special case of the `salary` class.

Rule: *the set of possible instances of a derived class is included in the set of possible instances for the base class(es). In the same way, when executing an application, the set of current instances for a derived class is included in the set of current instances for the base class.*

The `managerial_salary` and `non_managerial_salary` classes will now be defined and they will both inherit from the `salary` class. The set of instances for the above classes is shown graphically in Figure 4.3.

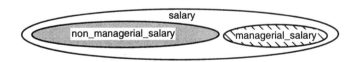

Figure 4.3 Set representation for the *salary* classes.

When expressed in terms of class properties, inheriting from class c1 is the equivalent of defining a new class c2 as a sub-class of c1. c2 can have additional properties or can further specify the properties of c1. Each representative of c2 can always be considered to be a representative of c1 (for example, a `managerial_salary` can be processed as if it were a `salary` in the most general sense of the term).

Rule: *all the properties defined for one class are also true for its sub-classes.*

When a new class C2 (inheriting from C1) is defined, the properties of class C1 are either extended, substituted or restricted; the set of elements in C2 is, therefore, systematically more restrictive than C1. For example:

- The specification that a given category of table is red (attribute) reduces the number of possible tables,
- If the set of persons who can read() (method addition) is considered, the number of valid persons is reduced,
- A subset of the delivery_service class, all members of which can deliver a given product to a given address, can be obtained by selecting reliable_delivery_services, the action of which is to deliver() an *undamaged* product on a fixed date (further method specification).

Definition: *inheritance systematically defines inclusion relations between classes, by adding or further specifying the properties of the base classes.*

Inheritance transmits all the properties of a base class to a derived class. If the sales_person_salary class inherits from the salary class, all the properties of the salary class are transmitted to the sales_person_salary class. Figure 4.4 shows the inheritance diagram and syntax of this relationship. These properties can then be extended using the techniques described later in this book (attribute, relation, method addition) or can be further specified by redefining or adding properties in that class.

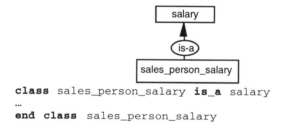

```
class sales_person_salary is_a salary
...
end class sales_person_salary
```

Figure 4.4 Inter-class inheritance diagram.

In the sales_person_salary class, further information is provided on the salary concept. For example, the sales_person_salary may be calculated in a different way, by adding a fixed part to a variable part depending on the sales volume generated by that person (method redefinition).

Such modelling requires that only the global properties of salary be expressed in the salary class. For example, the overall salary class cannot apply the *sales volume* concept to each person, as this concept is of no significance for non-sales personnel.

4.1.3 Abstract classes

The definition for a class may be too abstract for its representatives to be determined directly. Let us suppose that *animals* are exclusively made up of *fish, birds* and *reptiles*. A representative of *animal* cannot be distinguished directly, without specifying whether it is a representative of *bird, fish* or *reptile*. The animal class is therefore an **abstract class** (Figure 4.5).

To go back to the graphic software product, with which a graphic_form is modelled, the graphic_form can be drawn, has a surface area, can be increased in size and moved. Its purpose, however, is to define a more concrete element, such as a triangle or an ellipse, but its definition is too vague for it to be implemented in this way and for instances to be created. For example, it is not possible to implement the calculate_surface_area() method for a graphic_form, as there is no information on its shape or size. The graphic_form class is therefore another example of an abstract class.

In fact, all classes are potentially abstract; the fish class can be decomposed into tuna and salmon. The decision to create abstract classes depends on the problem to be modelled.

In an application, any instance of an abstract class C must be an instance of a class derived from C (an animal must be a bird, a fish or a reptile).

Rule: *In the set-based approach, an abstract class is strictly equal to the union of all its derived classes.*

Figure 4.5 Graphic view of abstract classes.

4.2 Class members

A class **member** corresponds to any property assigned to that class, whether this is a method, an attribute or a relation.

4.2.1 Methods

Overview

Definition: *the methods in a class correspond to the set of services to which the instances of that class can respond.*

The salary class, for example, is defined in terms of the actions that can be taken on each of its representatives and the specific values for each representative. This provides a mechanism to give a pay rise (increase()), automatically deduct a certain amount (deduct()), deposit the salary automatically into a bank account (pay()), calculate the gross monthly salary (calculate_gross_salary()), and allow cash advances to be made against the salary (give_cash_advance()). These actions on a salary correspond to the *methods* in the salary class. The corresponding graphic and syntax views are given in Figure 4.6.

```
method
    increase (amount : in dollars);
    deduct (amount : in dollars);
    calculate_gross_salary : in () return dollars;
    give_cash_advance (amount : in dollars);
    pay (amount : in dollars);
```

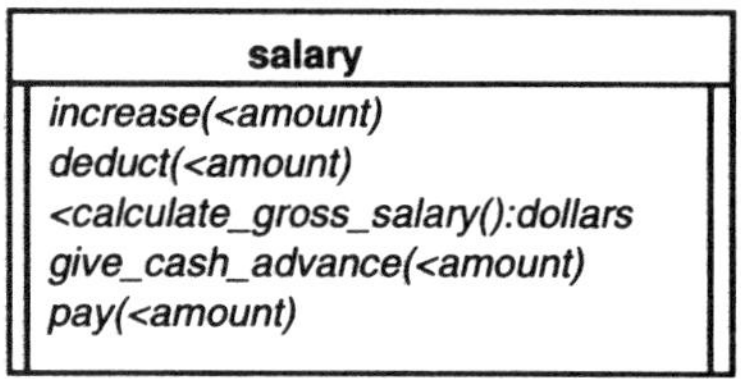

```
            ┌─────────────────────────────────────┐
            │              salary                 │
            ├─────────────────────────────────────┤
            │ increase(<amount)                   │
            │ deduct(<amount)                     │
            │ <calculate_gross_salary():dollars   │
            │ give_cash_advance(<amount)          │
            │ pay(<amount)                        │
            └─────────────────────────────────────┘
```

Figure 4.6 Expanded view of the `salary` class showing its methods.

Parameters

Overview

Each method can be assigned parameters and a single return value. A parameter is information transmitted to a method when a message is sent to a class representative. When a method is specified, parameters are used to indicate the information that must be provided by a class user when the method is invoked, as well as to distinguish between other methods. For example, if a user of the `salary` class sends the `smith_salary_increase(2000)` message to the `smith_salary` instance, the value of *$2000* will be passed to the `increase()` method for the `smith_salary` instance.

Parameter properties

A name, a **passing mode**, a class and a default value (optional) are defined for parameters. The syntax is shown below:

```
parameter_name : passing_mode class_name := default_value
```
There are three types of *passing modes*:

- *in*: ('<' symbol) Non-modifiable input parameter for a method,

- *out*: ('>' symbol) Output parameter for a method, its value being provided by the method. The *return value* for a method (*return* keyword) can be considered to be an unnamed output parameter,

- *inout*: ('<>' symbol) Modifiable input parameter for a method.

The parameter *class* indicates the type of information transmitted and provides all the means required to handle this information (class methods, attributes, and so on). If no default value is specified, a parameter value must be provided during method invocation. The method class definition (attributes, related classes) and method parameters provide all the information that can be handled when this method is invoked.

Special parameters

Return value

The return value for a method is indicated by the *return* keyword. It corresponds to an unnamed parameter in *out* mode; by default it is assigned the same name as the method.

Message receiver object

When a message is transmitted to an object, the corresponding method is invoked on the object itself. The attributes, methods and relations assigned to this object can thus be handled directly and implicitly within the method. The object itself is considered to be a default parameter of the method. This object can be:

- Modified by the method: *inout* mode,
- Left unchanged by the method: *in* mode.

By default, the current object is in *inout* mode. The following example specifies explicitly that the current object cannot be modified by the method:

        `calculate_gross_salary `**`:in`**` () `**`return`**` dollars;`

Graphic representation of a method

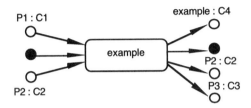

Figure 4.7 External representation of a method.

In chapter 6 (dynamic model), the reader will see that the processing performed by a method can be represented as an extension of the external method view presented above. Parameters are input/output data flows, a return value, which is an output data flow with the same name as the method, and the current object, which is represented by a black circle. Figure 4.7 illustrates the following instruction:

        `example (p1 : in C1, p2 : inout C2, p3 : out C3) return C4;`

4.2.2 Attributes

Overview

Definition: *an attribute characterizes a class property, for which a value is assigned. Each instance has its own set of class attributes. The combined set of class attributes represents the state of that object.*

An attribute is characterized by its class and default values. The `salary` class can have attributes, such as `amount`, last `pay_date`, last `payraise_date` and also `payraise_amount`.

    `attribute`
        `pay_date        : date;`
        `payraise_date   : date;`
        `payraise_amount : dollars;`

Default Value

Attribute default values are used to define the *class prototype* (see section 2.1.3). They are the typical values for all possible instances. The default value for an attribute is the value used systematically by all class instances when they are created, if no specific value is given. For example:

```
                    payraise_amount : dollars := 0;
```

4.2.3 Relations

Definition

Relation concept

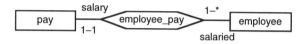

Figure 4.8 Representation of a relation between two classes.

Each `salary` concerns one `employee` (for example Smith's salary). Depending on employment legislation, an `employee` may have more than one `salary`. The `employee` (salaried worker) and `salary` concepts are therefore interrelated. It can be said that a *relation* exists between the `employee` concept and the *salary* concept (Figure 4.8).

The relation between an `employee` and a `salary` is used to retrieve the corresponding `salary` instances when an `employee` instance is accessed. Inversely, it is used to retrieve the corresponding `employee` instance when a `salary` instance is accessed.

Definition: *a relation is a stable link between two different classes; it can be used at any time to determine which representatives of one class are associated with a known representative of the other class.*

Relation stability

A link between two instances is *stable* when it can exist between two inactive objects (objects that are not currently processing a message).

Given a `person` who can `drink()` from a `glass`, `person` and `glass` are defined as classes. There is a link between an instance of `person` and an instance of `glass`, but it only exists when the `person` is drinking. In other words, it only exists while the `drink()` method is being processed. The `person/glass` link is a transient link, which only exists for the `drink()` method if a `glass` is passed as a parameter; it is not, therefore, a relation.

Conversely, if a guest at a cocktail party is modelled and it has been decided that any `guest` at this party will be given a single `glass`, the `guest/glass` link is a stable link (as `guests` keep their `glasses` even when they are not drinking); it is, therefore, a relation.

Inter-concept link definition

A relation is used to define a class in terms of other classes. For example, a `library` is defined in relation to the `books` it lends (`loan` relation) and to the `books` it owns (`availability` relation). The `books` are defined in relation to their `authors` (`creation` relation) and to their `publishers` (`publication` relation) (Figure 4.9).

Class members 49

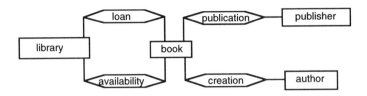

Figure 4.9 Relations linking library, book, publisher and author.

Definition: *a relation further defines the concept represented by a class.*

In the example of a man drinking from a glass, the glass notion does not need to be understood to define the man notion, and vice versa. A relation between these two concepts is therefore inappropriate, as it would infer interdependency.

On the other hand, the concept of a *guest at a cocktail party* is defined as being a person assigned a glass. The guest definition refers to the glass concept; therefore a relation must logically exist.

Inter-set relations

The relation, as defined in the class relation model, is closely correlated with the mathematical concept of inter-set relationship (Figure 4.10). A relation R between the sets defined by classes C1 and C2 is a sub-set of the Cartesian product C1 X C2.

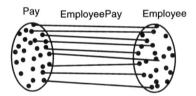

Figure 4.10 Relations defining links between instance sets as expressed by classes.

Role concept

The relation name does not indicate in which direction the relation exists. This orientation is expressed by class **roles** with respect to that relation.

In the example in Figure 4.11, parent and child correspond to two roles indicating the orientation of the relationship between two persons. If a person is called Smith, Smith is associated with two parents when assigned the child role, and with his or her children when assigned the parent role.

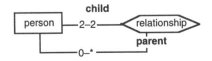

Figure 4.11 child and parent roles in the relationship relation.

Figure 4.12 (i–j) and (k–l) cardinalities for a relation.

Chapter 5 explains that roles are used to handle relations within methods. For example, the `smith child(n)` message is used to access the nth child of Smith, whereas the `smith parent(n)` message is used to access the nth parent of Smith.

The `parent` role is a mathematical relationship corresponding to the $\{x,y\}$ coordi-nates of `person X person`, where x represents the child and y one of the parents. The `child` role is an inverse mathematical relationship: `child = (parent)-1`.

In Figure 4.12, the `connection` relation is assigned the `computer→device` orientation by the `server` role (sub-set relation of `computer X device`), and the opposite orientation is indicated by the `client` role. When an instance of `computer` is known, it is thus possible to obtain the set of `servers` (that is, the set of `devices` linked with that instance and assigned the `server` role). The syntax for the relation from the `computer` class is as follows:

    connection : (i-j) as client to device (k-l) as server

Relation cardinality

The number of devices connected to a computer is in the *i–j* range of integer values. This range corresponds to the **cardinality** of `computer` for the `connection` relation. Cardinalities indicate the minimum and maximum number of representatives in the linked class that can be linked with one representative of the current class. Cardinality values can be:

- Unsigned integers (for example, 1–6),
- An unsigned integer constant to which a name is assigned (for example, 0–max),
- The value * in the right-hand part of the range, indicating an unlimited number (for example, 1–*),
- The *all* keyword specifying that each class instance is linked with all instances in the related class.

The *all* cardinality is a special case of *0–**. If a `car_registration_service` uses car registration numbers to handle a set of `cars`, the following syntax is used to express the relation from the `car_registration_service` class:

    control : (0-*) as controller to car (1-1) as controlled;

In an application, if the fact that the car registration service handles *all* cars is to be expressed, a special cardinality is used:

    control : (all) as controller to car (1-1) as controlled;

Relation orientation

In the class relation model, relations can be oriented. Given a relation R between two classes C1 and C2, if R is oriented from C1 to C2, the instances of C2 linked with instance I of C1 can be accessed directly via R, whereas the reverse is not necessarily possible. This also means that class C1 uses class C2.

Definition: *relation* **orientation** *provides a way of moving around a class relation diagram. It also determines inter-class usage.*

Orientation has both functional and conceptual implications. For example, the chances are that the transmission relation linking a car to its engine is oriented from car to engine as:

- The engine concept can be clearly defined without knowing anything about the car concept, whereas the car concept is based on the engine concept,
- When performing certain actions on a car instance, these actions have an impact on the engine (such as start(), accelerate()) via this relation. The orientation is therefore required on a functional basis, which is not necessarily true for the reverse orientation.

In another computing example concerning the Unix file management system, the file and directory notions exist. The access relation linking directory to file is oriented from directory to file, as a directory is based on the file concept, whereas a file can be defined independently of directory (conceptual impact of the orientation) (Figure 4.13). Moreover, a directory can be displayed to determine which files it contains (Unix *ls* command), whereas it is not possible to display a file in order to determine to which directories it belongs (functional impact). Finally, it can be seen that the Unix implementation of this relation (inode table) is oriented from directory to file (physical impact).

Figure 4.13 Oriented relation (black triangle) from directory to file.

The relation orientation is indicated on the diagram by a triangle leading out of the directory class. In a syntax description, only the source classes contain the relation definition. In this case, the access relation will be described within the directory class.

A relation can also be:

- Mutually oriented: mutual orientations must remain limited in number in a model, as they may cause problems when creating classes (see section 8.4),
- Non-oriented: arelation may be defined between two classes, without specifying the orientation and by assigning relation and role names (this is optional but highly recommended) in addition to cardinalities. This is often the case during the software analysis phase when non-oriented relations must be defined, as has often been done in the examples presented up to now.

Relations with attributes

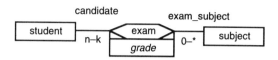

Figure 4.14 Relation with attributes.

Definition: *relation* R *can be assigned attributes when a value is associated with each couple of interrelated instances but is not directly linked with either of the two instances.*

In other words, the attribute does not directly concern either of the interrelated classes. For example, students are linked with the different subjects they study by their exams. For each of these subjects, the student receives a grade. The grade cannot be an attribute of the student class, as it depends on the subject. Inversely, it cannot be an attribute of the subject class, because it also depends on the student. The only possible solution is to define the grade as an attribute of the exam relation itself, so that it is associated with the student/subject couple (Figure 4.14).

```
class student ...
relation
    exam : (N-K) as candidate to subject (0-*) as exam_subject
attribute
    grade : integer;
```

Rule: *when at least one of the cardinalities of a relation with attributes is equal to 0–1 or 1–1, then its attributes can be assigned to one of the related classes.*

If each relation occurrence corresponds to the occurrence of one single instance in at least one of the related classes, the attributes can simply be assigned to that class (Figure 4.15).

Figure 4.15 Transfer of relation attributes to a linked class.

Composition relation

The composition 'red herring'

Rule: *A* **composition** *relation is simply a special case of a relation. More often than not, it corresponds to a trap in a particular view of the model and has no actual mathematical correspondence.*

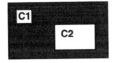

Figure 4.16 c2 is part of c1.

The traditional view of composition is as follows: if c1 encloses c2, then c2 is an integral part of c1 and is closely related to the structure of c1 (Figure 4.16). c1 must be referenced in order to access c2.

A composition relation may have a negative impact on a model. In Figure 4.17, two separate domains exist: first, *a company is made up of its employees* and second, *a football team is made up of its members*. These two domains cannot be merged, as elements that are both *members* and *employees* cannot be represented appropriately (Figure 4.17).

Rule: *to get around these disadvantages, only those attributes for which the class is an elementary class should be allowed for that class.*

This rule corresponds to the *first normal form law* in the entity-relationship model. When an attribute is not associated with an elementary class, a relation must be used to express it. Chapter 8 explains this rule in greater detail.

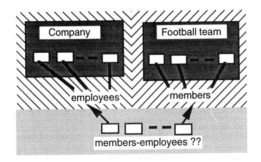

Figure 4.17 Composition hinders model development.

Notation

A composition relation is a frequently used special case. A specific graphic notation is used. Within this notation, the *comp* keyword enables names to be assigned to composition relations. The orientation of the triangle (Figure 4.18) indicates that c1 is the enclosing class and c2 is the component class.

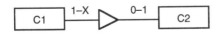

Figure 4.18 Composition relation.

Rule: *when a composition relation exists between two classes, the instances in the component class can only exist if the corresponding instances exist in the enclosing class.*

In the same way, when a representative of the enclosing class c1 is destroyed, all representatives of class c2 are also destroyed. The purpose of this mechanism is to simplify programming.

The cardinality of the component class (c2) must be 0–1 or 1–1, as an instance of c2 is not necessarily an instance of c1.

Composition relations have the following advantages:

- They provide a short-form notation of the traditional relation notation,
- They reinforce semantics for this special case.

Abstract relation

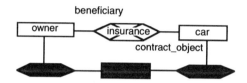

Figure 4.19 The *insurance* relation synthesizes a more detailed model.

A relation can always be specified as a composition or union of more detailed relations. It simply indicates that a link exists between instances, without specifying how they are accessed.

The *abstract* symbol (the cross covering the relation in Figure 4.19) is used to indicate that a relation will be specified explicitly by other relations.

4.2.4 Modelling example

Problem

In a 19th century human society, the laws governing relationships between people (women, men, children) were as follows:

(1) No person can be both a man and a woman,

(2) Each person must be either a man or a woman,

(3) Only women can have a husband, who must be a man,

(4) Women have only one husband,

(5) Husbands have only one wife,

(6) A mother must be a married woman,

(7) A married woman must be an adult,

(8) Each person has a given name.

Moreover, people have the following properties:

- They can get married or divorced, provided the above laws are respected,
- They die at a given age,

- Women are able to give birth to a child.

Solution

This short text can be considered to be the specifications for an application. These specifications are written in a natural language and as such are necessarily vague. Such specifications systematically allude to accepted concepts in the natural language. The description of a person is very succinct and the concepts such as adult_person are not defined at all. Figure 4.20 uses a class relation model to formalize the problem.

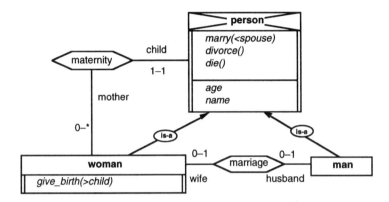

Figure 4.20 Model for a human society.

The information extrapolated from the text and provided in the class relation graphic view is as follows:

- Man and woman are two subsets of person, which was implicit in the text. The fact that person is an abstract class enables the following condition to be obtained (2): man ∪ woman = person,
- Law (1) has not been illustrated; it must be specified that: man ∩ woman = ∅,
- Laws (3), (4) and (5) have all been expressed via the marriage relation,
- Law (6) is a constraint imposed on the marriage and maternity relations. The schema does not express it. On the other hand, the schema does express the cardinalities of the maternity relation, which did not appear in the problem. Simply by applying the class relation formal representation, the analyst is required to provide further information which would probably not have been so clearly highlighted in a textual description (a woman can be the mother of 0 or an indefinite number of children, and a person is the child of only one woman).
- The husband role is a partial injective function of woman to man:

  husband: woman-> man.

  wife is the inverse function of husband: wife = (husband)-1.

Constraint (6) is expressed in the following form: `maternity` ∈ {f : `dom(wife)` -> `person`}. This means that the `maternity` relation only exists for women who have a husband (`dom(wife)` <=> definition domain for the `wife` function),

- Constraint (7) is also not defined in the schema. To express it, an `age` attribute must be assigned to `woman` and the range of possible values for this attribute must be restricted: `age` ≥ `18`,
- Constraint (8) is not covered in the schema. The name unicity rule must be explicitly set.

It can thus be seen that the initial class relation model enables further information to be given and the textual description of the problem to be expanded. It also illustrates that a graphic view alone does not give an adequate level of detail for the model. Constraints described in textual form (clauses to be respected) must be added so that they can be included in the class invariant (see section 4.5).

4.2.5 Class members

Definition: *a class member is a member shared by all instances in the class.*

A class member is accessed globally for the class rather than via a particular instance. When processed, it has an impact on all class instances. To specify that a member is of the *class* type in the syntax, the *class* keyword is used. In the graphic view, the *class* type is symbolized by <> in front of the member name.

salary
<> calculate_average_salary()
<> factor

```
class salary
   public
      method
         calculate_average_salary class () return dollars;
      attribute
         factor class : real;
```

Class attribute

In the following example, a health insurance contribution is deducted from salaries. This deduction corresponds to a factor applied to all salaries plus a fixed sum, as follows: *health insurance contribution = gross salary * factor + fixed sum*. The *factor* and *fixed sum* are the same for all representatives of the `salary` class.

These values are determined by the government, which can change them at any time, thereby modulating the health insurance contribution amount for all salaries.

From a programming point of view, it can be seen that the values of *factor* and *fixed sum* apply to the whole `salary` class, that is to all current and future instances of that class. If these values are considered to be attributes of `salary`, they are called class attributes for the `salary` class.

As a result, factor (class attribute) is shared by all instances of salary, whereas gross_salary (instance attribute) is specific to each instance.

Class method

Class methods are used to group together instances. They are defined for all current instances in the class. For example, the following methods concern the whole salary class, rather than any particular instance:

- get_highest_salary(): This method is used to look up current instances of salary and determine the highest gross salary,
- calculate_average_salary(): This method is used to calculate the average for all current instances of salary,
- calculate_total_salaries(): This method is used to add together all gross salaries for all current instances of salary.

A class method accesses class members directly. It cannot, however, access an instance member directly. It must do so via known instances of the class.

Class relations

All citizens in a given state are linked to one and the same head of state. The government relation, which links all citizens to one specific citizen (the head of state), is therefore of the *class* type, as far as the citizen class is concerned:

government **class** : (1-1) **as** elector **to** head_of_state (**all**) **as** administrator;

When a relation is of the *class* type for one of the related classes, the cardinality for the other class must be *all*.

4.3 Correspondence between attributes, methods, relations and classes

4.3.1 Correspondence between attributes and methods

Overview

An attribute is a property assigned to a class. This means that for a given class representative, a unique value is obtained for each of its attributes. Given attribute a for class C, a mathematical function f : C->Ca associates a representative of class Ca for a to each instance I of C, which corresponds to the value of attribute a for I.

Rule: *all attributes correspond to a method.*

a : Ca; <==> a () **return** Ca;

If, for each instance, a value can be defined for an attribute or a method which calculates the value dynamically, depending on how the instance is to be implemented, the two concepts of attribute and method can be advantageously represented in a single view. This allows a class to be specified without having to specify its implementation. The person responsible for implementing the class methods can then consider an attribute to be a data storage area, whereas the class user obtains an external view of the class methods.

The values of salary_deduction, gross_salary and net_salary can all be attributes of the salary class. However, the net_salary = gross_salary - salary_deduction formula indicates a *functional dependency* between the three attributes. If these three values are implemented as attributes, inconsistencies may arise, as a modification made to one of the three values must be passed on to the other two in order to maintain the integrity of the above equation. It is then probably worthwhile implementing one of the three attributes as a function in which its value is calculated from the other two.

This implementation issue does not however concern the users of the salary class, who want to have the same view of all three attributes.

Rule: *in the class relation model, an attribute is a special case of a method, and its value is accessed in exactly the same way as a method value.*

Objects communicate by sending messages, but never by accessing attributes.

4.3.2 Correspondence between relations and classes

Transformation principle

The difference between the relation and class concepts must be made very clear. All relations can in fact be transformed into classes, whereas the reverse is not always possible: only some classes can be transformed into relations.

Figure 4.21 Insurance relation.

If the example used in Figure 4.21, concerning the insurance relation between a car and an owner, is considered from the insurance company's point of view, the insurance relation is its prime concern. This relation thus becomes a fully-fledged concept to be linked with the car and owner classes via two new relations (Figure 4.22).

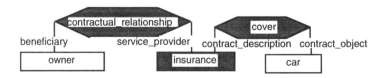

Figure 4.22 Transforming the *insurance* relation into a class.

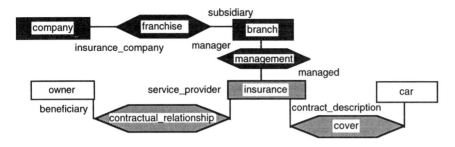

Figure 4.23 Extending the insurance model.

The insurance relation is therefore transformed into a class. In mathematical terms, the previous insurance relation is strictly equal to the composition of the contractual_relationship and cover relations (contractual_relationship ° cover).

If the problem is developed still further, the insurance concept can be expanded as shown in Figure 4.23. A new requirement covering a different viewpoint specifies that only the owner and company classes, and their relation need be represented. This new relation summarizes the contractual_relationship°management °franchise relation.

The principle highlighted here is general and respects the rules for transforming a relation into a class, as illustrated in Figure 4.24. This principle can be applied as often as required, thereby extending the model further by transforming relations into classes.

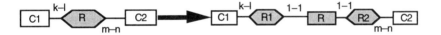

Figure 4.24 Transforming a relation into a class (R = R1°R2).

Case of multi-valued relations

The principle whereby relations are transformed into classes can be very useful when simplifying complex relations, particularly those with multiple values, as illustrated in Figure 4.25.

Several jobs may exist in a software project:

- Project manager,
- Configuration manager,
- Quality engineer,
- Designer,
- Developer,
- Quality inspector.

Structure model : basic notions

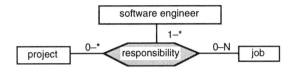

Figure 4.25 responsibility is a tertiary relation.

The same physical person (software engineer) may have different responsibilities within several projects.

There is a clear relation between software engineer and job, but this relation is also dependent on the software project.

To simplify modelling and implementation, simple relations (two values) will be systematically used by applying the transformation principle shown in Figure 4.26.

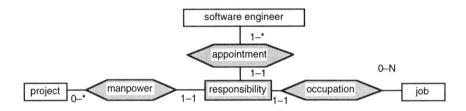

Figure 4.26 Removing tertiary relations.

Criterion for choosing between relations and classes

Rule: *a relation never has any methods. Its sole function is to interconnect classes.*

This clear-cut rule can be used to determine whether a notion in the modelled domain should become a class or a relation. If a concept does not provide any services (there are no methods) but links other key concepts together, it is represented by a relation. If this relation then plays a more active role in the model (it has methods), a class must be defined, as in the insurance example above.

As a result, the rule whereby a class must be a key notion in the problem to be solved is once again applicable. *Insurance*, *marriage* and *electrical_connection* are typical examples of relations which may become classes, depending on which viewpoint is adopted and which domain is of particular importance in the modelling process.

4.3.3 Transforming relations into attributes

Overview

The attribute notion is also linked with relations. The fact that a *person* has a *name* can be expressed in two ways as shown in Figure 4.27.

Figure 4.27 Attribute/relation equivalence.

Attribute/relation equivalence is systematic: the attribute notation A : Ca; is a short-hand notation for **comp** : (1-1) **to** Ca (x-1) **as** A;, which indicates a composition relation.

Definition: *an attribute is a specific implementation of a composition relation.*

Note that the attribute notion is less precise than the relation notation, as the cardinality, for example, has been lost in the attribute→class direction. However, from the programming point of view, A is accessed in exactly the same way, regardless of whether it is a role of the composition relation or an attribute of class c.

4.4 Inter-class dependency

4.4.1 Example of inter-class usage

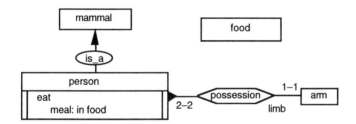

Figure 4.28 Model for the *person* class.

In Figure 4.28, a model is created and a specific method is assigned to person. This method performs the following processing:

```
eat (meal : in food)
    processing
        text : language_code
              take(knife)
              take(fork)
              cut food with knife and fork
              WHILE food remains :
                   pick up a piece of food with the fork
                   put the food in the mouth
                   chew and swallow the piece of food
              END WHILE
    end text
```

This example sets up a usage diagram for the person class, shown in Figure 4.29. The person class uses:

62 Structure model : basic notions

- A `mammal`, from which it inherits,
- Its `arms` as they are an integral part of its structure,
- `Food` as a parameter for the `eat()` method,
- A `knife` and `fork` during the execution of the `eat()` method.

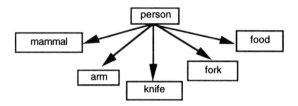

Figure 4.29 Classes used by the *person* class.

4.4.2 Use categories

Operational use

The various uses of the `person` class are not seen from the same modelling viewpoint. As a result, the model remains unchanged even if `person` changes the type of eating implement from a `knife` and `fork` (for example to `chop-sticks`). The specification of the `person` class has in no way been changed. The type of use between `person` and `knife` and `fork` is called an *operational use*.

Definition: *the use of one class by another is said to be* operational, *when the used class simply enables a user class method to be invoked.*

Operational uses are highlighted very late in the development cycle when coding a class or more frequently when coding implicit methods. For example, when coding a method for which a dataset must be stored temporarily, a programmer may decide to use a `stack` or `list` class, without impacting the processing logic or class definitions.

Contextual use

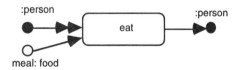

Figure 4.30 Contextual use of *food*.

Another use category is between the `person` and `food` classes (Figure 4.30). These two concepts are completely independent, as one can be defined without the other and their structures have nothing in common. This category is called a **contextual use**.

Definition: *a use is said to be* contextual *when the used class can be considered to be a method parameter for the using class. Contextual uses are characterized by the data flows handled by a class.*

Conceptual use

The last use category is one between the person and mammal classes or between the person and arm classes. The very concept of person is defined using concepts in mammal and arm. The definitions of mammal and arm have a direct influence on the structure of person. This category is called a **conceptual use**.

Definition: *a use is said to be* conceptual, *when it defines a stable link between the using class or its instances and the used class or its instances.*

4.4.3 Importance of each use category

Order of appearance

Conceptual uses are discovered first when setting up the model. They define the connections between the represented concepts and remain stable, even when the model is extended. Any modification made to a conceptual use has a direct impact on the definitions of the concepts handled by the application.

Contextual uses are based on the flow of information between classes (method input/output parameters). They are less stable than conceptual uses as they are affected by the dynamic behaviour of classes. Any modification made to a contextual use in a class definition only affects the use of the corresponding methods.

Operational uses are discovered last. They play no role in concept definition. Most of them are brought to light only when the methods are implemented (coding). Neither the class definition nor the application itself is affected by any modifications made to the operational use.

Syntax description

Conceptual and contextual uses are implicit in the class relation model, whereas operational uses must be specified when a method is implemented using the **use** keyword.

```
eat (meal : in food)
    description
        text
            This method enables a person to be fed.
            It must be activated several times a day.
            First, the food is found and second,
            it is absorbed.
        end text
    use knife, fork; ...
    pre ...
    processing ...
```

4.5 Application invariants

4.5.1 Definition

Definition: *a class is the set of all known possible instances.*
This definition of a class in terms of a set is developed using the properties described on the class level (attributes, methods, relations, inheritance), but must be further specified in order to determine the necessary and sufficient conditions characterizing its instances. In this approach:

- The properties which must be systematically respected by class objects will be listed,
- The criteria used to decide whether a given object belongs to one or the other of the classes will be determined.

Figure 4.20 illustrates a 19th century society made up of men and women, but does not represent all specification constraints. For example, the fact that only married women can be mothers (dom(child) ≠ dom(husband)) must be expressed. If it is accepted that all women must be adults, an additional constraint must be added: age ≥ 18. To set up a precise model for the specification, additional information must be provided and integrated into the graphic model.

Definition: *a class invariant is the set of properties that must be respected by all class instances at any given moment in time.*

If I *is the invariant for class* C, *then* C *can be defined by the following formula:*

C = {x / I(x)} *(that is the set of objects respecting the class invariant).*

The invariant for a class is, therefore, made up of the properties highlighted in the model (for example, relation cardinalities are invariant constraints), in addition to any other specific constraints.

By definition, an object is valid when it conforms to the invariant for its class. If a program no longer complies with its specifications, a bug exists in the processing. As the specification is defined via class invariants, method pre- and post-conditions, a method contains a bug if an object no longer complies with its invariant after the method has been invoked or a result that does not comply with the method's post-conditions is obtained (see chapter 5).

The invariant pre- and post-condition concepts are taken from the Hoare logic (Hoare, 1985), used to specify a program mathematically (algebraic specifications). These concepts are used particularly in the Eiffel language.

An invariant is used to specify a class as fully as possible and also to provide a way of ensuring that the software complies with its specifications. When a class is defined you must also declare the properties to be respected, and develop as precise an invariant as possible.

4.5.2 Expressing an invariant

In the class relation model, the invariant can be expressed either in a natural language (freeform text) or as a clause. A clause is a logical formula in the programming language used and must always be true. For example, in the expression:

```
text : language_name
```

```
        ==> condition1
        ==> condition2
    end text
```
`condition1` and `condition2` must always be true for any application instance.

Example

In this example, which goes back to the 19th century society, the clauses are expressed in C++:

```
class woman
    is-a human;
    invariant
        text
            Only married women can have children.
            A woman is always an adult.
        end text
    --conversion of constraints into C++ code
        text : C++
        ==>child_card()==0 || husband_card()>0
        ==>age ≥ 18
        end text
```

4.6 Visibility

4.6.1 Encapsulation

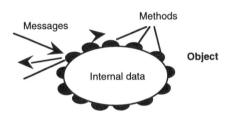

Figure 4.31 The data internal to an object can only be accessed via its methods.

Rules: *each object handles its own set of data. Objects intercommunicate exclusively by exchanging messages. An object can never modify another object by directly accessing the information handled by that object.*

These rules ensure object independence and integrity.

Encapsulation exists in the real world

The following example concerns a company which manufactures both *washing machines* and *cassette recorders*. Identical electronic components, such as resistors, are used in both machines. In order to reduce costs, both machines share a resistor.

Two machines using the same component would be an unsatisfactory solution, as conflicts would occur when they were both used at the same time. It would be possible to prohibit the use of both machines at the same time, but the risk of error would become too great. This principle is neither economically nor industrially viable, as it links together two elements which have nothing in common; they would have to be sold together. Any technical improvement made to one machine would be dependent on those made to the other.

If such a principle were generalized, excessive compatibility constraints would exist when each machine sharing common components with other machines (*digger, word processor, refrigerator, television*) is implemented. Absurd questions would arise, such as, *if a worker is using a digger, does this iprevent my secretary to work on the word processor?*

Negative side-effects

Surprisingly, such absurd problems often arise during application development projects, particularly when no specific programming method has been adopted. The result is of course chaotic. The system reacts randomly and the developers do not understand the interference and thus the cause of the detected anomaly.

When the internal state of an object is affected in an uncontrolled way by outside intervention, it can be said that there is a *side-effect*. Side-effects also exist in the real world. For example, a machine controlled remotely via a radio transmitter can be adversely affected by other transmitters. Side-effects are extremely dangerous in the software field and are minimized by using a masking mechanism for the data specific to each object. This mechanism is called **encapsulation**.

Definition: *encapsulation restricts the visibility of each item used by a program (methods, attributes, constants, and so on) to a limited part of that program.*

More specifically, the use of shared data (global variables) must be prohibited. According to the encapsulation principle, the encapsulation units (classes, methods and the schemas described in chapter 7) only make visible what is strictly necessary, and hide all other items.

Basic computer language types are encapsulated

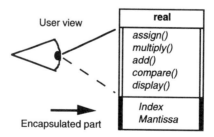

Figure 4.32 Real number class.

Basic computer language types, such as the *real* type, have an equivalent encapsulated class. For the *real* type, programmers do not handle the internal binary structure (which is complex and decomposed into *indexes* and *mantissas*). They simply handle an object of this type using predefined methods, such as `assign()`, `multiply()`, `add()`, `compare()` and `display()`. Figure 4.32 demonstrates the principle of encapsulation.

Guaranteeing software reliability and solidity

If tests or formal mechanisms are used to prove that an individual object class operates correctly, it cannot be assumed that it will still operate correctly when integrated with other classes, unless it is fully encapsulated. Otherwise, any external intervention may have an impact on the consistency of the class without it being aware of this situation. In this case, when it is integrated with other classes, it is not possible to guarantee its validity.

For example, a cassette recorder manufacturer guarantees that its machine is fault-free and will repair any fault detected during the warranty period. A label on the rear of the machine stipulates however that this warranty is null and void if a user opens the casing and tampers with the cassette recorder components. As a result, the manufacturer only guarantees the machine if encapsulation is respected.

It will be seen in section 5.1.5 that class encapsulation does not in itself guarantee that the class will be integrated correctly with other classes. It must also be proved that the classes that use it do so correctly. This result can only be achieved by defining a class *invariant* and method *pre-* and *post-conditions*.

4.6.2 Interface and body

Interface and body concepts

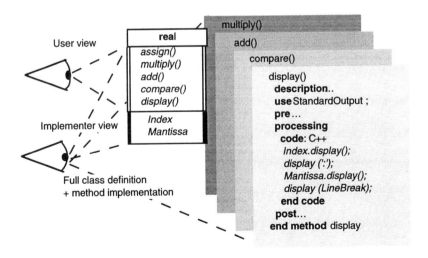

Figure 4.33 Class interface and body.

Structure model : basic notions

A class is decomposed into an **interface** and a **body** which provide two different views (Figure 4.33):

- The external view, as seen by the class user (interface): in this view, only the services provided by the class are defined and made visible,
- The internal view, as seen by the class implementer (body): the whole class structure and coding, that is the class processing mechanisms, can be accessed.

Advantages of encapsulation

For the reasons mentioned above, it must be possible to maximize class encapsulation. Other quality factors are also guaranteed by encapsulation:

- Masking of internal class complexity: Encapsulation provides the user with only the information necessary when using a class; it simplifies not only general software implementation, but also testing and maintenance,
- Specifications independent of class implementation: The way in which a class provides the expected services can be modified for optimization purposes or because the technology has changed (for example, when a class is ported to different environments). In this case, encapsulation protects the user against the effects of class upgrading and limits the impact of these modifications.

In the example in Figure 4.34, a *cassette recorder* user is not expected to be an experienced electronics engineer and simply needs to know which buttons are to be pressed to play and record on this sophisticated machine. As a result, even young children can use this machine (complexity masking).

```
class example …
--"example" interface description
body example …
--"example" body description
end class example
```

Moreover, the development technique adopted is of little importance (specification/ implementation independency). The fact that the cassette recorder contains *transistors* or *integrated circuits* has no impact whatsoever on the way it is used.

Finally, it is possible to develop more complex systems (sound-recording studios) in which the *cassette recorder* is considered to be a simple component, the implementation of which must be as straightforward as that of any of its internal components, such as a *resistor*.

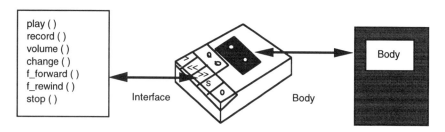

Figure 4.34 Cassette recorder interface and body.

The following syntax is used to define such a class. In this class, the specification of the class interface is separated from the implementation in the class body:

```
class cassette_recorder                    --interface
    method
        f_rewind ();
        play ();
        record ();
        f_forward ();
body cassette_recorder ...         --body
f_rewind () ...
    description ...
    use resistor, transistor ;
    pre ...
    processing ...
    post ...
end method f_rewind ...
end class cassette_recorder
```

4.6.3 Defining access rights

Member visibility

Visibility categories

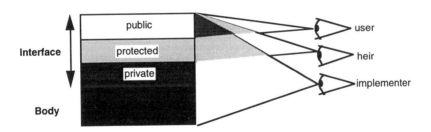

Figure 4.35 User, heir and implementer.

Three different viewpoints can be adopted when looking at a class (Figure 4.35). They correspond respectively to:

- The *user* who only has access to the specifications for the services required to use the class,

- The *heir* who is concerned with the class specifications in order to set up a specific case, has privileged access to class information, but does not necessarily have all the privileges of the implementer,

- The *implementer* who is concerned with the operating mechanisms and has access to all class information.

The visible parts of a class are defined when specifying the class. Each class must specify the **visibility** of each property. For the three allowed access categories, this specification is set up using three keywords: *private, protected* and *public*. Member visibility is indicated graphically by the colour of the side bars (Figure 4.36).

```
class cassette_recorder
  public
    method
          record ();
          play ();
          f_forward ();
          f_rewind ();
  protected
    method
          move_read_head();
  private
    attribute
          R1 : resistor;
          T2 : transistor;
```

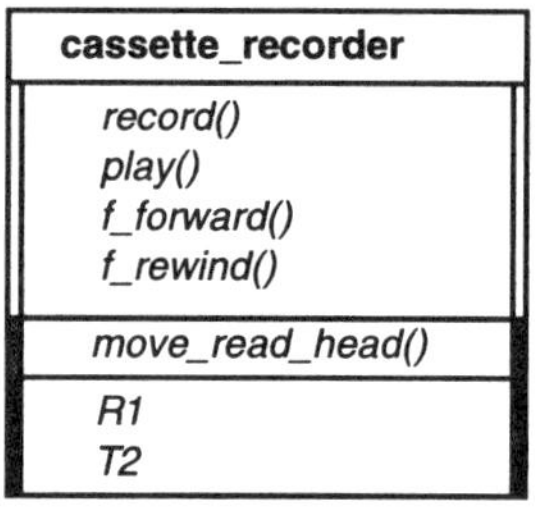

cassette_recorder
record()
play()
f_forward()
f_rewind()
move_read_head()
R1
T2

Figure 4.36 Expanded class view: member visibility.

Each keyword corresponds to a heading under which the properties are described for the corresponding visibility (relations, methods or attributes). The order in which these properties are declared is of significance. Public information is presented first, as it concerns the greatest number of users, whereas private information, which only concerns the class implementers, is provided last.

Visibility rules

The following visibility rules exist:

- The *user* only accesses public properties,
- The *heir* only accesses public and protected properties,
- The *implementer* accesses all private, protected and public properties.

Method visibility (public, protected or private) is used to define which user categories can invoke the method. As a result, a user can only send messages to a class object to invoke a public method (for example, `my_cassette_recorder play()`).

Protected and private attributes can be accessed in both read and write modes by heirs and implementers, whereas class users can only access public attributes in read mode by sending the appropriate messages.

In this manner, a user can access all class methods, attributes or relations in the same way, since all properties are handled by the same message transmission mechanism. Only class implementers can access the internal class view to modify an attribute value, for example.

A class user does not, therefore, have a direct impact on the internal structure of handled objects. Moreover, it will be seen later that this rule is used to create a reliable class invariant control mechanism.

Over and above guaranteeing class integrity, this mechanism is used to encapsulate attribute value retrieval without the user being aware of any change in the class implementation. In the *gross salary* example for an employee (see section 4.3.1), this salary can be implemented as an attribute or a calculation (functional dependency); the `salary` class user does not, however, see any difference in the way it accesses this information.

Relation visibility

The same visibility rules are applied to relations. When class `c1` is linked to class `c2` via relation `R` assigned public visibility, all users of `c1` can access the instances of `c2` linked with a given instance of `c1` via `R`. Users have no impact on the relations for class `c1`, that is, they cannot handle linked objects directly to *detach* or *attach* them to an instance of `c1` via a relation.

Relation visibilities are only significant when expressed in terms of the source classes of the relation; they are expressed graphically using triangles to symbolize their direction:

- ▶ : The relation is *private*,
- ▷ : The relation is *protected*,
- ▷ : The relation is *public*.

In the case of *relations with attributes*, these attributes have no specific visibility; they are assigned the relation visibility. When a relation has public visibility, the attributes for this relation can be accessed in read mode only by user classes.

A `driver` who uses the `car` class (Figure 4.37) has access to the `steering_wheel` via the `direction` relation, as it is public; he or she cannot, however, access the `engine` via the `transmission` relation, as this relation is private.

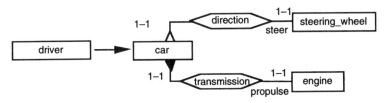

Figure 4.37 The class relation view determines which information can be accessed.

72 Structure model : basic notions

Accessing information in a class relation diagram

Information accessed from a class

The relation and inheritance links on a diagram are used to determine all the information that can be accessed within a class relation model. Relation orientation and visibility are used to determine how to move around the diagram and what its limits are.

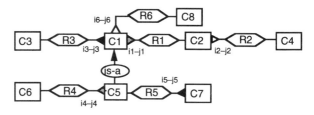

Figure 4.38 Example of a class relation diagram.

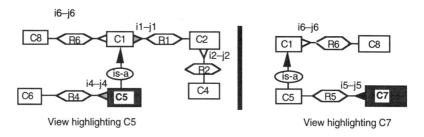

Figure 4.39 Detailed views of classes C5 and C7.

It is thus determined which implementation can be accessed by each class. When a *detailed view* is set up for an individual class, only those classes accessed by the class concerned are highlighted (Figures 4.38 and 4.39).

The class relation model is used to define access to all information in the system.

Information accessed from a method

A method belonging to class c accesses information on:

- Member attributes and relations for the current instance, as defined in class c itself or in its base classes (if the corresponding visibility is other than private).
- The *parameter* instances for the methods.
- The instances that can be accessed via the relations, either for the current instance or for one of the instances defined above.
- The instances created within the method itself; they may be class instances with a conceptual, contextual or operational use.

4.7 Decomposition by inheritance

4.7.1 Overview

The definition of class c' inheriting from class c is used to create a sub-set of class c, by adding further information. This can be done either by defining new properties for c' (new methods, relations or attributes), by further specifying properties that already exist in the base class using the *redefines* keyword or by adding new conditions to the invariant.

4.7.2 Inheritance and invariant

Rule: *a class invariant must be reinforced by inheritance.*
If c2 inherits from c1, then any instance of c2 is also an instance of c1 and must comply with the invariant in c1. The inverse situation does not, however, apply. The invariant for a derived class always includes the invariant for its base class implicitly.

The adult_woman class inheriting from the woman class can thus be defined, with the following additional invariant constraint: age ≥ 18. Each instance of adult_woman must comply with the properties of the woman class, in addition to the age constraint in the derived class.

Class invariant extension is the most precise way of defining the sub-set in a derived class.

4.7.3 Additional visibility specifications

A class can restrict the visibility of properties in the base class using inheritance and by transforming public visibility into protected or private visibility or protected visibility into private visibility. This mechanism concerns relations, methods and attributes.

Example using a cassette recorder

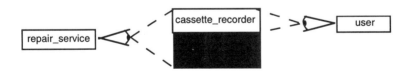

Figure 4.40 Different views of the same class.

In the example in Figure 4.40, the viewpoint adopted by the machine manufacturer, or the repair service who *repairs* it, is such that they must be able to access the contents of the cassette recorder freely. The repair service sees this machine as if it were an electronic appliance to be mended as required. It understands its internal structure and how it works. On the other hand, the user only accesses the essential operating functions provided by the cassette recorder.

Structure model : basic notions

Here, there are two contradictory standpoints: the first one allows a repair service to access the cassette recorder freely, whereas the other one provides only restricted access.

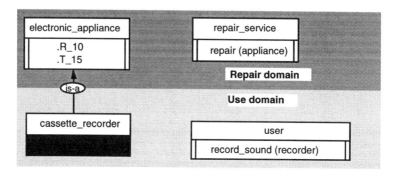

Figure 4.41 Restricted class visibility.

The schema notion described in section 7.3 shows how this problem can be solved globally. This principle is illustrated in the model in Figure 4.41. An `electronic_ appliance` is defined in which its components can be accessed freely, and then a user class is created. It inherits from the `electronic_appliance` class but restricts component visibility.

Inheritance is thus used to restrict class component visibility. Starting with the `electronic_appliance` class:

    class electronic_appliance
        public :
            attribute
                R_10 : resistor;
                T_15 : transistor; ...

the visibility of its attributes is defined in the following way:

    class cassette_recorder
    is_a electronic_appliance; ...
        private :
            attribute
                redefines R_10 : resistor;
                redefines T_15 : transistor;

Rule: *derived class visibility can only be made more restrictive to prevent that class from violating base class encapsulation.*

Gradual masking of base class properties

Depending on whether the same object is considered to be an `electronic_ appliance` or a `cassette_recorder`, its components may or may not be accessed. This specification rule enables class member visibility to be restricted by providing additional information. Several goals are thus achieved:

- Visibility is not increased by inheritance, as this would violate base class encapsulation,
- Definition details in a base class are masked. They are then no longer known to the derived class. This layer-by-layer encapsulation approach makes it possible to process a high-level class (end derived class), without accumulating the properties of all the base classes used to create it.

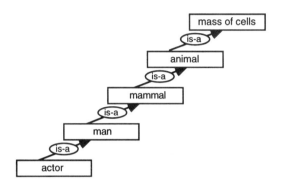

Figure 4.42 An actor is a mass of cells!

When considering an *actor*, his *background* as expressed in the inheritance diagram, and his properties as a *man*, and particularly as a *mammal*, *animal* or *mass of cells*, are forgotten (see Figure 4.42). Thus, the further a base class is away from the derived class in an inheritance diagram, the more properties must be masked.

4.7.4 Specifying properties by inheritance

All properties can be specified by inheritance.

Specifying methods

The *redefines* keyword is used to specify method processing further, simply by adding a new definition to the derived class.

Pre- and post-conditions rules (see chapter 5) indicate how the processing can be specified:

- By extending the cases in which a method can be used (pre-condition reduction),
- By increasing the number of services provided by the methods (post-condition extension).

Specifying attributes

Attributes can be further specified by restricting their definition domains (Figure 4.43).

In the class relation model, this specification is not set up on an attribute level, rather invariant constraints are used:

76 Structure model : basic notions

```
class dwarf
    is-a man
    invariant
        text : C++
            ==>size < 3 ...
```

```
┌──────────┐         ┌──────────┐
│   man    │◄──is-a──│  dwarf   │
├──────────┤         ├──────────┤
│size: 1.5...6│       │size: 1.5...3│
└──────────┘         └──────────┘
```

Figure 4.43 Restriction of the attribute definition domain.

Specifying relations

Further specifications can be given for relations on the following levels (Figure 4.44):

- Cardinalities, by restricting the intervals,
- Linked classes, by restricting the relation target set.

Such specifications cannot be defined on the relation level. The only way to do so is to reinforce the invariant for the derived class.

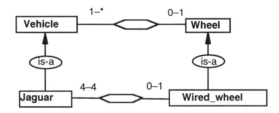

Figure 4.44 Cardinality and target set specification using inheritance.

4.8 Objects

An *object* is an independent operational element defined by its class. It changes within an application when it receives messages. When it changes, it updates its internal values which must comply with the class definition at all times.

Each object is unique within an application. The fact that two objects have the same values or state does not mean that they are identical. Furthermore, an object is not necessarily assigned an identifier, as each one is identified by its own specific existence.

The class relation model represents objects in the following diagrams (Figure 4.45):

- Scenario diagrams (see Figure 4.46 and section 6.3.2) used to represent the order in which messages are exchanged between instances,

- Data flow diagrams in which a data flow is an object exchanged between modelling items; **data flows** are also represented in flow diagrams, scenarios and object flow diagrams.

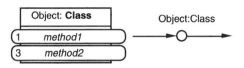

Figure 4.45 Representing an object (scenario) and a data flow (scenario, flow diagram, object flow).

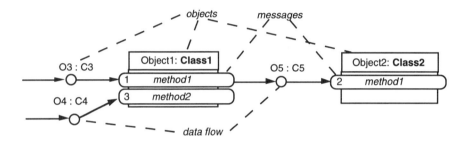

Figure 4.46 Scenario representing the messages transmitted between two objects and data flow communication.

4.8.1 Object lifecycle

Constructor and destructor

Two specific methods are used to create and delete an instance:

- The create() constructor,
- The delete() destructor.

When an object is instantiated, processing can be defined within the *constructor* method to specify that object further, to pass an initial value in compliance with the class definition, or to create specific conditions in compliance with the class invariant. In the same way, when an object is destroyed, a *destructor* method can be defined so as to delete an object and inform its environment, so that consistency is maintained at all times.

Constructors and destructors indicate the start and end of the object's *semantic* existence, as shown in Figure 4.47.

78 Structure model : basic notions

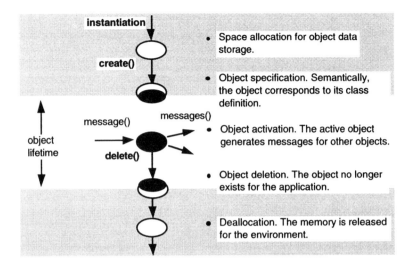

Figure 4.47 Object lifecycle.

Example

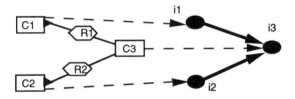

Figure 4.48 Links with the same object (i1->i3, i2->i3).

In Figure 4.48, if instance i3 in C3 is linked simultaneously to instance i1 in C1 and instance i2 in C2, and if i1 destroys i3, then i2 must be informed that i3 no longer exists. When i3 is deleted, actions must therefore be taken to inform the system that i3 no longer exists.

For example, the bank_account class defines objects which are identified when they are created; they are declared in the banking system, have a manager, a holder and an initial balance. The role of the constructor is to guarantee that any instance of the bank_account class complies with these properties.

In the same way, when a bank_account is deleted, it must be archived, the banking system must recognize that it is no longer an active bank account and must first check whether the bank account balance is equal to zero. The destructor must ensure that these requirements are met.

4.8.2 Activating a method on an object

Once created, an object is *alive* and is ready at all times to receive a message. When it receives a message, it becomes *active* and performs the necessary processing, using its internal data and activating any other objects required. When a message is received, the corresponding method is triggered and accesses the internal object structure directly. The `cassette_recorder` class is defined as follows:

```
class cassette-recorder
    public
        method
            play ();
    private
        method
            move_read_head();
        attribute
            R_10 : resistor;
            T_15 : transistor; ...
```

The body of the method handles the attributes, relations and methods of the activated instance:

```
play () ...
    processing
        text : C++
            R_10 = value1;
            move_read_head(); ...
```

Traditionally, a method uses a keyword (*self* in Smalltalk, *this* in C++) to reference the current object (receiver of the handled message).

From the analysis point of view, the fact that objects are executed in parallel (multi-tasking environment, parallel systems) or sequentially (traditional systems) is of little importance. An object is still an independent element activated when a message is received.

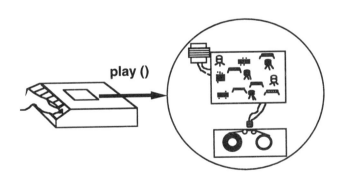

Figure 4.49 A method accesses the object structure directly.

5 Operating model

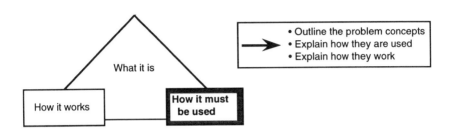

5.1 Introduction

5.1.1 What is the operating model?

Each class specifies one software component that can be integrated into several different systems.

Definition: *Components are implemented via the services they provide and in compliance with the usage rules they enforce. The operating model specifies these services and rules, but does not cover processing sequences.*

The operating model includes a description and a mechanism for applying these rules, thus guaranteeing that a class is used correctly within an application.

The model enables class usage modes and rules to be defined and the services provided by the methods to be specified. The modelling mechanisms inherent in this model take the form of pre-conditions, post-conditions and control automata.

5.1.2 Defining methods

Initially, a straightforward description will be given to define each method; this description includes:

- The data sent and received (1),
- Its purpose or function (2),
- The conditions that must exist before it is executed (3),
- The conditions that must exist after it has been executed (4).

Note: *The numbers in parentheses refer to the following syntax examples.*

For example, the syntax description corresponding to the `take_off()` method in the `airliner` class is as follows:

    class airliner ...
    body plane ...

```
(1) take_off (runway_number : in integer,
              cruise_altitude : in altitude)
description
(2)
text
    The take_off method causes a plane to leave the ground and
    climb to the cruise_altitude.
end text
pre
(3)
  text
      The plane is on the ground.
      Pre-take-off checks have been conducted.
      Air traffic control has cleared it for take-off.
  end text
processing ...
post
(4)
  text
      The plane's altitude is equal to cruise_altitude.
      The landing gear is retracted.
  end text
end method take_off ...
end class plane
```

The pre- and post-conditions thus provide the most global specification possible for the `take_off()` method, that is: *action whereby a plane progresses from the* `on_ground` *state to the* `in_air` *state at a given altitude.*

5.2 Pre- and post-conditions

5.2.1 Definitions

Pre-condition

Definition: *The pre-conditions for a method are the set of conditions that must exist before that method is executed.*

Pre-conditions always include the class invariant – with the exception of the `create()` method. More specifically, they include the conditions to be checked using parameter values and thus constitute the *terms of contract* which the calling element must follow.

Before sending a message to an object, the appropriate context must be set and the usage rules followed. Using the `cassette_recorder` class as an example, before transmitting the `one_cassette_recorder play()` message:

- The cassette must be correctly inserted in the cassette recorder,
- The cassette recorder must be switched on,
- The end of the cassette must not have been reached,

- The cassette recorder must be stopped,
- The cassette recorder invariant must be checked (voltage, temperature).

```
play ()
    pre
        text
            The cassette is correctly inserted.
            The cassette recorder is switched on.
            The end of the cassette has not been reached.
            The cassette recorder must be stopped.
        end text
```

Post-condition

Definition: *The post-conditions for a method are the set of conditions defining the expected results when a method has been executed correctly.*

Post-conditions always include the class invariant – with the exception of the `delete()` method. More specifically, they indicate what a method must do.

Given a `delivery_service` class with the `deliver(package)` method, the post-conditions for that method are as follows:

The package to be delivered is taken to the indicated address.

Going back to the example of a 19th century human society (Section 4.2.4), the `give_birth()` method for the woman class has the following pre-condition:

`cardinality of husband = 1`

and the following post-conditions:

`cardinality of husband = 1`
`cardinality of child = previous cardinality + 1`

5.2.2 Inheritance rules

Pre-condition constraints can be reduced by inheritance

Counter-example using the `cook` *class*

A `person` class contains the `eat(food)` method and the following pre-condition: *The food is edible.*

The cook's job is to feed all members of the `person` class. The `eat(food)` message is sent to each person to be fed, after having checked that the food meets the pre-conditions set for this method.

The cook prepares a hamburger and transmits this food to the first instance of `person`, but an error is generated as this instance belongs to the `vegetarian` derived class (and so does not eat meat). The following clause must consequently be added to the pre-conditions for the `eat()` method: *The food is not meat.* The cook then prepares a pasta dish.

Unfortunately, as the person who is to eat this dish is an instance of `baby`, the following clause must be added: *The food must be milk-based.* But all persons cannot just drink milk: some find it hard to digest and it is not a balanced diet.

Conclusion: *The cook decides that the* `eat()` *method cannot be applied globally to the* `person` *class.*

Rules for using pre-conditions

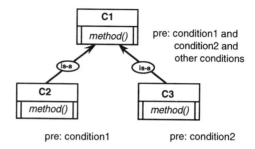

Figure 5.1 Base class pre-conditions are the most restrictive.

In this example, the `eat()` method cannot be applied globally to the `person` class, as the union of the conditions required for each instance (each person) to eat, systematically generates an invalid condition. The `eat()` message will never be sent to a `person`; it is, however, possible to send it to each of its derived classes (`vegetarian`, `baby`).

The pre-conditions for the `method()` method in the base class are more limitative than the union of all the pre-conditions in the redefined `method()` method (Figure 5.1). When a method is redefined, the pre-conditions in the base class can be made more flexible but never more restrictive.

A redefined method can be invoked in more cases, as there are fewer restrictions on its usage (pre-conditions). It can thus be seen that inheritance increases the scope of the derived class, as compared with the base class itself.

A class derived from `person`, in which all members eat any type of food, could have been defined.

Example using the `plane` class

The pre-conditions for the `take_off()` method applied to the `plane` class include the following clauses:

- The plane is on the ground,
- The pre-flight checks have been conducted,
- The runway is more than 1 mile long.

The runway constraint exists because long-haul airliners require a long runway to be able to take off. As the pre-condition must specify the initial conditions applicable to **all** planes, the most restrictive case must be taken into account.

The `private_plane` class which inherits from `plane` may redefine the pre-condition for the `take_off()` method to make the runway clause less restrictive:

- The plane is on the ground,
- The pre-flight checks have been conducted,
- The runway is more than 500 yards long.

To go even further, the `helicopter` class, which also inherits from the `plane` class, can delete the runway clause altogether.

Inheritance reinforces post-conditions

The redefinition rule for post-conditions is the exact opposite of the one for pre-conditions. For example, when the `deliver()` method for the `delivery_service` class is redefined in a derived class, this new method must provide services that are at least equivalent to those of its base class.

The `reliable_delivery_service` class can be defined with a new `deliver()` method to reinforce the existing post-conditions:

> The package to be delivered is taken to the indicated address
> The package is in good condition
> The actual delivery date is equal to the scheduled date

Any user of the `deliver()` method obtains at least the same results as those defined by the post-conditions for this method.

Rule: *The post-conditions for the `m()` method applied to class `C2`, which redefines the `m()` method for base class `C1` by inheritance, reinforces those for `C1`. The post-condition clauses for the `m()` method, as applied to `C1`, are implicitly present in those for the `m()` method in `C2`.*

Example using the `plane` class

The post-conditions for the `take_off()` method in the `plane` class include the following clauses:

- The plane is in flight,
- Its altitude has been stabilized,
- Its altitude is greater than 600 feet.

The altitude constraint is based on the lowest altitude at which planes are allowed to fly.

The post-condition for the `take_off()` method applicable to the `airliner` class which inherits from `plane` can be redefined to make the altitude clause more restrictive and to add a constraint for the landing gear:

- Implicit conditions
    - The plane is in flight,
    - Its altitude has been stabilized.
- New conditions
    - Its altitude is greater than 3000 feet,
    - The landing gear has been retracted.

5.2.3 Security provided by the invariant, pre-conditions and post-conditions

Inheritance cannot add exceptions

Kiki the ostrich is often used as an example in artificial intelligence. When defining birds, it is stated that all birds fly. If additional information is given on different bird species, it can be seen that there are exceptions. Such is the case for Kiki the ostrich who does not know how to fly. This exception can be specified in the `ostrich` class. While this solution is of use when representing vague areas in our understanding, it cannot be permitted when specifying an application.

If the `bird` class is considered as a whole, one of its members can be treated abstractly by throwing it out of the window so that it can fly away. If the poor bird thrown out of the window happens to be an `ostrich`, our feathered friend will simply crash to the ground, bringing to light what computer engineers call more prosaically a *bug*.

This sample model is invalid for one of the following reasons:

- The bird concept has not been correctly defined (all birds do not fly), or
- The ostrich should not be called a bird, as defined in this problem.

Defining validity conditions

The invariant defines the normal conditions in which objects exist in a class. The advantages of declaring an invariant are two-fold: firstly, it gives a more precise definition of a class and secondly, it ensures that the objects systematically meet the invariant conditions, thus enabling bugs to be detected immediately.

In the cassette recorder example (Section 4.6.3), the following conditions in which the machine is to be used were not specified:

- Power supply voltage,
- Temperature,
- Relative humidity.

The warranty, however, is only applicable if the machine is used in specific conditions. This example shows that the invariant, over and above encapsulation (see Section 4.6), contributes to reliability and safety.

Guaranteeing model extensibility

Rule: *If class `C1` is used by one software module and a new class, `C2`, inheriting from `C1` is defined, all the software using `C1` must be retested* (Figure 5.2)

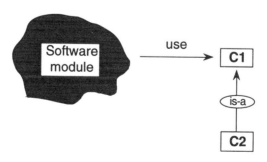

Figure 5.2 Extending an application by inheritance.

In fact, there is no way of guaranteeing that an instance handled by the software reacts correctly when that instance is really an instance of class c2.

Method post-conditions and class invariants can, however, be used to prevent class redefinition errors from occurring.

If an application uses a delivery_service class, from which a dishonest_delivery_service class inherits with a deliver() method stipulating that the packages are in fact to be stolen, then the application will not run correctly as it handles an instance of dishonest_delivery_service in the same way as a delivery_service. In this specific case, the use of post-conditions for the delivery_service class forces each derived class to respect these conditions and to provide a service which is at least equal to that of the base class, when the deliver() method is invoked.

On the other hand, the reliable_delivery_service is a valid heir of the delivery_service class; it has no adverse effects on the application. The dishonest_delivery_service class must be prevented from being defined by the post-conditions, as the inheritance, and thus the application itself, is invalid.

Here is a second example which defines a class called person_of_responsibility, the members of which hold positions of importance. The invariant for this class specifies that the mental age of all its instances must be greater than 18. A class, called senile_person and inheriting from person_of_responsibility, whose mental age can be reduced by a method called regress(), has an adverse impact on the application. This is because the application generally confers responsibilities on members of the person_of_responsibility class, but one of them may, by inheritance, have a mental age of less than 18. The invariant is then used to ensure that no heir can violate the conditions stipulated in the base class.

This clearly shows that invariants, pre-conditions and post-conditions are a fundamental way of guaranteeing application reliability, both when it is validated and when it is extended. These concepts reinforce the notion that a class is a collection of possible instances. It is a key addition to encapsulation.

5.3 Specifying the object lifecycle: control automaton

5.3.1 What is an automaton

Overview

Automata, which are used frequently in information processing, express allowed transitions between two defined states. One of the main applications of automata is with compiler lexical analysis.

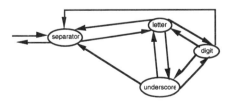

Figure 5.3 Automaton specifying variable name formats.

88   Operating model

The **automaton** in Figure 5.3 shows the possible combinations (arrows or transitions) between different character types (circles of states). It stipulates that a valid identifier for a given computer language must start with a letter and be made up of a series of characters, that can be either letters, digits or the underscore character (_). The identifier must also be delimited by two separators. A state is represented by the name of the identifier in a circle, and a transition is represented by an arrow linking two states together.

States and transitions

Two key concepts are applied when defining an automaton: **state** and **transition**.

It is assumed that the modelled element has a finite number of states, each of which represents a typical situation. States are mutually-exclusive, that is the modelled element can be in one single state at any given time.

Transitions represent all the possible ways in which the modelled element can progress from one state to another.

Abstract states and sub-states

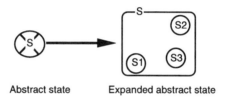

Abstract state   Expanded abstract state

Figure 5.4 Representation of a collapsed or expanded abstract state.

With this basic representation, automata can quickly become overly complex. As a result, **abstract states** can be used to split automaton models up and present several simplified views (Figure 5.4). This concept is based on the Hyper-graph and state-chart principle developed by Harel (1988).

If a state can be divided up into sub-states, it is called an *abstract state*. If S is an abstract state, made up of sub-states S1, S2 and S3, and the current state is S, it can be said that S is equal to S1, S2 or S3. Conversely, if the current state is S1, it can be said that S1 is equal to S.

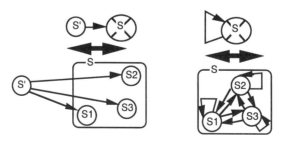

Figure 5.5 Examples showing the simplified views possible with abstract states.

Specifying the object lifecycle : control automaton 89

For example, a `pendulum` can either be in the `Stopped` or `Started` state. When `Stopped`, it can be in one of the following sub-states: `StoppedAtTop` or `StoppedAtBottom`. If the current state is `StoppedAtTop`, it is also equal to `Stopped`. If it is `Stopped`, it is in fact equal to either `StoppedAtTop` or `StoppedAtBottom`.

The advantage of this system is that it greatly simplifies complex automaton diagrams, as shown by the equivalences in Figures 5.5 and 5.6.

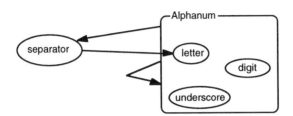

Figure 5.6 Simplified view of the automaton in Figure 5.3.

A **terminal state** represents a value, whereas an abstract state is not actually a value but a group of possible elementary values. The abstract class (see Section 8.1.1) called *state*, from which all specific state classes inherit, enforces these rules.

For example, the following pseudo-code shows which operations are allowed and which are not:

```
current_state := S1;        -- Variable assigned a value
current_state := S ;        -- INVALID: S represents a group of values
IF (current_state = S) ...  -- This means  = S1 or = S2 or = S3
```

5.3.2 States, transitions and control automata for a class

What is an object state

Definition: *An object state is a predefined value characterizing one of its possible stable situations.*

The notion of *stability* is similar to the one used to define relations (Section 4.2.3). It can be said that an object is in an unstable situation when it is processing a message (active) and in a stable situation when it is waiting for a message (passive).

In Figure 5.7, for example, each object called `dice` has six known states corresponding to the six sides on which it can come to rest.

Figure 5.7 The `my_dice` object is in a stable situation followed by an unstable situation.

Transition on an object

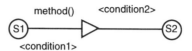

Figure 5.8 Graphic representation for a transition.

A transition is a means whereby an object moves from one state to another. It can be associated with pre- and post-conditions (Figure 5.8). The functions of the triangle on the transition are two-fold:

- It indicates the transition direction (starting_state → ending_state),
- It delimits the before and after elements, such as the pre- and post-conditions (Figure 5.9).

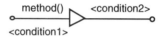

Figure 5.9 Transition without a mandatory starting or ending state.

When a transition occurs, the corresponding object state becomes unstable since it is processing a message. A transition is always based upon a class method. The same method can define several transitions, as determined by the pre-conditions, and the value of the state before the method is invoked.

A transition does not necessarily have a starting or ending state, in which case it can be triggered from any starting state and lead to any ending state.

For example, the create() method triggers transitions from any starting state to one or more ending states, whereas the delete() method triggers transitions from one or more starting states to any ending state.

Control automata

For a given class instance, messages cannot always be sent in any order. A protocol can be defined to set up specific call sequences. In this manner, an instance *lifecycle* can be created for a class, by specifying the order in which the methods can be activated and the states through which an object progresses during its existence.

This lifecycle is represented in the form of a *control automaton*, which defines all allowed transitions for each method. For example, Figure 5.8 above shows that the method() method can cause an object to move from state S1 to state S2 when condition condition1 is met, resulting in condition condition2. The control automaton must represent all methods that can generate a given change of state for a class. Those methods that do not generate a transition (as in the case of *in* mode methods – see Section 4.2.1) are not represented in the control automaton.

Specifying the object lifecycle : control automaton

This technique enables a method invocation order to be set up and also identifies the way in which a class is to be used. Moreover, it helps highlight the mandatory nature of some methods, as an object should not have states from which it cannot exit.

Rule: *A control automaton must be set up for any class, whose methods cannot be activated in any random order.*

In the graphic views, the automata appearing with the methods and attributes are considered to be special class members and are assigned a name (see the *:A* notation in Figure 5.10).

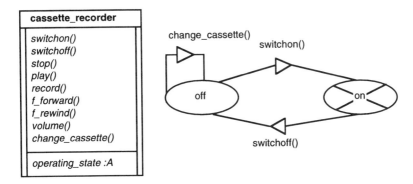

Figure 5.10 Top-level control automaton for the cassette_recorder class.

The cassette recorder described in Section 4.6.3 has a series of methods that cannot be invoked in any order for a class. Figures 5.10 and 5.11 illustrate this example with a control automaton.

In Figure 5.11, the on state is abstract. Instead of providing for all the possibilities on the same diagram, it has been structured in such a way that the details for this particular state can be defined in a separate diagram.

Note two special cases: the `change_cassette()` method can be activated either from the stopped state or from the off state, and the `stop()` method can be activated from any sub-state of on.

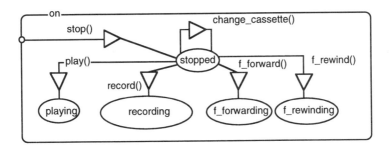

Figure 5.11 Details of the control automaton for the *on* state.

The `switchon()` and `switchoff()` methods trigger a transition between the `off` and `on` states, irrespective of the `on` sub-states. A transition does not, therefore, have to be defined for each of these sub-states.

Associating control automata and pre- and post-conditions

Pre- and post-condition rules are implicit for transition-triggering methods. For example, the `play()` method can only be activated if the cassette recorder is in the `stopped` state. Pre-conditions specifying that the cassette recorder must be in the `stopped` state, do not, therefore, have to be defined for this method. Once the method has been executed, implicit post-conditions specify that the machine must be in the `playing` state.

Property: *Control automata are used to control run-time ordering of methods by determining equivalent pre- and post-conditions.*

Specific states

Figure 5.12 Representation of a starting or ending state.

Some of the possible states for a class can be considered to be starting or ending states for an instance. They are indicated by a double circle around the name (Figure 5.12); they are the destination point for the `create()` method or the departure point for the `delete()` method.

Case of multiple control states in a class

Example

A class can contain several control automata. For example, a `person` can have both the `single, married, divorced` or `widowed` state and the `asleep` or `awake` state. It would be a mistake to merge these two automata into one, as there is no correlation between the two categories (that is, it is not possible to move from the `married` state to the `asleep` state). If these two automata were merged, the result would be both complex and unrealistic: for example, `doze()` would trigger a transition between `widow awake` and `widow asleep`, and also between `married awake` and `married asleep`.

Rules for use

When a class has several automata, these automata can generally be divided up between several different classes using an inheritance diagram. The inheriting class adds an automaton to the one in the base class. For example, the `person` class used in the above example can be divided up as follows:

- `biological_person` with the `asleep` and `awake` states and main methods (`go_to_sleep()`, `wake_up()`, `eat()`, and so on).

- `person − is-a biological_person` − adding the characteristics for a member of society and defining a `social_status` control automaton with the associated states and methods (`married, marry()`, and so on).

Parallelism

A control automaton defines the mandatory sequences to be followed when certain messages are sent. If the methods are defined in a control automaton, several messages cannot be processed at the same time on the same object. For example, a person cannot go to sleep and wake up at the same time.

On the other hand, a parallel structure may exist between methods that exist within or are external to a control automaton, or between methods defined in two different automata. A person can thus go to sleep and get married at the same time.

Control automaton definition syntax

A syntax-based notation can also be used to define control automata in the **automaton** section, which specifies the allowed states and transitions.

```
class Cassette_Recorder ...
  automaton
    operating_state
      state
        off, on:stopped, on:f_rewinding,
        on:f_forwarding, on:recording,
        on:playing;
      control
        off        ==> off          change_cassette;
        stopped    ==> stopped      change_cassette;
        off        ==> on           switchon;
        on         ==> off          switchoff;
        on         ==> stopped      stop;
        stopped    ==> playing      play;
        stopped    ==> recording    record;
        stopped    ==> f_forwarding f_forward;
        stopped    ==> f_rewinding  f_rewind;
      end state ...
```

5.3.3 Decomposing a control automaton by inheritance

Rules for transforming an automaton by inheritance

The derived classes inherit the states defined for a base class. The derived class can further specify or decompose the states in the base classes, as well as add other automata. The methods triggering transitions between these states can also be modified. These changes must, however, respect the pre- and post-condition laws laid down for cases of inheritance.

These rules must be taken into account for the automaton model to be applied to the object model correctly.

The following naming convention is used to designate starting and ending states:

- sS: Starting state,
- eS: Ending state,
- NsS: New starting state,

- NeS: New ending state.

For a given base class called C, with a control automaton called A, the inheriting class can:

- Add new automata to C.
- Convert a terminal state in A into an abstract state and decompose it into sub-states, in which case any method in C generating a transition to eS must be redefined.
- Increase the number of starting states accepted by a redefined method of C, by creating a new transition for this method.
- Specify the ending states for the redefined methods of C, when and only when new starting states have been added.

Demonstration of specification rules

When method m() in class C is defined as triggering a transition from state S1 to state S2 and from S3 to S4, the following pre- and post-conditions are established (where sS is the starting state and eS the ending state):

- Pre- conditions: (sS = S1) **or** (sS = S3), that is the state of the object before method m() is triggered must be either S1 or S3.
- Post-conditions: ((sS = S1) => (eS = S2)) **and** ((sS = S3) => (eS = S4)), that is, if the starting state is S1, then the ending state must be equal to S2; otherwise, the starting state is S3 and the ending state must be equal to S4.

As inheritance is used to make the pre-conditions less restrictive, the starting states can be increased in number when redefining a method in the derived class, as in the (sS = S1) or (sS = S3) **or (sS = S5)** formula. On the other hand, a starting state must not be deleted from a method, as this makes the pre-conditions more restrictive.

Conversely, the post-conditions in redefined methods must be made more restrictive, that is it must be possible to add new conditions (logical *and*). In this manner, if a new method, m'(), is applied with a starting state allowed by the redefined method m(), then the ending state of m'() must be one of the states allowed for m(). For example, if the transition S1->S5 m'() were to be authorized, the following post-conditions would have been defined:

((sS = S1) => (eS = S2)) and ((sS = S3) => (eS = S4))
and **((sS = S1) => (eS = S5))**

This condition is always false when sS = S1.

On the other hand, when a new starting state, NsS, is defined for method m'(), complete freedom is maintained with respect to the ending state, NeS:

((sS = S1) => (eS = S2)) and ((sS = S3) => (eS = S4)) **and ((sS = NsS) => (eS = NeS))**

Transforming a terminal state into an abstract state

It has been shown that inheritance enables an automaton to be extended by transforming terminal states into abstract states and by defining sub-states. The *redefines* keyword (Section 4.7) is used for this purpose. For example, a new class called `programmable_cassette_recorder` can be defined to transform the `on:stopped` and `on:recording` states in the `cassette_recorder` class into abstract states:

    class programmable_cassette_recorder **is_a** cassette_recorder ...
        automaton
            redefines operating_state
                state stopped:normal, stopped:ready,
                      on:recording:programmed,
                      on:recording:immediate ; ...

Such a transformation does not change the pre- and post-condition rules for the base class and is, therefore, valid. However, any method in the base class that triggers a transition to these decomposed states, must be redefined for the derived class. This is because such methods handle a state that has become abstract, and the sub-states actually generated must be specified.

Example

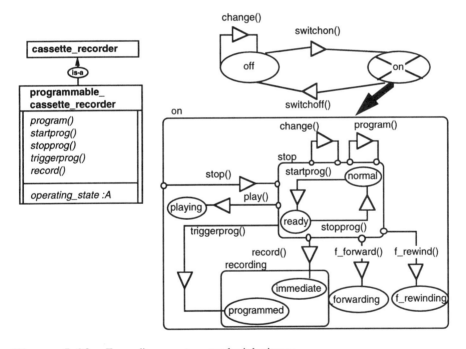

Figure 5.13 Expanding an automaton by inheritance.

The `programmable_cassette_recorder` class (Figure 5.13) represents cassette recorders on which it is possible to program the recording start and end times. It adds specific programming and program activation methods. The `recording` state is decomposed in order to differentiate between the `programmed` recording state when a program has been activated and the `immediate` recording state. The `stopped` state is also decomposed, in order to add the `ready` sub-state defined above. In this model,

96 Operating model

the `record()` method must be redefined, to indicate that it triggers the `on:recording: immediate` sub-state.

5.4 Exception programming: pre- and post-condition extension

5.4.1 Pre- and post-condition applicability

There are two ways of handling pre- and post-conditions:

- Software validity checks: the invariants, pre- and post-conditions generate an error when they are not met. The fact that they are not met enables internal software errors to be detected, which is of great use during the test and validation phases.
- Specification of normal operating conditions for an object or method, in which case, pre- and post-condition errors corresponding to unexpected anomalies must be handled.

In this latter case, the types of anomalies to be handled must be specified, together with the corresponding error clause.

5.4.2 Usage combined with the exception mechanism

Exceptions principle

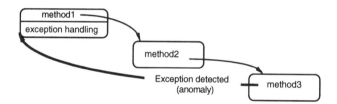

Figure 5.14 Exception handling.

Various programming languages, such as Ada and C++, use the **exceptions** principle, as described below (Figure 5.14):

- A series of exception conditions is declared,
- The processes whereby these exceptions are detected are also specified,
- When handling a method, if an anomaly is detected (no memory, division by zero, and so on), an exception is returned,
- If necessary, the current process is aborted and the process to which the exception is returned is activated.

The advantage of such a principle is that it avoids having to program a complex conditional routine to handle all exceptions likely to occur within an application.

Exception programming: pre- and post-condition extension

Combining with the pre- and post-condition mechanism

The invariant, pre- and post-condition principle is extended to take into account the exception handling mechanism and create a global specification for exception conditions (equivalent to an anomaly or error to be processed).

In the class relation model, exceptions are declared in schema or class *contexts*:

```
context :
    exception : Ex1, Ex2, Ex3;
```

These exception conditions can then be returned to the methods:

```
example () …
    processing    -- Definition of method processing
        text : C++
            Final programming language code
        end text
    exception    -- Definition of exception handling routines
        text : C++:Ex1
            Code returning exception Ex1
        end text
        text : C++:Ex2
            Code returning exception Ex2
        end text …
end method example ;
```

Finally, the invariant, pre- and post-condition clauses are used to specify that an exception is returned when given rules are not followed:

```
example2 () …
pre -- pre-conditions for method example2
    text : C++ -- Normal pre-condition clause
        ==> Boolean expression to be checked
        ==> Boolean expression to be checked
    end text
    text : C++:Ex1 -- Conditions in which exception Ex1 is returned
        ==> Boolean expression to be checked
        ==> Boolean expression to be checked
    end text
    text : C++:Ex2 -- Conditions in which exception Ex2 is returned
        ==> Boolean expression to be checked
    end text…
```

The clause definition syntax is the same for post-conditions or invariants. As a result, it is possible to define the conditions in which a method is operating correctly and the exception handling process.

When a clause that does not have an associated exception is executed, it is considered to be an unknown error not handled by the software, and the program is aborted.

6 Dynamic model

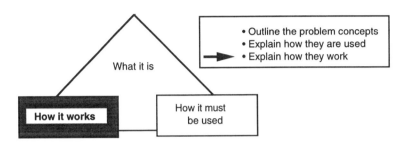

6.1 Overview

6.1.1 Dynamic model: lowest modelling level

Flow diagrams (Section 7.5.2) and *scenarios* (Section 6.3) are used early in the modelling process to obtain both an initial view of system dynamics and a processing overview. *Events* (Section 6.5) can also be brought to light at this stage in the structure model diagrams.

Each class is described in the *structure model* in terms of system components, which are the links between the various classes being represented. A representation of the services provided by the classes with the different kinds of links and the way they are implemented can be found in the *operating model*.

A more detailed use is made of the dynamic model during the final modeling phase – *object flow model* (Section 6.2) and *trigger automata* (Section 6.4). To obtain a full and accurate description of system dynamics for each of the classes and methods, the operating principles adopted for the classes must be formalized, which requires that the model be both stable and precise.

6.1.2 Links with classes and methods

Like all elements in the class relation model, the dynamic model is strongly coupled with the structure model. The dynamic model is based both on *trigger automata* (defined at class level) which describe how given objects react to external stimuli or specific conditions, and on *object flow* diagrams (defined at the method level) which represent the method processing order.

The dynamic model continues to apply object encapsulation and independency principles to remain perfectly consistent with the object-oriented approach.

Object independency properties are, to a certain extent, incompatible with the following requirements:

- An overall view of the application must be provided,
- These objects must cooperate together and coordinate their actions within the system.

100 Dynamic model

Flow diagrams and *scenarios* are used to solve these problems.

Finally, *events* provide a way of establishing inter-class communication and control based on the reactive behaviour of the classes, without one class needing to know that the other exists.

6.2 Representing the processing sequence (object flow)

6.2.1 Principles of the data flow model

Data flow diagram

A data flow diagram does not provide a detailed description of how processing is sequenced, nor when it occurs. It simply describes the possible processing paths and the information that can be transmitted.

The data flow diagram helps obtain an initial understanding of the problem, but the actual processing must still be specified. This solution is not applicable to all types of problems (for example, it would be difficult to imagine how such a diagram could help specify the X-Window system).

Data flow

A *data flow* represents the flow of information between two processing units. It is assigned a name to identify the type of information transmitted.

Process

Figure 6.1 A process handles input data and generates output data.

A **process** is a sequence used to transform input data values into output data values (requirement specification and product, respectively in Figure 6.1). In data flow models, the processes can themselves be decomposed into a hierarchy, using a recursive approach, until the processing has been defined in a detailed text description. Thus, the data flows link several processes together by transporting output data from one to another (Figure 6.2).

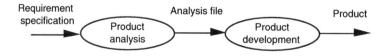

Figure 6.2 Data flow transporting information from one process to another.

Storage

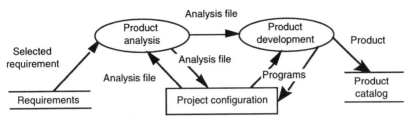

Figure 6.3 Data storage: sources and sinks.

Data storage units are passive units in which data can be stored or retrieved (Figure 6.3). *Data sources* and *sinks* are two special cases. A data storage unit often represents connection points with external systems. This is systematically the case for sources and sinks.

Data sources are storage units from which the modelled system will extract information but in which it will never store data. *Data sinks* are storage units in which the system stores information but from which it will never extract data.

6.2.2 Object flow model

Adapting the data flow model to objects

Data flows and objects

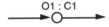

Figure 6.4 Data flow *o1* for class *C1*.

Data flows reference objects, that is, the class representatives defined in the model (Figure 6.4). As a result, a data flow can be sent a message, passed as a parameter, created or destroyed.

A data flow represents the state of a referenced object during processing. For example, in Figure 6.5, two different flows concern the same object, o. One of them represents the object before processing P is performed, and the other represents the same object transformed by P. The data flow is identified by its position, which may be indicated by a sequence number (see the sub-section on symbolic data linking later in this Section). Its identifier is therefore made up of the name of the referenced object and its sequence number.

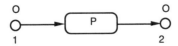

Figure 6.5 Different data flows (1 and 2) referencing the same object (o).

102 Dynamic model

Processes and methods

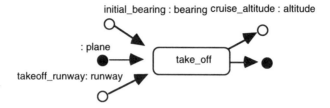

Figure 6.6 External view of the `take_off()` method in the `plane` class.

Processes are either methods or part of the processing in the methods which decompose them. Each method has an external view describing its parameters and an internal view corresponding to the Object Flow diagram. Figure 6.6 illustrates the external view for the following method:

```
take_off (takeoff_runway: in runway, initial_bearing: in bearing,
         cruise_altitude: out altitude)
```

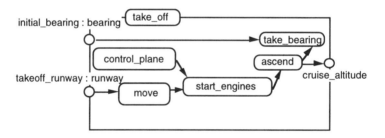

Figure 6.7 Internal view of the `take_off()` method.

The internal view for this method will be similar to the one illustrated in Figure 6.7. It is used to order the processes or invoke other methods.

Object flow model components

Data flows

Figure 6.8 illustrates the various types of data flows in the object flow model. The *current object* is the object for which the method has been invoked.

Figure 6.8 Data flow representations.

Representing the processing sequence (object flow)

Each object can be represented in two ways:

- Expanded form: the object label is *object_name:class_name*.
- Collapsed form: the label is *object_name*.

Sets are frequently used in a model and provide element insertion, extraction or selection mechanisms.

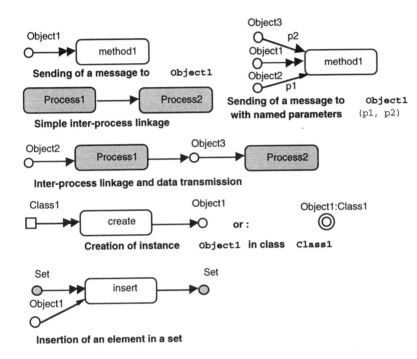

Figure 6.9 Usage examples for methods and processes.

A *class* is itself a data flow. It represents all current instances and is an element to which class methods can be applied. Figure 6.9 shows the way in which a class instance is created; it is the same as applying the create() class method to that instance and passing any instantiation parameters required. The class, when seen as a set of current instances, is modified by the processing.

Events are described in greater detail later in this book. The event symbol is used here to indicate that an event is transmitted or a given event is received and triggers a reaction.

Using methods and processes

When a message is activated for a specific instance, a link is created between a data flow and that message; this link is represented by a double arrowhead. Data flows can be used as *parameters*, to which names can be assigned to avoid ambiguity.

Class methods are invoked for the flows defining classes.

104 Dynamic model

Non-interconnected messages and processes can be activated in any sequence, parallel or otherwise.

Procedural linkages (single arrowhead) between processes or methods are used to define the order in which they are executed; no data is transferred.

Each method is made up of a series of internal processes which can, in turn, be further decomposed into other processes. By expanding the method invocation diagram, a tree structure or acyclic diagram is obtained.

Defining control structures

Control structures are used to provide a detailed definition of how a method behaves. They are made up of *decision operator structures* (equivalent to the `if` instruction) or *multiple choice structures* (equivalent to the `case` instruction).

Looped processing (the `while` structure) is defined by creating a process within which the loop instructions and the exit condition (`condition1`) are specified. The loop only appears in the decomposed process.

The *exclusion operator* is used to ensure that multiple branches leading to or from the same flow are mutually exclusive. In Figure 6.10, if `process1` is executed, `process2` will not be executed.

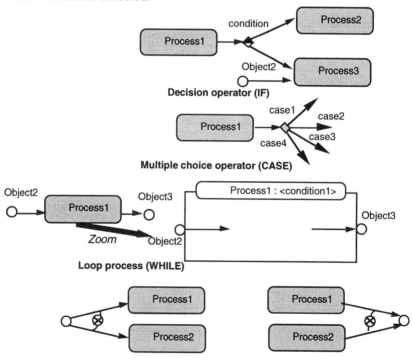

Figure 6.10 Control structure examples.

Handling relations and attributes

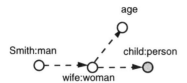

Figure 6.11 Relation handling examples (using the 19th century human society model from Section 4.2.4).

The following items can be accessed from a method: the current instance, method parameters, current class attributes, locally-created data flows and objects linked with any accessible instance.

A dotted arrow is used to symbolize that a relation is handled or that an attribute is accessed. The data flow is then assigned either the name of the *role* played by the accessed item for that relation (for example, wife), or the name of the *attribute* (for example age). Depending on relation cardinality, the accessed item is either an object (0–1 or 1–1 cardinality), or a set (k–n cardinality). Figure 6.11 shows how to access the children belonging to Smith's wife and to determine the age of his wife. A shortform notation can replace the dotted arrow (Smith.wife).

When handling the current instance of a method, the associated items are accessed directly using the role names. For example, within a method of the man class, the data flow called wife indicates the woman related via marriage and playing the role of wife (see Section 4.2.4).

Symbolic data linking

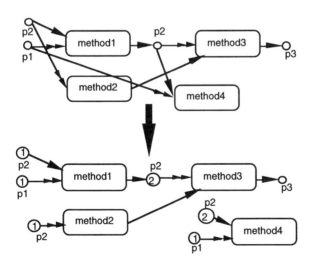

Figure 6.12 Using symbolic links to avoid cross-over links.

106 Dynamic model

The same data flow can be used as input for several processes. As a result, the arrows in an object flow diagram may cross over one another, which reduces legibility. To simplify the diagram, a data flow can be referenced by number and retrieved later (Figure 6.12). A data flow is therefore identified by:

- The name of the object with which it is linked,
- Its sequence number.

Describing end processes
Level of detail in object flow diagrams

Processing can be described at great length; a description as detailed as the actual programming can be provided. The purpose of the object flow model is not, however, to replace programming languages but rather to summarize the processing principle adopted, represent information circulation graphically and ensure that no information has been lost or inconsistencies left.

When the graphic view describes the processing in sufficient detail, additional information may be provided using a programming language during the development phase, or a simple text description in a **pseudo-language**.

Pseudo-language

Processing can in fact be expressed using a natural language. To do so, the modelling terminology must be used:

- Modelled classes,
- Inter-class relations between classes, particularly as expressed by the roles,
- Attributes,
- Methods,

and so on.

The pseudo-language is used to provide natural language processing descriptions for the various modelling items. The use of pseudo-syntax formulae, instead of freeform text, can be justified by the need to:

- Specify items more accurately and concisely,
- Formulate an expression, which would have been difficult to describe in a natural language,
- Provide notation conventions, thus making the specification easier to express and to understand.

In no circumstances must the pseudo-syntax expression duplicate the final code, as this negates all the advantages of such a system.

Modelling example

In Figure 6.13, the following method is defined:

```
give_birth : in (baby : out person)
```

It applies to the woman class, described in the 19th century human society example (see Section 4.2.4).

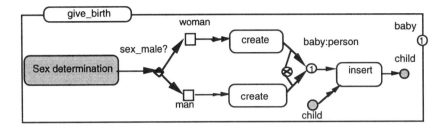

Figure 6.13 Object flow for the give_birth method.

It can be seen that the method uses the man class (operational use) and accesses the elements linked with an instance of woman directly (child). The output value (baby) is an example of a symbolic link.

The processing expresses the following formula:

```
IF sex is male
    Instantiate a woman (baby)
ELSE
    Instantiate a man
END
Add baby to the current woman's children.
```

6.2.3 Starting up an application

A model frequently only concerns part of an application and does not represent how execution starts. However, an application always has a starting point from which all other operations stem.

In the class relation model, the following items can be specified:

- Any objects that already exist when the system is instantiated are called *pre-existing objects*.

- The object from which the startup is performed is called the *main object*.

Pre-existing objects are declared within the schemas to which their respective classes belong, using the **instance** object1 (instantiation_parameters), object2 (instantiation_parameters), ... instruction. The preexisting objects are created before the application is instantiated. In this way, the initial state of the system can be defined prior to execution.

The *main object* is the sole instance in a class representing the application. This class is called the *main class* (**main** keyword) (Figure 6.14). The main class defines all possible application executions, whereas the main object represents a specific execution. For example, a main class frequently corresponds to the current task or process; multi-tasking applications can thus have several main classes. Its purpose is to centralize global data concerning execution contexts (current process identifier, start-up options, and so on) and to define general methods, such as sequencing methods for the whole application (class main sequencer...).

This principle is similar to the *root* class principle in the Eiffel language. The default method for the main class is called **start()**. The *main object* (its sole instance) is implicitly present when the application starts up. A start() message is

108 Dynamic model

automatically sent to this instance when the system is invoked. The `start()` method for the main class is therefore the application entry point.

A class that inherits from the main class can be created to define the structure of those applications which have properties in common. Any class derived from the main class is also a main class, the instance representing the application then being an instance of the end class on the corresponding inheritance diagram.

If, for example, a task is to be defined in abstract terms in a multi-tasking application, the main class `task` would be created and used to specify each separate task by inheritance.

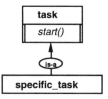

Figure 6.14 Definition of application structures based on the `main` class.

6.3 Processing scenarios

6.3.1 Purpose

Limits of the previous approaches

Comprehensive, detailed modelling...

On the one hand, the object flow model gives a detailed view of processing and is well-suited to the structure of object-oriented modelling. As a result, processing can be defined comprehensively, using the structure model to define methods and the object flow model to describe them.

...but no overall processing view

On the other hand, an overall view of all processing sequences cannot be represented, other than in functional models, such as the data flow model or the SADT model. These models have the following disadvantages:

- A hierarchical functional model is difficult to expand as it is relatively inflexible. Although it is apparently simple, it is difficult to control for large-scale applications. Minor modifications to the functional specifications require significant reworking in the functional model.

- It is extremely difficult to define processing comprehensively, using such an approach.

- These models are not compatible with the object model. A model must be significantly reworked to mould it to the object model, or the resulting model is deformed by the functional approach imposed on it.

Processing scenarios

It can be seen that when applied to domains, system *flow diagrams* provide a way of representing system information exchanges on a general level (see Section 7.5.2). However, some processing sequences must be defined on the highest system level and it is at this stage that scenarios can be useful.

Scenario development approach

The following approach is retained:

- The processing sequences, considered to be of importance in the modelled system, are determined. These sequences are often called *procedures* when a company is modelled. In this book, they will be called *scenarios*.

- These sequences are modelled using the classes created, the methods they contain and *flow diagrams* if necessary (see Section 7.5.2).

  The represented sequences are mere examples of how the system operates. Their usefulness stems from the fact that they:

- Enable users to understand how the classes cooperate when a given system function is executed

- Ascertain that the resulting model actually enables all *key* functions to be performed

6.3.2 Scenario modelling

Formal representation

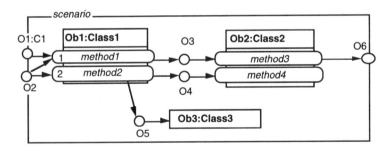

Figure 6.15 Scenario diagram.

Scenario definitions are based on the classes and methods in the structure model. In addition to the classes and methods that enable a given system function to be executed, this model highlights the input, output or input/output data flows. In Chapter 7, it will be seen that *domains* and *schemas* can be used via scenarios to give a more general point of view.

Figure 6.15 illustrates a scenario in which the following items are known:

- Classes
- Implied methods

110 Dynamic model

- Input or input/output data flows
- Processing sequences (arrows and/or numbering)

A scenario corresponds to a sequence of *messages* (identified by the name of the corresponding method) sent to class *instances* (identified by the *object_name: class_name* notation in Figure 6.16). In this manner, if a method is activated several times during a scenario, its name appears several times for the same instance and for each represented message.

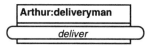

Figure 6.16 Object called Arthur in the deliveryman class.

Scenarios are not deterministic. For example:

- These diagrams do not define which instances are activated (for example, it is not known whether a relation is implemented, and so on).
- A data flow to be transmitted to a class instance can be defined without specifying which method is concerned (for example, Ob3:Class3).
- Input or output flows can be represented without specifying the source or target (for example O6).

A scenario can be decomposed into *sub-scenarios*, thereby establishing a tree-form structure for complex cases.

Message receiver objects can be designated on a general level (any instance of the selected class) using the :class_name form, or can be explicitly named using the object_name:class_name notation. If a class is designated globally, several of its potential representatives are selected. Object *attribute* values can also be included in scenario diagrams.

Modelling example

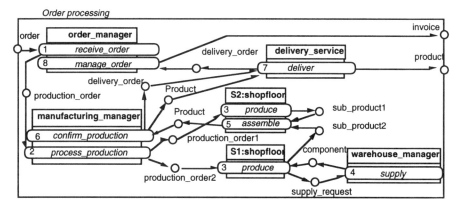

Figure 6.17 Order processing scenario.

An order starts being processed when the receive_order() method is invoked for an instance of order_manager. The order_manager generates a production_order and activates process_production() for an instance of manufacturing_manager. The manufacturing_manager divides the work by distributing production_orders to shopfloors S1 and S2, and so on (Figure 6.17).

Starting with the input order, the procedure used to manufacture a product and generate an invoice is defined by determining the messages transmitted to system objects and the flow of data exchanged.

6.4 Trigger automata

6.4.1 Definition

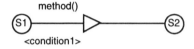

Figure 6.18 Graphic view of a transition.

Control automata, presented in Section 5.3.2, are used to specify the order in which class methods can be invoked. They do not however describe class dynamics.

Trigger automata are used to describe the cases in which a transition is systematically triggered. For example:

- When a specific state is obtained,
- When a specific condition is met,
- When an *event* occurs.

They further specify the *control automata* and are applied to the system's *reactive objects*.

The *states* defined for a trigger automaton are the same as for the control automaton. Those used in a trigger automaton must be declared in the associated control automaton.

On the other hand, *transitions* are interpreted differently. The transition in Figure 6.18 is interpreted as follows:

- For a *control automaton*, method() can be invoked when the object is in state S1 and meets condition condition1. It then generates the transition represented in Figure 6.18 and sets the object to state S2.
- For a *trigger automaton*, method() is triggered as soon as state S1 exists and condition condition1 is met, and the transition in Figure 6.18 is generated.

Trigger and control automata are declared in the same **automaton** syntax section:

```
automaton
    example : state ...
        control ...
```

112 Dynamic model

```
        trigger ...
end     state
```

6.4.2 Special modelling cases

Trigger indeterminacy

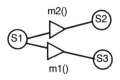

Figure 6.19 Invalid case for a trigger automaton.

Cases that are valid for control automata may not be valid for trigger automata. They are always *indeterminate* cases, that is when it is not possible to decide which transition is to be activated in a given state, as illustrated in Figure 6.19.

Trigger based on a single condition

The case in Figure 6.20 is valid. It is more like a declarative programming system, in which processing is activated when a given condition is met. Such modelling must be fully optimized for efficient code to be generated, and so must be used with care.

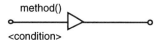

Figure 6.20 Triggering a method when a single condition is met.

6.5 Events

6.5.1 What is an event?

Definition: *an event corresponds to an occurrence of a signal (from the software point of view) at a given moment in time. It is different from a state which corresponds to a predefined configuration of a stable object, which lasts for a given length of time.*

An event must meet the following criteria:

- It corresponds to exceptional circumstances. It is not part of a regular communication or exchange procedure. More importantly, it is not a predefined method invocation.

- It can be ignored. Its role is simply to indicate that a new condition has occurred, without requiring that it be processed by other specific elements in the system.
- It does not imply that the transmitter or receiver know each other. This mechanism is required when two independent systems inter-communicate.

Events are generated when external signals occur or internal events disappear. Events are neither messages, nor interrupts: an event does not necessarily interrupt the message being processed by the object to which it is addressed. They do, however, enable interrupts to be modelled. The receiver object processes the event as soon as it has completed the current transition (see Section 6.4 on trigger automata).

An event is an object.

Event class

A special class, called event, is used to represent events. The send() method is used to send an event instance. All events are instances of this class.

Event diagram

An event belongs to a specific *event class*, which must be declared (**class event** plane_arrival…). Event classes all inherit from the *event* class. Any class inheriting from another event class is also an event class. Events can thus be grouped together logically and event categories created (Figure 6.21).

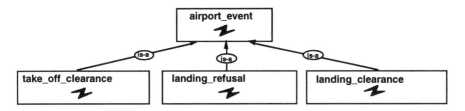

Figure 6.21 Event inheritance diagram.

Event classes are no different from other classes, except that they inherit from the event class. A lightening symbol is used to indicate their specific characteristics.

The **event** keyword is used in the class relation syntax to indicate that a class is an event class:

    class event airport_event…
    class event landing_clearance **is-a** airport_event…

When to use events

The following example concerns a ship in distress which sends out SOS signals. From a programming point of view, this case is difficult to handle as the ship class does not know *beforehand* which type of element will react to the SOS signal. Various ship instances are capable of receiving it and each will react according to its current state or specific conditions (some ships are too far away, they themselves are in distress or being rescued and thus cannot intervene); a given maritime protocol

114 Dynamic model

may also be applied. On the other hand, instances of `bird` or `fish` will not detect this signal and will not react.

Events can be usefully employed in the following cases:

- The information can be processed later, once the related objects have completed their current tasks. For example, the *receipt of an invoice* by a company is an external event, which is not necessarily processed immediately.
- The exception event occurs and anomaly processing is performed. For example, an event can be used to send a *reset* or *power failure* signal to a system.
- Several systems use events to intercommunicate without requiring much information about each other (for example, they do not know how the receiving classes are defined). A signal can also be sent to a set of objects without knowing exactly which set of objects will process that signal.

  This case corresponds to a typical requirement for process control systems, when *transducers* or *other external physical devices* interact with the software product.

  This is also a key requirement for *multi-tasking* applications, in which the tasks are physically independent and therefore have little information about each other. This property is used to ensure a high level of *encapsulation* between two parts of a system which have little need to communicate.

- Several systems inter-communicate in an *asynchronous* mode: this is also a typical requirement for multi-tasking applications, but it can also concern mono-tasking applications using a sequencer.

6.5.2 Reactive objects: events and trigger automata

Event transmission or reception declarations

Figure 6.22 Graphic representation of event-based communication.

Each object class declares both the events that it is likely to receive (`receives`) and the events that it may transmit (`sends`).

From a graphic point of view, the event sends and receives are part of the structure model. They are represented with the sending or receiving classes (Figure 6.22).

```
class airport ...
    receives airport_event;
    sends plane_event; ...
```

Rule: *When class C2 inherits from class C1, then C2 transmits and receives all events transmitted and received by C1.*

Synchronous and asynchronous events

Figure 6.23 Synchronous event symbol.

By default, events are asynchronous, but they can be declared as being synchronous:
 `class event synchronous` information_request ...

When an event is asynchronous, the sender does not need to be informed whether it has been processed. On the other hand, when an event is synchronous, the sender may use the `wait()` method in order to synchronize with the end of event processing (Figure 6.23).

Event-based communication

Sending/receiving events

The `send` message can be used by an instance to send events declared in the corresponding class:

- To a specific object (`my_plane_arrival send(JFK_airport)`).
- To a class (`my_plane_arrival send (airport)`). In this case, the receiving class sends the event to each instance, which then reacts according to its specific state.
- By broadcast: This is the same as sending the event to the object class (`my_plane_arrival send()`). Each object affected by the event then reacts. This communication mechanism has two main advantages:
  - The sender does not necessarily know who the receiver is. An event can be sent globally to a set of objects.
  - Unlike a message which, when sent to an object, imposes the action to be taken, an event allows the object to determine the appropriate action, given its current state and existing conditions. The target object contains the behavior pattern (automaton management).

Events and object flows

An event sends a given flow of data, the target for which may be:

- A class,
- An object,
- All classes.

In an *object flow* diagram, the receipt of an event is a special condition which may be taken into account by one or more processes. In Figure 6.24, process P1 is only activated if event `<<E1>>` is received.

116 Dynamic model

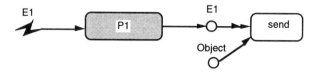

Figure 6.24 Triggering a process when an event is received, and retransmitting the same event.

An event is an object like any other and is processed in the same way. Figure 6.24 represents how an event is transmitted (`E1 send (Object)`).

Scenario diagrams can also use events in the same way as data flows. This is useful, for example, when a data flow is sent without specifying a given method or target (object or class).

Events and trigger automata

How instances react to an event

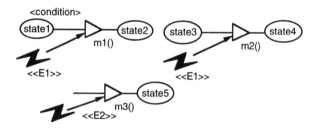

Figure 6.25 Trigger automaton taking events into account.

When a class receives an event, it must specify how it will react. This is equivalent to specifying which methods will be invoked for the current state of an instance.

A *trigger automaton* is used to describe how an object reacts to an event, depending on its state (Figure 6.25).

```
class example ...
   automaton
      example_state : state
   state1, state2, state3, state4, state5 ;
         control ...
         trigger
               state1   ==> state2   /@ condition @/    <<E1>> m1;
               state3   ==> state4                      <<E1>> m2;
                        ==> state5                      <<E2>> m3;
   end automaton ...
```

The above automaton determines which actions are taken by an object in a given class, when event `E1` occurs. It should be interpreted in the following way: '*when* `E1` *occurs, if the receiving object is in state* `state1` *and* `condition` *is true, then* `m1()` *is invoked; if the object is in state* `state3`, *then* `m2()` *is invoked. If event* `E2` *occurs, method* `m3()` *is systematically invoked and the object is set to* `state5`'.

No method is invoked for the object if it is not in one of the states or preliminary conditions explicitly specified.

Sending events from a trigger automaton

Events can be sent from trigger automata (Figure 6.26), before or after a transition occurs or when a specific state exists.

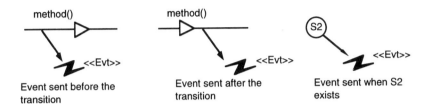

Figure 6.26   Various cases specifying event transmission.

Effect on inheritance

Class c2 inherits from class c1 and an automaton is used to define its behaviour when event E is received. If the states/conditions defined do not cover all possible cases, the actions taken in response to event E for states not defined in the c1 automaton can be specified on class c2.

For example, the ship class does not necessarily react when it receives an SOS event, whereas its derived class, life_boat, does.

6.5.3 Example using the cassette recorder class

Going back to the example using the *programmable_cassette_recorder* class described in Sections 4.6.3 and 5.3.2, Figure 6.27 represents the corresponding trigger automaton and behaviour when certain events occur. Two events are taken into account by the trigger automaton:

- *End_of_cassette*, which is triggered when the cassette can no longer be wound forward (end of cassette, jam, and so on) and causes the cassette recorder to stop immediately
- *Power_failure*, which switches off the device

The way these events are taken into account is specified by the automaton illustrated in Figure 6.27.

Automatic operations corresponding to the start of the record program have been fully specified by the trigger automaton (start of recording and stop when given conditions are met). The other operations (*play*, *f_forward*, and so on), which are neither systematic nor automatic, take place when a specific method is invoked. They are not, therefore, part of the trigger automaton.

All possible states are represented in the control automaton, whereas the trigger automaton only represents the states it handles.

118 Dynamic model

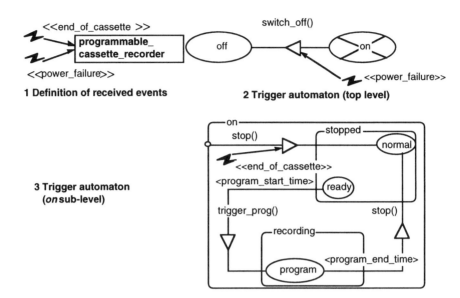

Figure 6.27 Diagrams using triggers.

7 Structuring

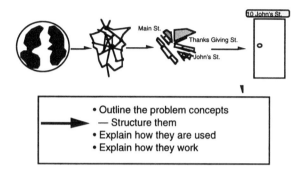

7.1 Concepts

7.1.1 Overview

The class relation method uses the *schema* and *domain* concepts to structure an application of any size (Figure 7.1).

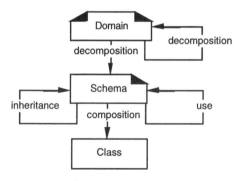

Figure 7.1 Class relation structuring.

Schemas define consistent groups of classes that have strong coupling and cannot be separated. *Domains* provide a way of presenting a problem, by gradually breaking it down into smaller units. Their purpose is three-fold: they present application components, they gradually decompose the application as problem analysis progresses, and they provide a series of general views. Both concepts are based on the domain notion enabling concepts to be structured (see Section 2.1).

When analysing large-scale systems, the *class* concept becomes useful only at a low level of detail.

7.1.2 Example

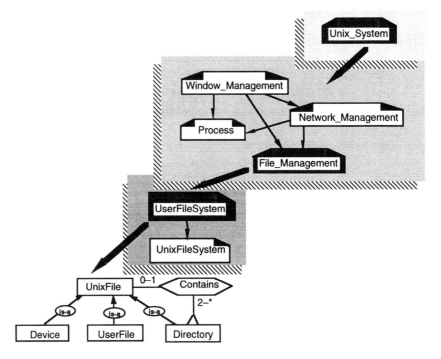

Figure 7.2 Structuring the Unix system into domains and schemas.

The Unix operating system (Unix_System in Figure 7.2) consists of the following domains:

- File_Management, which is the file management system.
- Process, which is the domain used to handle processes.
- Network_Management, which handles Unix networks.
- Window_Management, which controls the multi-windowing system.

The File_Management domain is itself divided into two schemas:

- UserFileSystem representing the concepts handled by the user.
- UnixFileSystem representing the internal file management structure.

Finally, the UserFileSystem schema is broken down into several classes for files (UnixFile) and directories (Directory).

It should be noted that a *detailed class view* (Figure 7.3) highlighting the appropriate elements is provided for each class.

At this stage, the structuring domain is put aside so as to provide a detailed definition of these classes, using a structure model (attribute, relation, invariant, and so on), an operating model (control automata, pre- and post-conditions) and a dynamic model.

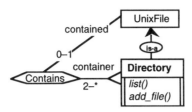

Figure 7.3 Detailed view of the Directory class.

The *dynamic model* may be based on the structure so as to provide general views of inter-class cooperation, using *automaton diagrams* or *scenarios* (see Sections 6.3 and 11.3.4).

7.2 Software structuring

7.2.1 Changes in software structuring techniques

For a long time, programming methods and languages were guided by the need to organize processing and data.

The significant increase in the size of applications, in terms of the number of programming instructions, meant that data processing concepts had to evolve to enable the code to be structured. Each time the size of a software application is multiplied by 10, a new concept must be implemented. Software structuring concepts are:

- *Instruction*: This is of course the most basic concept and is used when the program does not exceed 10 lines.
- *Instruction block*: Structured programming introduced this concept (control structures: *if*, *while*), which segregated different programming areas and enabled up to 100 lines of code to be handled more easily.
- *Sub-program* (method): Software applications consist of a series of sub-program calls, where each sub-program performs specific independent processing; this enables more complex applications to be handled (up to 1000 lines of code), as each problem is handled individually in separate sub-programs.
- *Module*: This concept gave birth to languages such as Modula and Ada. A module is used to handle encapsulation and decompose large-scale applications. It is backed up by the use of object-oriented languages to apply the *class* concept. When the module concept is applied, programs containing 10 000 instructions can be developed relatively easily.

The increase in software complexity and computing requirements therefore led to the development of computer-based facilities, the purpose of which was to structure this software. If the number of lines of code is again multiplied by 10, a great many classes must be handled (in the region of 500 classes for 100 000 lines of code).

Note: *Programming languages do not include a concept, whereby a series of classes can be grouped together to structure large-scale applications.*

7.2.2 Decomposing a large-scale application

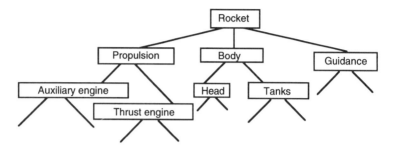

Figure 7.4 Structuring a large-scale project.

Large-scale software development projects must be decomposable and, therefore, must also be structured.

Structuring is multi-faceted:

- An *application* is decomposed into structuring units down to modules.
- The *various issues* addressed by an application are *differentiated*.
- A recursive process is used to move from application specification through to determination of the required classes.
- A *synthetic*, top-down *approach* is applied to development decomposition.
- A software project is divided into *management units*, each unit defining the work to be performed by the developers.
- Software *usable and reusable units*, such as *libraries* or *processes*, are defined.

Structuring can be applied to a software project of any size. In Figure 7.4, the main contractor of a complex system, such as a `rocket`, will use the particular fields of expertise concerned and the components distinguished when defining the `propulsion`, `body` and `guidance` parts to decompose the system. These parts can then be further decomposed until they are divided up into separate projects or subprojects.

7.2.3 Learning rules

Overview

When structuring a model, the issues addressed can be distinguished and the main concepts gradually brought into focus. The software structuring problem is similar to the one met by a teacher wishing to structure a topic, regardless of its nature: a teacher must not give out a whole string of information in a linear manner, but must find a way of separating this information and presenting it comprehensively, consecutively and gradually.

The basic principle behind structuring is, therefore, the ability to split problems gradually into elements that can be easily assimilated by a human. The ideal size has been given by Miller: '*A person knows how to rapidly assimilate and understand seven (plus or minus two) elements simultaneously*'.

Note: *A model is a dialogue tool used to help people understand the problem to be solved. The development of a good model, and more importantly a good structure, is therefore essentially a learning problem.*

The concepts inherent in the problem must be presented gradually by building them one by one and defining them with precision. Each new class corresponds to a concept which must be both situated within its environment and defined in terms of what is already known.

Order in which concepts are presented

The first basic learning rule is that concepts which have not yet been introduced must not be referenced. If notion A is explained in terms of notion B which is not yet known, it is obvious that the audience will have no reference on which to base their understanding of A. For example, the meaning of the sine and cosine functions cannot be explained unless the angle notion is previously understood. Furthermore, to understand these notions, the audience must first assimilate the meaning of a real value, and so on.

Breaking a presentation down into paragraphs

The second rule is that a complex topic is presented by decomposing it into several parts which may be called *paragraphs*. Each paragraph explains a limited number of related concepts, all of which concern the same type of problem. For example, it would be absurd to try to explain the salary and angle concepts simultaneously in the same paragraph, as there is absolutely no relation between the two.

The Miller rule, mentioned earlier, defines the maximum number of ideas per paragraph. Two concepts may have to be presented together in the same paragraph. On the other hand, two paragraphs cannot be presented simultaneously. In the example, a paragraph called trigonometry can be created, in which the teacher starts by explaining the angle concept, followed by the sine and cosine concepts (Figure 7.5). The last two notions are explained together. Obviously, the teacher will avoid presenting the theory of real_numbers at the same time as trigonometry, as this may hinder assimilation by the students.

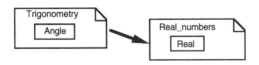

Figure 7.5 Presenting several concepts in schemas.

In the class relation model, these paragraphs are called *schemas*. The key concepts correspond to *classes*, whereas concepts of lesser importance become *relations*, *attributes*, *roles* or *methods*. A schema, therefore, groups together a given number of classes. The rule defined above implies that two classes within the same schema can be used at the same time, whereas two schemas cannot.

Higher-order structuring units (chapters, volumes, and so on)

Paragraphs explain concepts in clearly-defined, consistent contexts. Of course, when a large number of paragraphs exist, they too must be structured. Paragraphs are not, however, concepts and thus cannot be structured iteratively using other paragraphs. A more flexible higher-level structuring unit must then be used; this unit may be called a *chapter*, a *volume* or a *book*, and so on. A concept cannot be dissociated from the specific context in which it was defined, that is, its paragraph, whereas the same paragraph may appear in several different chapters. For example, each book in a publisher's catalogue may contain identical paragraphs, such as the copyright or a list of related publications.

It is important to recognize that paragraphs are almost independent of each other, as they themselves determine which interlinks exist. Chapters merely bring together a series of paragraphs in a given order. Finally, paragraphs can contain complex or specific explanations which are not handled elsewhere. This corresponds to the encapsulation mechanism provided by schemas.

The principle used to structure paragraphs into chapters is iterative. For example, chapters can be structured into other chapters, using a referencing or presentation sequencing mechanism. In this book, chapters will be called *structuring domains*. As a result, just as chapters are decomposed into other chapters or paragraphs, which, in turn, describe a series of concepts, so a model is decomposed into *domains*, which are, in turn, decomposed into other domains or schemas. Schemas terminate model decomposition as they contain the actual classes (Figure 7.1).

It is never easy to set up the perfect structure to solve a problem. There is an intermediary stage when the structure is not yet finalized as not all concepts have been defined and some still need reworking. At this stage, it is accepted that structuring is still relatively vague, that concepts are presented directly in chapters and that paragraphs have yet to be written. This means that, during the intermediary stages, a structuring domain can reference classes directly. It, therefore, represents a chapter, a volume or a book as required.

Developing an explanation

Two approaches can be adopted when organizing a presentation:

- The first approach, a gradual or top-down approach, which is applied to each of the represented domains. An overall view of the problem is presented, which is then further decomposed to a finer level of detail.

- The second approach identifies the most basic, initial concepts and then gradually builds up new concepts, each of which stems from previously defined concepts. This bottom-up approach builds up the solution.

When developing a presentation, a mixed approach is usually adopted (top-down and bottom-up). The final presentation must consist of either one of the two possibilities. When developing software, the solution is built using a mixed approach, but the application is always presented using the top-down approach.

7.2.4 Controlling software development

Software project management

Distributing development tasks

Software development can be decomposed into independent parts to be distributed between the various team members. The OBS (organization breakdown structure) presented in Figure 7.6 uses a matrix to determine which person will perform which activity.

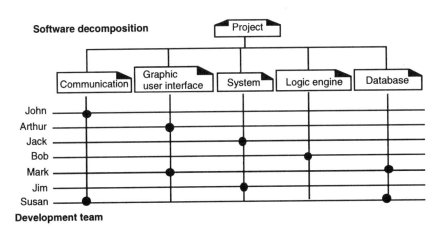

Figure 7.6 Example of an OBS.

Software decomposition is a complex task which can only be done gradually. The project team must first study what the system is intended to do (specification), and then how it is to do it (design) before a detailed structure can be obtained.

Estimation

Activity	Man/months
Communication	10
Graphic user interface	15
System	7
Logic engine	12
Database	23
Project	**67**

It should be noted that the estimated workload is based on the structure and is divided into activities, which are easier to estimate and total. The complete software structure is not known at the beginning of the project. Initially, only the major domains in the project have been identified and, as development progresses, the structure is developed and becomes more precise, enabling a more accurate estimate to be made.

Technical project control

Using and reusing software components

During software development, sub-components used by other software components can be defined. Sub-components generally correspond to the lower layers of the application and take the form of *utilities* or *libraries*. They are potentially reuseable and may be extracted from a specific software development project so as to be reused in other projects.

Schemas enable these sub-components to be represented as groups of classes which are used together, plus a clearly defined handling interface (Figure 7.7).

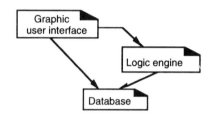

Figure 7.7 The Database schema is required by both the Logic engine and Graphic user interface schemas and as such may be reused.

Integration

The software components developed by each person or group of persons are finally assembled to obtain the actual software product. A strategy must be defined in order to determine:

- The order in which the components are to be assembled, which, in turn, defines development priorities and schedules,
- How the components are to be tested during assembly.

Domain and schema diagrams indicate the dependencies and flows of information, and provide solid foundations when developing this strategy (see Section 11.5). Using the inter-schema dependency diagram illustrated in Figure 7.7 as an example, the deduced integration order may be:

- Database,
- Database + logic engine,
- Database + logic engine + GUI.

Code production

When developing software, the code is based on a specific structure used by production tools (compilers, link editors, *MakeFiles*, and so on), the aim being to obtain a final executable application. It is important that a good code production structure be defined, as it helps implement a production schema, enables independent development projects to be conducted and facilitates integration, configuration management, and so on. This task is part of software structuring and uses the domain, schema and class definitions (Figure 7.8), to set up the groups required to obtain final code.

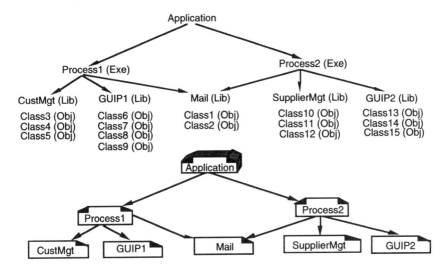

Figure 7.8 Composition diagram and equivalent structure diagram for reusable binary files (Obj), libraries (Lib) and executable files (Exe), required by the final application.

Version management

If version c.1 is created for class c, then version c'.1 must be created for c' which is closely coupled to c; it is dependent on c.1. If a software product is poorly structured, any change in version for one class often means that the versions for all classes in the application must be changed. Structuring is used to define categories of classes with low coupling, so that limited versions can be defined for each class category (schema or domain).

7.3 Schemas

7.3.1 Overview

Definition

Section 2.1 explained that concepts are not all handled on the same level and that humans structure concepts in terms of the *applicable domain*. The *domain* concept is, therefore, the basis for the schema concept (conceptual domains).

Definition: *Just as a class is the computer representation of a concept, a schema is the computer representation of a domain.*

128 Structuring

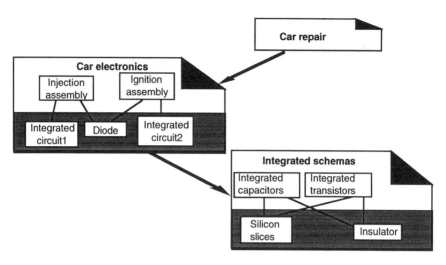

Figure 7.9 Domains are based on concepts taken from other domains.

By definition, a schema is a finite group of classes. It concerns a specific conceptual domain. Each class belongs to one and only one schema. An application is therefore *partitioned* into schemas.

Various real-world domains have been studied by experts. Each domain is based on other domains and uses concepts from them. For a given domain, two viewpoints exist:

- That of the domain *specialist*, who has an in-depth understanding of the concepts and mechanisms,
- That of the domain *user*, who is only concerned with some of its concepts.

For example, the graphic in Figure 7.9 represents the `car repair` domain, where a `garage_mechanic` is a specialist. This domain uses concepts taken from other domains, such as the `ignition assembly` or `injection assembly` concepts in the `car electronics` field. The `garage_mechanic` knows the components, but does not know how they work or are repaired. This more specific level of detail is the responsibility of `electronic experts`. They can repair or put together these assemblies, using `electronic components` such as `diodes` or `integrated circuits`. The `electronics specialist` does not have a detailed understanding of how these electronic components are manufactured, as this information concerns a different area of expertise, the `integrated circuit` domain, where the composition of these components (`silicon slices`, `insulators`, `integrated transistors` and `integrated capacitors`) is described in detail. Domains are therefore gradually conceptualized, each of which contains both very specific concepts for specialists alone and other more general concepts to be used by other domains.

Domains are represented by class relation *schemas*. A schema is a finite set of classes with an *interface* and a *body*. The interface and body are themselves two separate sub-sets of classes within the schema. The concepts not known to external schemas are defined as **body classes** in the schema, whereas those concepts handled by other domains (schemas) become **interface classes**.

Representing a schema

Schemas are defined in the class relation model using a specific syntax and graphic representation. Figure 7.10 shows a schema diagram for a signal processor and Figure 7.11 shows an internal schema view.

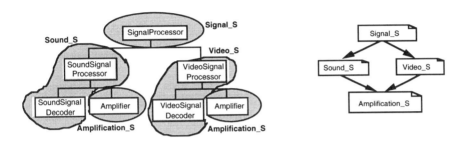

Figure 7.10 Tree-form decomposition for a signal processor and corresponding inter-schema usage diagram.

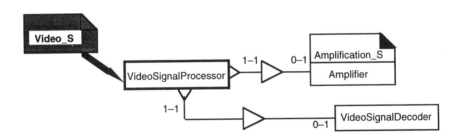

Figure 7.11 Description of the video_s schema (internal view).

A tree-form decomposition is very suitable for hardware requirements, in which each function is implemented in the form of sub-functions, which, in turn, correspond to electronic components when the lowest level is reached.

The hierarchical structure is however unsuitable for software, as component duplication, a natural phenomenon in the hardware field (Amplifier for example), must be avoided.

The following elements exist within a schema:

- *Body classes* (for example, VideoSignalDecoder), which cannot be accessed from outside the schema.

- *Interface classes* (for example, VideoSignalProcessor), which can be accessed from outside the schema.

130 Structuring

- *External classes* (for example, `Amplifier`), which are taken from other schemas.

  schema `Video_S`
      use `Amplification_S;`
      interface `VideoSignalProcessor ;`
      body `VideoSignalDecoder; ...`

7.3.2 Inter-schema links

Usage link

Schemas can be interconnected by *usage links*. It is said that schema `s1` has a usage link with schema `s2` when at least one of the classes in `s1` uses at least one of the classes in `s2`. Figure 7.10 shows an example of an inter-schema usage diagram.

When schema `s1` uses schema `s2`, the classes in `s1` can access the `s2` interface classes, but not the body classes.

For each schema, a graphic view can indicate the classes it contains and the associated external classes. An *external class* is one which does not belong to the current schema, but which is nevertheless part of the graphic view. In Figure 7.11, the `amplifier` class is an external class for the `Video_S` schema and an interface class for the `Amplification_S` schema.

Inheritance link

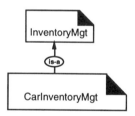

Figure 7.12 Example of inter-schema inheritance.

Schemas can also be interconnected by *inheritance links* (Figure 7.12). Thus, schema `s2` inherits from schema `s1` when an item provided by `s2` is a special case of an item provided by `s1`. The domain represented by `s2` further specifies the domain represented by `s1`. For example, the car inventory management domain for a car manufacturer further specifies the general inventory management domain.

Inheritance example: chess and draughts

The chess and draughts games can be modelled using two schemas. The first schema concerns the game of *chess,* its classes represent the `board`, the `squares` and the types of `chessmen`. The second schema is for the game of *draughts*; its classes also represent the `board`, the `squares` and the two types of `draughts`.

These two schemas have several important points in common. It is, therefore, quite natural to try and factorize them. A schema called `BoardGame` can thus be defined to represent the `board`, the `squares` on the board, the game `tokens`, the `players`, the `colors`, the `moves` and other more general interactions.

Schemas 131

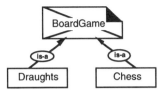

Figure 7.13 BoardGame schema inheritance.

In this case, the Draughts and Chess schemas inherit from the BoardGame schema (Figure 7.13). It is quite easy to define the general use of the BoardGame schema, where two players have a game and one is the winner.

In such a case, the *abstract schema* concept (see Section 4.1.3), whereby a schema is not implemented directly, is of significance. The BoardGame schema cannot be implemented as such, since its definition is too general. On the other hand, it is quite possible to use a BoardGame in the abstract sense.

Definition of inter-schema inheritance

Definition: *A schema specifies a domain and defines all computer implementations that meet this specification. Inter-schema inheritance exists when the various possible implementation sets can be inclusive.*

In this way, the Chess schema defines possible implementations (which can be further specified for each chessboard model). These implementations also correspond to specific aspects of the BoardGame schema. The Bishop, Knight and King concepts in the Chess schema inherit from the more general concept of Token in the BoardGame schema (Figure 7.14).

Rule: *If inter-schema inheritance exists, all classes in the base schema are reused or redefined by inheritance.*

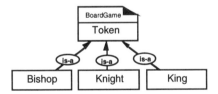

Figure 7.14 Partial view of the Chess schema.

7.3.3 Schema properties

A schema contains the definition context for its classes

The meaning of each class name is specific to its schema, whereas the name of a schema is relative to the whole application.

It can be said that the *ball* concept is defined in the general *ball game* domain, whereas in the *football* and *basketball* domains, more specific concepts are associated

132 Structuring

with the general *ball* notion and are assigned specific meanings. The meaning of the word *ball* is therefore related to one of three domains. Consequently, the definition of a class is dependent on the other classes visible from the associated schema.

Rule: *when a class is defined within a schema, its usage cannot be dissociated from that particular schema.*

Dependency properties

Note: *a schema is a group of classes. Schemas structure classes and determine visibility in the same way as classes structure methods and visibilities. A schema can be considered to be a* super-class, *the properties of which are its classes (Figure 7.15).*

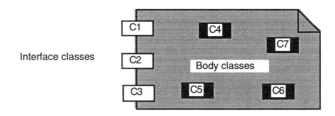

Figure 7.15 A schema can be considered to be a *super-class*.

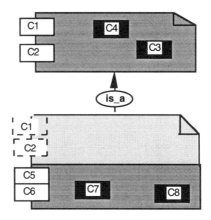

Figure 7.16 The derived schema reuses and expands the interface for the base schema.

Inter-schema inheritance and usage determine access rights to the classes within one schema in relation to those within other schemas (Figure 7.16). Given two schemas S1 and S2:

- If S1 is not linked to S2, then the classes in S1 cannot access the classes in S2.

- If S1 uses S2, then the classes in S1 can access the interface classes in S2.
- If S1 inherits from S2, then classes in S1 can access all classes in S2 and the S1 interface implicitly contains all classes in the S2 interface.

Rule: *The class relation model allows mutual inter-class usage, but prohibits mutual inter-schema usage.*

Section 8.4.1 describes the techniques used to avoid mutual inter-schema usage systematically.

Schema context

A schema can define the information shared by all classes within that schema (for example, *constants*). For instance, if a geometry schema is defined, in which shapes such as polygons or ellipses are handled, types in the appropriate programming language may be imported. These types may be distance or surface, and constants like PI or MAXIMUM_SURFACE_AREA. All schema classes must access this information and there is no reason why one of them should be given precedence over all others. In this way, the schema *context* is defined, as illustrated in the example below:

```
schema geometry ...
interface distance, surface, graphic_form;
   context
      enumerate form_intersection (contiguous, included, disjointed) ;
      const PI : real := 3.1416;
end schema geometry
```

All schema classes access the context information in that schema. When class C1 uses class C2, it accesses the context information in the schema corresponding to C2.

If schema S2 inherits from schema S1, the context for S2 contains the context for S1, in addition to its own.

Schema-based structuring

Each schema provides a summarized view of the final application, obtained by implementing the class relation synthesis mechanism (Figure 7.17). Each limited view can be associated with its own definition or based on those provided by other views.

This decomposition, which is more flexible than a hierarchical decomposition, ensures systematic direct access between classes when required.

A schema may have an empty interface or body. An empty schema uses and summarizes the concepts defined in other schemas, but does not set up any of its own specific concepts. From a developer's point of view, an empty schema may be used to integrate several other schemas in the application.

134 Structuring

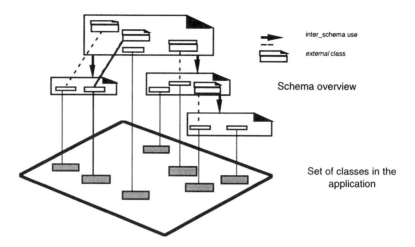

Figure 7.17 Schemas representing a partial view of an application.

Schema invariant

A schema corresponds to a consistent group of classes. Thus, its main role is to define and ensure this consistency.

Definition: *A schema invariant is the union of all invariants in its classes, together with any general clauses.*

When invariant clauses are written for an application, they need not be specific to one class, but may concern several classes. This second type of clause is defined on the schema invariant level.

In the example of the 19th century human society, given in Section 4.2.4, Figure 4.20, which represents the links between the man and woman classes, the following clause must be represented: $man \cap woman = \emptyset$. This clause cannot be defined on the human class level, because it is unaware of its derived classes, nor can it be defined on the woman or man class level, as they only handle part of the required elements. It must therefore be specified in the HumanSociety schema.

The schema invariant is applied to each class in the schema in addition to all those defined for the class itself. Each instance in schema s must meet the clauses of the class invariant and the more general clauses defined in the schema invariant.

Rule: *When a schema inherits from another schema, it reuses and, if necessary, extends the schema invariant.*

This last rule is similar to the one for invariants in derived classes. In the following example, a society schema reuses the example mentioned above, but does not apply the intersection constraint existing between man and woman. The following schemas can inherit from the society schema:

- A human_society schema does not add any classes, but includes the intersection constraint between man and woman.

- A society_from_outer_space schema provides an additional class called android, inheriting both from man and woman, but does not extend the invariant constraints (there is no constraint concerning the intersection between man and woman).

Library **schemas**

Application development is always based on existing elements, such as the operating system, the windowing system, a database management system, a driver, and so on. These existing elements take the form of *libraries*, which are generally not part of the class relation model. During modelling, and more importantly during the design phase, it is worthwhile including these libraries, particularly when visualizing the dependencies on them. These external libraries are modelled using specific schemas, as illustrated in Figure 7.18. They make up the **virtual machine** for the application (see Chapter 11).

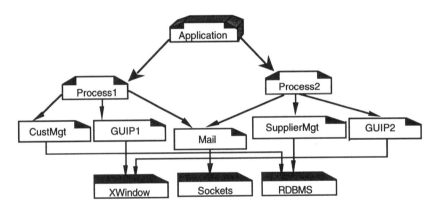

Figure 7.18 Representing the libraries on which an application is based.

7.4 Structuring domains

7.4.1 Structuring a large number of schemas

Schemas are used to structure an application regardless of its size, as they provide local summarized views. A presentation problem may however arise when an overview is to be created for an application with a large number of schemas (Figure 7.19).

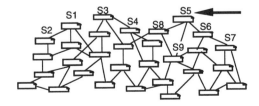

Figure 7.19 The schemas must in turn be structured.

136 Structuring

To solve this problem, a schema may be represented with only those schemas (used or inherited) required to define it. This part of the schema diagram is called the *external view* (Figure 7.20) as compared with the class diagram which corresponds to its *internal view*.

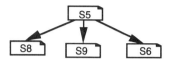

Figure 7.20 External view of S5.

7.4.2 Structuring domain concept

Overview

The external schema view does not provide an overall view of the application; the schemas must, therefore, be grouped together into units on the next higher level. These new units may, in turn, be structured.

This new grouping unit is called a **structuring domain**. For example, when developing a compiler, the domains represented in Figure 7.21 can be defined; the CodeGeneration domain is then decomposed into domains and schemas, as is the GeneratedLanguage domain.

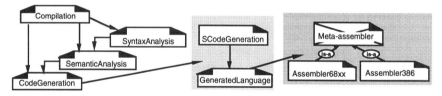

Figure 7.21 Domains in a compiler.

Inter-domain links

Inter-domain links are referencing links used to denote *decomposition* or *recomposition*. Unlike schemas, for which the link with their composing classes is fixed, a domain represents one *aspect* of an application, corresponding to the elements to which it refers.

Thus, a class, once fully defined, belongs to one and only one schema. Two different schemas cannot contain the same class. When a class is used, the corresponding schema must also be used. Different domains, however, can reference the same schemas (Figure 7.22). They are used to recompose a view by assembling schemas or classes in a different way. This mechanism is used to define domains with different purposes (functional view, specific documentation set, software architecture, specific version, specific application, integration plan, and so on).

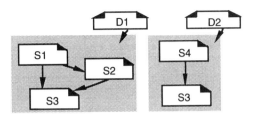

Figure 7.22 D1 and D2 are two different domains, each referencing S3.

Inter-schema dependencies must be acyclic, whereas inter-domain dependencies can be cyclic.

Definition: *A domain is a structuring unit which references part of the application.*

Unlike schemas, a domain is not part of the definition context for a class. As a result, a class can be used without knowing to which domains it belongs, but the schema which contains it must, however, be known.

For example, the transistor, capacitor and resistor classes are defined in a schema called ElectronicComponent. The SignalProcessing and PowerSupply domains use these concepts. This type of model requires that the ElectronicComponent schema be used whenever transistor is used, but does not mean that either the SignalProcessing or PowerSupply domain must be applied.

Project domain

A *project* is a specific domain which corresponds to the root of the domain diagram and represents an application.

A large-scale application is broken down into different projects, each of which corresponds to a domain. A project diagram is then set up to decompose each project into individual domains (Figure 7.23).

Project diagrams must be acyclic.

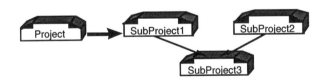

Figure 7.23 Decomposing the *Project* domain into three sub-projects.

7.4.3 Global structuring approach

Domains are used to apply an *immediate* structure to a problem

The initial structure of an application can be defined immediately using domains. This is because the classes must be clearly understood before an application can be

138 Structuring

structured into schemas (the class context must be fully defined), whereas it is easy to decompose an application into domains, using a global top-down approach. For example, if it is known that an application has a *graphic interface*, *operating system* interface and *database* management parts, these three parts can be immediately represented as domains (Graphics, System, Database in Figure 7.24). The specification and design activities can then be started using these domains as a basis.

Figure 7.24 *Immediate* application structuring.

Overview of the modelled parts

Schemas give a detailed view of each sub-problem handled by the application. They concentrate on the classes they contain or those accessed directly by classes in the schema.

A domain view can illustrate all elements referenced either directly or indirectly. It can, therefore, present schemas or the classes which belong to the referenced schemas.

This enables certain classes belonging to different schemas to be highlighted in order to present an overall model and place emphasis on cooperation aspects which do not appear locally in schemas. For example, *scenarios* (see Chapter 6) are generally defined on domain level and situate all classes concerned on the same level (Figure 7.25).

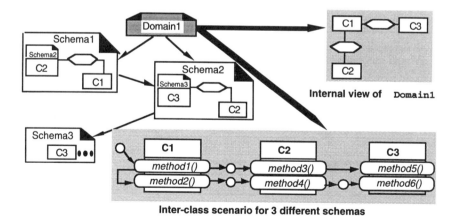

Figure 7.25 Domains are used to represent the classes in the composing schemas on the same level in order to set up several overviews.

Need for multi-view modelling

Another advantage of using domains is the ability to present several partial views, each structured differently.

The same modelling items (classes, schemas, and so on) can be presented in different views for the following reasons:

- Presentation of the same problem from different points of view. For example, one representation can concern the specification or design of a specific part of the system.
- Global or local view of a model. The above example presented both views specific to each schema and a general domain-level view.
- Representation of different modelling aspects. For example, some domain diagrams can represent the static software structure (domain and schema diagrams), a *flow diagram*, or *scenarios* showing how several classes cooperate.

Gradual problem structuring

The final specification of the schemas is not known until the composing classes have been defined with the appropriate context.

Initially, the model is defined using a trial – and error – principle to detect the correct concepts, consolidate them and then structure them. At the beginning of the analysis phase, only one domain exists: the *project*. The first domains can be immediately identified, particularly when modelling the key entities in a system.

Within these initial domains, a class determination approach is applied, whereby the classes are represented directly in internal domain views. They can then be structured in a more detailed manner, by defining the domains specific to each type of problem.

During the design phase, other more technical classes and domains are discovered via a similar class determination and structuring process. When structuring is finalized, the lowest level domains become schemas. During this same phase, the schema structure must be organized, taking care to avoid dependency loops.

To conclude, the following structuring approach is applied:

- Initial domains are defined (the application being the first),
- Classes in these domains are determined,
- Class model is consolidated,
- Classes are grouped together into problem categories (new domains are defined),
- Model is checked for redundancy between specific classes in each domain (duplicate definition),
- *End* domains are defined (domains referencing the classes directly),
- Dependency loops between end domains are removed,
- End domains are transformed into schemas.

140 Structuring

Rule: *For a given problem, the structure is complete when every class belongs to one schema.*

Chapters 8 and 9 give a detailed explanation of the class determination approach.

Example: Using a multi-tasking application

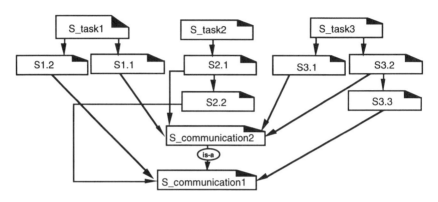

Figure 7.26 Schema diagram from a multi-tasking application.

The following example (using specific structuring domains) concerns a multi-tasking or multi-process application. Each task corresponds to an executable binary file and is described using a specific schema diagram. A root schema forms the entry point when the task is executed. Several tasks can share schemas corresponding to shared code libraries. This is typically the case for low-level utility libraries, such as those for inter-task communication management. As a result, a schema diagram of the type illustrated in Figure 7.26 is obtained.

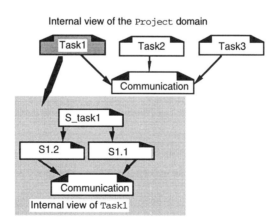

Figure 7.27 Structuring of a multi-tasking application into domains.

The domains used to represent this type of diagram, in which one domain is defined per task, each present a specific point of view.

The internal view of the `Project` domain may simply present the *task1*, *task2* and *task3* domains. The `Communication` domain is then defined locally for each of the *taskX* domains.

In this example, domains are used to represent how each of the tasks and the parts shared by these tasks are composed (Figure 7.27).

7.5 System modelling

7.5.1 Overview

It has been shown that domains and schemas are useful in that they provide a general overview of the software, regardless of its size. Domain views, however, are a static view of the system and do not provide any indication regarding its operation.

The *data flows* between domains or schemas are, therefore, represented to give a macroscopic understanding of how these entities cooperate. In this manner, it will be seen that an existing or new system can be quickly represented from a functional point of view, and architecture diagrams can be easily set up during the technical analysis phase.

Finally, a top-down class determination approach is also possible, using the flow diagrams as a starting point.

7.5.2 Flow diagrams

A *flow diagram* is used to review the data exchanged between different entities:

- Domains,
- Schemas,
- Classes.

It does not define processing or sequences, but parts of the information communicated between classes or groups of classes.

A first draft can be obtained immediately, using the synopses defined spontaneously when representing any system.

Flow diagrams provide a general view of the system (Figure 7.28) and are used to derive system functions and execution scenarios. Details on the information receiver or sender classes can also be included.

Events can appear on a flow diagram in order to highlight exceptional situations (for example, << budget_deficit >>).

Here, the fact that a communicating entity (domain, schema or class) is not a function or a process must be emphasized. It is a unit capable of receiving, processing or sending information. It summarizes the active elements processing the information flows, as represented by the instances of the referenced classes.

142 Structuring

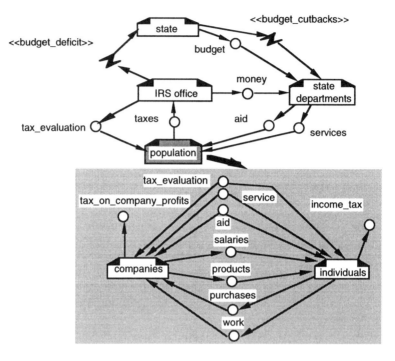

Figure 7.28 Financial flow diagrams for a state.

7.5.3 Combining flow diagrams with scenarios

The *scenarios* defined in Section 6.3 are based on flow diagrams. Unlike flow diagrams, which express the information that can be exchanged in a general way, scenarios express a typical information exchange sequence. Flow diagrams concern domains, schemas or classes, whereas scenarios concern instances. Scenarios can, however, be defined on a more general level, by taking into account the information exchanged with domains or schemas. In Figure 7.29, the scenario concerns a specific employee, without taking into account the members of the companies domain. Unlike flow diagrams, scenarios describe sequences.

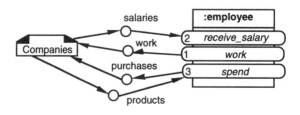

Figure 7.29 Scenario between a class and a domain.

7.5.4 Gradual class determination

Flow diagrams enable classes to be determined in a top-down approach by applying the following rules:

- Each data flow is generally a class representative (it can also correspond to message passing). When describing the more complex data flows, an inter-class inheritance diagram must be set up. For example, Figure 7.30 is used to obtain the tax_on_company_profits and income_tax classes which inherit from the tax class.

- It is possible to determine the actual entities that handle each data flow, that is the classes for which one or more methods can handle the data flow in input or output mode, as in the case of the employee class.

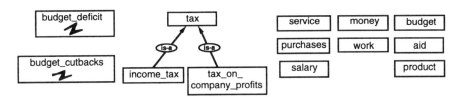

Figure 7.30 Classes extracted from the flow diagram in Figure 7.28, the definition for which must be reworked.

This approach is therefore used to determine the initial classes for a system. It complements the class determination approach, described in Chapter 9.

8 Modelling rules

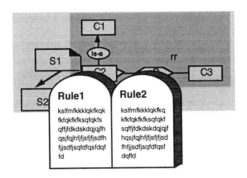

This chapter provides further information on the model (**elementary classes**), the traps to be avoided and the rules to be applied. The purpose of these rules is to obtain an *ideal* modelling form when a problem is being analysed, so that it can be easily implemented during the design phase.

8.1 Handling instances

8.1.1 Elementary and non-elementary classes

Overview

In the example below, the code is written in a pseudo-language:

```
-- Declaration of three instances in the 'integer' class
i : integer ;
j : integer ;
k : integer ; -- Intermediary variable
k := j ;
j := i ;
i := k ;
```

This code is fairly standard and contains apparently nothing out of the ordinary. But if the same code is looked at again and a different object class selected, the following result is obtained:

```
-- Declaration of three instances in the 'person' class
John   : person ;
Smith  : person ;
Arthur : person ; -- Intermediary variable
Arthur := Smith ;
Smith  := John ;
John   := Arthur ;
```

This new version, which applies the same structure, is more surprising: if a human society were the problem domain and humans corresponded to `customers`, `citizens`, and so on, the creation of a `person` instance is an important act.

This act cannot be represented by defining a temporary variable.

Moreover, the `Smith := John` assignment has no meaning when talking about humans:

```
Can one person be replaced by another?
Can several instances represent the same person?
```

These problems do not exist for `integer` instances: integers can be created and copied, as required, without taking into account existing instances, duplicates or temporary items. If new classes, such as `complex` for complex numbers or `cartesian` for two-dimensional point coordinates, are defined, they will have the same characteristics as the `integer` class.

On the other hand, classes such as `insurance` and `bank account` cannot be instantiated temporarily, as is the case of the `person` class.

Thus, it can be said that some classes have instances that are controlled by the application, whereas others can have any number of instances. This second type of class is called an *elementary class*.

Definition

Any class for which the identities, the number of instances or their very existence have an impact on the application, are considered to be non-elementary. For example, company management identifies and attaches great importance to each of the `invoice`, `order` and `customer` elements, whereas the `string`, `boolean` or `integer` concepts are simply used to handle or store information.

An elementary class has the following two characteristics:

- Its instances are not controlled by the application (the existence of a new instance is of little importance),
- The values of its instances are considered to be non-decomposable.

The users of this class are not concerned with the individual properties of its instances, but with a global value. For example, the `real` class (Figure 8.1) is decomposed internally into *index* and *mantissa*. It is an elementary class, as only the overall value of `real` is of interest.

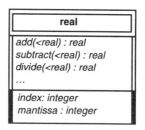

Figure 8.1 Any external user of real does not access its indexes and mantissas.

When classes are modelled, a distinction is made between elementary and non-elementary classes, as illustrated in Figure 8.2.

Abstract classes are, however, an exception to this rule, as it is not necessary to decide whether they are elementary. For example, the `object` class (which groups together all classes) is an abstract class for which some derived classes are non-elementary.

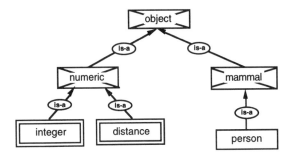

Figure 8.2 Examples of elementary, non-elementary and abstract classes.

Rules for elementary classes

- A relation cannot lead to an elementary class.
- A class attribute must concern an elementary class (first normal form in this case).
- An elementary class has no identifier.
- An elementary class cannot inherit from a non-elementary class (non abstract), and vice versa.
- An elementary class never has control or trigger automata.

Note: *The elementary class notion is fundamental to modelling, as it has a direct impact on what must be represented in attribute or relation form. It gives additional meaning to class instances and indicates their relative importance.*

The elementary class notion is apparent during programming, particularly when using C++: only this type of class can have temporary instances. For example, only an elementary class instance can be an attribute or passed by value when sending a message.

Predefined elementary classes

The following predefined elementary classes exist in the class relation model:

- `integer`: set of natural integers.
- `boolean`: set of *TRUE, FALSE* values.
- `char`: set of defined characters ({a,b....}).
- `real`: set of real values.
- `string`: character string.
- `enumerate`: finite subset of `integers`, where each integer value is a literal. An enumerated class called `traffic_lights`, with three possible literal values `red`, `green` and `orange`, is declared in the following manner: 'enumerate traffic_lights (red, green, orange);'.
- `state`: possible states for a class.
- `exception`: exceptions that can be sent or received by methods.

8.1.2 Object identifier

Each object is identified by the fact that it exists. This definition is not, however, sufficient in most cases, as the object must be identified by a value. For example, a *house* must be identified by its *address* so as to be able to mail a letter to it. Each *car* must be identified by a *registration number*, in case a traffic ticket has to be issued.

From a technical point of view, the need for an **identifier** is seen particularly in database management applications, or when objects are shared by several tasks.

Definition: *The identifier for an entity is the minimal number of assigned values (attributes) required to characterize each of its representatives.*

In a simple model, the `person` class can be assigned its `name` as an identifier, but this is insufficient when processing bank customers or social security files. In the banking example, references to '`Lastname, Firstname, Date of birth` and `Place of birth`' may be sufficient to characterize the individual (Figure 8.3), but they are not enough for the social security example, which requires a specific identifier to ensure unicity (`social security number`).

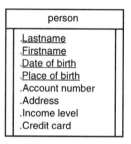

Figure 8.3 Identifiers (underlined attributes) for the `person` entity in a banking application.

The fact that an identifier is required to characterize each of the representatives in a class means that administrative bodies often assign numbers (*military ID, bank account number, car registration number*).

The existence of an identifier in a database enables one entity to be referenced by another. The `bank account number` attribute defined for the `person` entity is used to establish a link between a `person` and his or her `bank account`. This corresponds to a reference and the pointer notion in programming languages.

Rule: *An elementary class never has an identifier.*

8.1.3 Handling instance sets

The way in which a class relation model is implemented determines how relations and some classes are transformed into programming structures, enabling links between elements (access keys, pointers), or sets of links (lists, arrays, and so on) to be managed. The instance set notion should never be represented in either way in the class relation model. However before discussing this statement further, a technique whereby a class is considered to be a set, is reviewed and a modelling counter-example is given.

Technique for accessing class instances

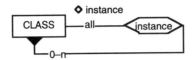

Figure 8.4 Representation of a class handling its instances.

Class instances can be accessed by considering the class to be a set of its current instances. By default, a class contains an unlimited number of instances. The model in Figure 8.4 is used to specify that the number of instances is limited and to indicate systematically the way in which class instances are accessed. For example, the third instance of person can be accessed in the following way: person instance (3).

Single-instance classes, which can have a maximum of one instance within an application, are of particular importance. This may be the case for classes representing a *sequencer, centralized handling device* or *system*, and so on.

This mechanism for accessing class instances is a special case of *class relations*. In other words, there is a class relation called instance between the class set and its instances, each of which plays the role of instance. The relation cardinality in the class→instance direction is *0–n* and the reverse cardinality is *all*.

8.1.4 Class relation modelling counter-example

All sets in a model result from defining a class or relation. Lists, arrays and other set structures simply implement a class or relation. Set structures are never concepts.

Rule: *The terms 'list', 'array' or 'set' must never appear in a class relation model, as they indicate incorrect use of the modelled classes or the existence of non-modelled relations.*

As a result, in the example concerning the 19th century human society in Section 4.2.4, Figure 4.20, the woman set is accessed via the woman class and the set of wives for Mr. Smith is accessed via the wife role in the marriage relation: smith wife().

The following problem highlights a case where it may be tempting to use such terms in a model. This problem is taken from specifications for a programming language compiler, as it analyses input text, stores the terms in this text and then processes them. Its exact description is given below.

> The symbol table stores each occurrence of a symbol in the source text to be analysed. A symbol is identified by a unique name-type combination specified when it is declared. Several symbols can be declared with the same name, but they must be of different types: the symbol first defined with a given name is then masked by the current symbol with the same name.
> The names are stored as the declaration is analysed. Given storage space restrictions, the name of duplicate symbols is stored only once in the symbol table.
> A declared symbol will then be used in the text: it references the symbol currently visible. Each time a symbol is used, its occurrence is stored and identified by the line number on which it appears. The symbol table is built when analysing the input source. The list of symbols, their types and occurrences is updated when the entire text has been analysed.

The analyst given this problem immediately produced the model in Figure 8.5.

150 Modelling rules

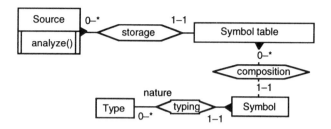

Figure 8.5 Incorrect class relation model.

Such a model is incorrect as it models a set-based structure, where the symbol table is represented as a class. The error was made because the above problem combined different conceptual, logical and physical levels (see the software lifecycle in Section 7.1) and *immediately* introduced the table notion which in fact corresponds to a possible technical solution. In the same way, constraints of the type *symbols with the same names must not be of the same type* should not appear at this stage, as they will be handled during implementation.

All declared symbols are handled, which means that the symbol class defined must handle its set of instances. The above symbol table is the symbol class itself. The class relation model provides a way of declaring this fact (instance relation), and it will be seen in Chapter 13 that primitives can be used to handle the set of current instances in a class. The solution to this problem should therefore be based on a model similar to the one illustrated in Figure 8.6.

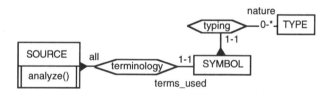

Figure 8.6 The symbol table is the symbol class itself.

If only some of the symbols were to be handled in the table by the application, this would indicate that a specific relation exists between the source and symbol classes. It does not, however, imply that a symbol table class must be represented.

Going back to the problem description, constraints such as symbol identification by name and type will be expressed as a symbol class invariant. The declaration line number is an attribute of symbol and depending on the importance attached to how a symbol is used, each symbol will be linked to its *users* or will have a set of *use* line numbers as an attribute. Class methods will be defined for the symbol class in order to retrieve other symbols and control symbol masking.

8.2 Normal form laws

8.2.1 Advantage of normal forms

The class relation structure model is heavily based on the entity-relationship model, frequently used when modelling databases.

During database design, information redundancy is a key problem.

If, however, a `person` is linked to a `car` as its owner and the age of the owner is declared as an attribute of the `car`, problems are systematically generated in the database. The information is not in the right place (as the age is relative to the `person` and not to the `car`). Moreover, this generates absurd queries if the age of a `person` is to be determined (as his or her `cars` must be consulted). It also duplicates information in the database (if the `person` has several `cars`, the age is duplicated for each `car`); moreover, the age of the `person` may also be defined as an attribute of `person`. All this leads to an incoherent database: if the age of a `person` changes, all attributes storing the age must then be updated.

To solve this type of problem, rules called *normal form laws* have been defined to characterize correct entity-relationship modelling. To obtain standard modelling, these normal form laws must be respected.

These laws are also very interesting in that they help determine which concepts are to be defined and where each piece of information is to be placed within the context of the model. They help clarify a model and define consistent concepts.

Duplicate information and consistency problems exist for all applications, as all application data must be stored.

There are five normal forms which guarantee application consistency. In this book, only the first three, most commonly used forms will be discussed. These laws must be applied on the model in turn (for the third normal form to be respected, the second one must be respected and to respect the second, the first must be respected).

8.2.2 Functional dependency

Not all values in an application are necessarily mutually independent. **Functional dependency** is therefore declared between attribute A1 and attributes A2, ..., An, to indicate that the value of A1 depends solely on the values of attributes A2, ..., An. In other words, a mathematical function f, such that $A1=f(A2, ...,An)$, exists.

Functional dependency may sometimes be expressed by a formula, but is often semantic and inherent in the problem studied. It cannot, therefore, be expressed as a compute function. For example:

- A nickname given to a person depends on that person's first name.

- The type of product purchased determines the tax rate applied.

- An employee's salary may depend on that person's category, degree or experience.

A functional dependency diagram can thus be defined for all information handled by the application. The normal form laws are based on these functional dependencies and govern how entities are defined and how attributes are assigned to these entities.

8.2.3 First normal form

The first normal form (Figure 8.7) stipulates that no attribute can be defined as a data structure or a set of values (array, list). Class or relation properties must be elementary.

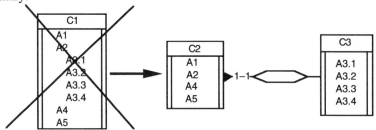

Figure 8.7 Application of the first normal form.

The purpose of this rule is to avoid defining nested or hidden classes, or nesting the same occurrences in different locations.

Rule: *Only non-decomposable values can be class attributes. This means that attributes are always associated with an elementary class.*

Moreover, the following inheritance-based rule can be added:

Rule: *Each class property must be significant for all instances (Figure 8.8).*

In the class relation model, attributes can also be a set of elementary classes.

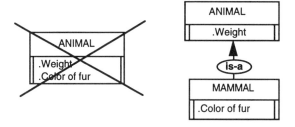

Figure 8.8 Some animals do not have fur.

8.2.4 Second normal form

The second normal form ensures that each entity has an identifier and that each attribute that is not part of the identifier is dependent on the whole identifier. For example, the model in Figure 8.9 does not comply with the second normal form.

Rule: *The value of an attribute must depend wholly on the value of the corresponding instance.*

Normal form laws   153

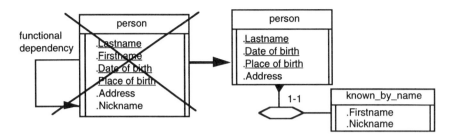

Figure 8.9 Application of the second normal form.

The following rules are applied in Figure 8.10. When attributes are assigned to a relation, its properties must depend individually on all aspects of that relation. If there is partial dependency on a sub-relation, the relation must be decomposed into two sub-relations, or the relation attribute must be transferred to one of the classes concerned.

CASE N°1: THE COEFFICIENT DOES NOT APPLY TO ALL EXAMS TAKEN BY THE STUDENT

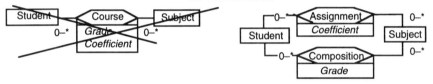

CASE N°2: THE BUILDING NUMBER DOES NOT DEPEND ON THE STUDENT

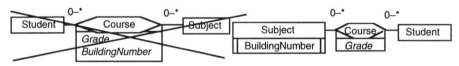

Figure 8.10 Violation of the second normal form.

8.2.5 Third normal form

The third normal form stipulates that any attribute assigned to an entity must depend *directly* on the identifier. The model in Figure 8.11 is invalid, as the `policy date` attribute does not depend directly on the `policy_holder` identifier, but more immediately on the `policy number` attribute. The consequence of this error is that a hidden class (the `insurance_policy` class) is nested in the `policy_holder` class definition.

Rule: *The value of an attribute must depend solely on the value of the instance with which it is associated. It must never depend on another class attribute unless that attribute is the whole class identifier.*

154 Modelling rules

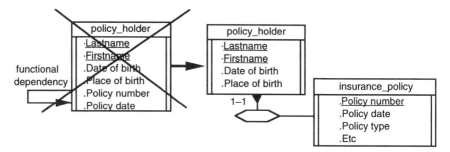

Figure 8.11 Application of the third normal form.

When a model has been finalized (particularly during the analysis phase), it must be checked to ensure that it complies with the first three normal form laws. Model standardization helps to identify certain classes, the definition of which may be hidden in the model. For a given problem, the possible solutions must converge towards a single ideal model, when the normal form laws are applied.

Any duplicate relation must be deleted or simply summarize a series of other relations. If all employees in a division must be assigned to a project within that division, the `administrative dependency` relation shown in Figure 8.12 should not exist. In fact, this `administrative dependency` relation is simply composed of the `assignment` and `responsibility` relations.

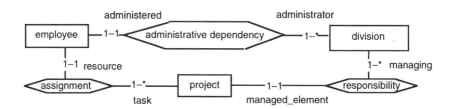

Figure 8.12 Possible relation redundancy.

8.3 Correct and valid modelling

A model is an abstraction of the *real-world*. It is quite possible to define a model which complies with all modelling rules, but which does not reflect the real world. The model is then said to be correct, but invalid. The software developed will not provide the necessary services. Rules enable the development team to ensure that the model is correct, whereas only a specific methodological approach can ensure its validity.

8.3.1 Counter-examples: correct but invalid models

Absurd models

In the following example, novice analysts wish to model the elements that exist on Earth (`minerals`, `vegetables`, `animals`, and so on). It is, of course, obvious how these elements should be classified (using the `animal`, `mammal`, `dog` concepts for example), but the novices must make their own decisions.

Correct and valid modelling

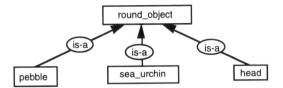

Figure 8.13 An absurd model.

By trial and error, they may discover any number of different classifications, which are mathematically sound, but which would be immediately dismissed by specialists (Figure 8.13). Such a classification, even if true, would not allow the novices to define a good model. This is because they do not know which criteria are pertinent when classifying these elements. In other words, everything can be expressed using a model, but the most demanding task is to determine the correct relationship required by that domain.

The quest for factorization

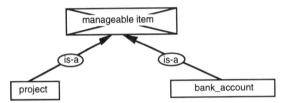

Figure 8.14 Factorization by inheritance.

The fact that a model contains multiple levels of inheritance does not necessarily mean that it is good. A typical mistake made by novices in object-oriented modelling is that they attempt to apply this exciting new technique to every conceivable situation.

The novice approach is as follows: *if two classes have a property in common, a base class should be defined to factorize it*. Although the principle is correct, care must be taken to avoid excessive use of inheritance. For example, if a project class is defined and contains a manage() method, and a bank_account class has the same method, it is both possible and tempting to create the model in Figure 8.14.

In theory, this model is not wrong; unfortunately it has very little meaning. Upon inspection of this model, a project management specialist or a banker would be taken aback. In this case, the following questions must be asked:

- Does the manage() method in the manageable_item class really factorize something? In other words, can some of the functions performed by the manage() method be described at this level?

- If the manage() method is defined at this level, does it have any meaning? Is it now possible to express the pre-conditions, and more importantly the post-conditions for this method?

- Does the manageable_item class really factorize something? In other words, do we need to handle a project or a bank_account in a transparent way? More importantly, does the application actually handle the manageable_item concept?

- Is the `manageable_item` concept important to the user?

Some cases are more ambiguous: it may be possible to factorize part of the code, but the resulting base class definition would be limited and its presence may hinder or complicate structuring into classes and schemas. This can lead, for example, to multiple inheritance or, during design, to a model that is difficult to integrate (see Section 11.5.3).

In such ambiguous cases, it is probably worthwhile duplicating part of the description in order to simplify the structure.

8.3.2 Rules determining correctness

For a model to be correct, the following properties must be respected:

- A class is a stable category in the application,
- All the properties defined for the class (attributes, methods, relations, and so on) are true for each instance, including those in the derived classes,
- An instance in a derived class can always be considered to be an instance of the base class,
- The relations represent stable links between instances,
- Class states are stable states for its instances,
- The pre- and post-condition and invariant rules are respected (extension of post-conditions, restriction of pre-conditions, extension of invariants between derived classes, and so on),
- The trigger automata respect the rules defined in the corresponding control automata,
- Any automaton specified by inheritance respects the laws defined in Chapter 5,
- The normal form laws are respected,
- The class and member names are unique.

8.3.3 Techniques for defining a valid model

A model is valid if it suitably reflects the *real world* with which it is concerned. To do so, several techniques must be used in conjunction.

Using a dictionary

A **dictionary** contains all the terminology used in the *real-world* and thus in the problem statements. It comprises all common names, proper names and verbs used in that domain. It helps:

- Define the initial modelling items. Common names can be modelled in terms of:
    - Classes,
    - Roles,
    - Relations,
    - Attributes.

Proper names can be expressed in terms of:

- Parameters,
- Data flows.

The verbs may correspond to methods.

This correspondence depends on the importance and role of each item. Each term must be carefully analysed, particular care being taken with *synonyms* (different names designating the same thing) and with *polysemes* (words with more than one meaning).

- Check that each of the terms is represented in the model and, if necessary, justify any omission.

Avoiding any preconceived abstraction

Initially, the model must adhere to the *real-world* information. Any material likely to contain worthwhile information must be used. For example, forms, factsheets, procedures and invoices are valuable sources of information when computerizing a company.

The same terminology must be used systematically. The initial concepts modelled must be familiar to all, since new abstractions can evolve only after obtaining an in-depth understanding of the domain and after an initial model has been created for the information gathered. In the same way, inheritance can only be declared if it is self-evident in the problem description.

For each class, it must be possible to define the meaning of an instance and its role in the *real world*.

Using a need to justify a class definition

Chapter 9 explains the class determination approach. When a new class is defined, or more importantly when an existing class is decomposed by inheritance, this choice must be backed up by requirements in the real environment (other classes, users). For example, the *mammal* concept does not have to exist, but is made necessary by handling requirements.

Using the overall system model or architecture diagram

It will be seen later in this book, when discussing system definition (Section 10.2) or software **architecture** representation (Section 11.1.2), that flow diagrams are used to define initial models. Using this source of information, classes can be determined in two additional ways:

- Each data flow is related to a class which determines its type (invoice, payment, and so on) or to a class method,

- The system can be decomposed (sub-domains), until the active elements (objects) that process input and output flows have been determined.

This approach reinforces the previous ones.

8.4 Design rules

8.4.1 Avoiding mutual dependency

Drawbacks of mutual dependency

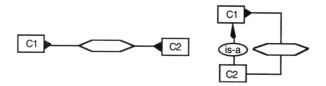

Figure 8.15 Examples of mutual conceptual use.

Mutual use between two classes must be minimized (Figure 8.15), as it reflects **unit test** and **integration** difficulties, which could be fatal to the software development project. It should be noted that mutual use between two classes belonging to different schemas is not permitted. Mutual use is of increasing gravity, depending on whether the use is *operational*, *contextual* or *conceptual* respectively. Mutual use also indicates high model complexity and an insufficient level of encapsulation.

The various techniques described in the following paragraphs demonstrate how to avoid mutual dependency.

Generalizing a property

Example: box/link dependency

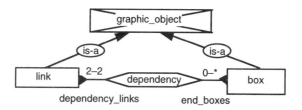

Figure 8.16 Mutual box/link use.

In an interactive graphic application, the notions of box and link are defined. Both are special cases of a more general concept called graphic_object. A link is attached to a box. When a box is moved, the dependency_links also move. Moreover, the appropriate end_boxes must be informed when a link is deleted or created. Finally, to be able to calculate where a link intersects with its end_boxes, the link must be aware of the box frame. An initial schema is therefore created (shown in Figure 8.16).

By observing this mutual dependency more closely, it can be seen that the link is only dependent on the graphic_object part of the box when it interacts with it and vice versa Moreover, the box/link dependency can be generalized to many other graphic_objects. The model can thus be improved as shown in Figure 8.17.

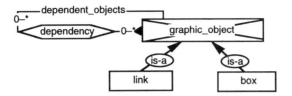

Figure 8.17 Generalizing a dependency relation.

This new model, however, has a drawback: specifically the fact that the object dependent on a box must be a link and that the object dependent on a link must be a box is no longer expressed in this model, nor is the fact that a link connects two boxes. This problem is solved by expressing these constraints as class invariants. On the other hand, this more general model enables software to be upgraded in that a link can be connected to another link, for example. The decision to select one model rather than another must be made by evaluating the comparative advantages of precision and extensibility.

Decomposing into general and specific parts

Principle

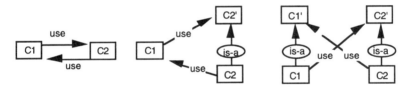

Figure 8.18 Removing a mutual dependency by decomposing one or two classes

A general technique based on inheritance can be applied to remove mutual uses (Figure 8.18). When a mutual use exists between two classes C1 and C2, the following question must be asked: *Does the use between C1 and C2 (or vice versa) need to be integral, that is, does C1 need to access all of C2 or can it just access a subset (C2') of C2?* Depending on the answer, C2 can be decomposed into two classes, thereby removing the the mutual use. Ideally, the opposite should also hold true (C1 can be decomposed into two derived classes). In the latter case, three possibilities exist: either one or the other of the classes can be decomposed, or they can be both decomposed. Unfortunately, such a situation is very rare, as it would mean that C1 and C2 are closely interlinked. The following question must then be asked: *Can C1 and C2 be grouped together into a single class?*

This mechanism will now be demonstrated using two examples.

Example 1: Using a plumber and a grocery_store

Two classes are defined: a plumber and a grocery_store (Figure 8.19). In the corresponding problem, the plumber purchases food at the grocery_store and the grocery_store has its plumbing repaired by the plumber.

160 Modelling rules

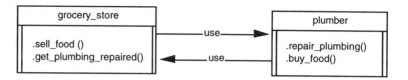

Figure 8.19 Mutual use between a plumber and a grocery_store.

In this real-life situation, mutual usage exists between the two classes, but in fact can be avoided. By observing this dependency in greater detail, it can be seen that the dependency is not integral; only part of the plumber class definition needs to use the grocery_store class (buy_food()) and similarly, only part of the grocery_store class definition causes the plumber class to be implemented (get_plumbing_repaired()). Moreover, when looking at the plumber and grocery_store more closely, it can be seen that the plumber concept is not required to define the grocery_store concept, and vice versa.

In Figure 8.20, the general concepts of grocery_store and plumber are defined with the respective methods of sell_food() and repair_plumbing(). In the application, they will be further specified by adding get_plumbing_repaired() and buy_food() methods to the general classes by inheritance. This requires inter-dependency. Thus, two schemas, one called small_store and the other called small_store_application, can be created, the first one defining the general grocery_store and plumber notions, while the second provides more specific information. In this way, mutual usage is deleted (coupling between grocery_store and plumber is minimized) and the problem can be decomposed into two separate schemas.

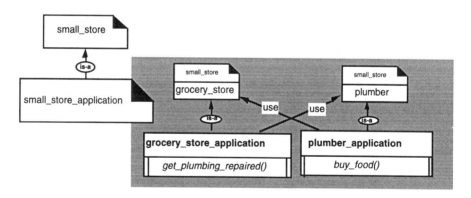

Figure 8.20 Deleting mutual grocery_store/plumber dependencies.

Example 2: Schema using its own users
The technique demonstrated here is of particular interest when designing a schema that uses the services of its users. The following example concerns the well-known concept of toolkits defined for the X-Windows multi-windowing software, such as Motif or Open Look. This type of application is specific in that it provides services to

Design rules 161

programmers (the means to create graphic windows), and also informs them when external actions (mouse click) are performed on these windows.

When a widget (window object – a basic toolkit component) is used, its callbacks must be defined. Callbacks are application functions that are triggered when the application user interacts with the widget. Depending on the type of window (button, scroll bar, menu, and so on), the user can perform a finite number of actions via the mouse or keyboard (click, drag, keystroke). All the actions permitted for a specific widget are declared in callbacks. The programmer using a toolkit determines which widgets are to be used – the windows to be displayed – and for each of them defines the actions to be taken on user request. In other words, for the selected widgets, the programmer declares the functions performed by the program in callback form. When the software is executed, the toolkit system recognizes the user actions on the displayed windows and invokes the appropriate callback functions (Figure 8.21).

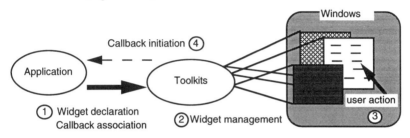

Figure 8.21 The Toolkit library transmits the user actions to the application.

Thus, the toolkit system can be described as a library which uses callbacks to execute an application, regardless of the application's nature.

The callback technique uses C *function pointers* to call a function without knowing whether it exists. Although this principle is very elegant, it is based more on a programming *trick of the trade* than on real object-oriented modelling. It will now be seen how such a mechanism can be defined within the context of a class relation model.

This case constitutes a mechanism for avoiding mutual use (between the application and the toolkit library), for which the general solution has already been given. A widget class does not need a full definition of the application that invokes it (where the callbacks are defined), but merely a sub-set indicating all possible reactions (actions resulting from each keyboard or mouse event generated by the final user). A widget_user class can then be created for all objects handling widgets in the applications that implement toolkits (Figure 8.22).

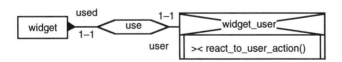

Figure 8.22 Defining a widget and its possible users.

162 Modelling rules

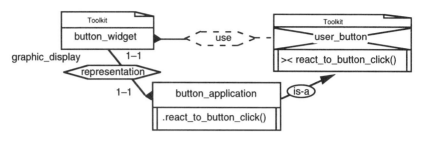

Figure 8.23 Implementing a button_widget.

An abstract user is therefore defined, thus modelling the basic behaviour expected from all widget users. When a real user of the widget class is defined, it must inherit from the widget_user class in order to implement its behaviour by redefining the react_to_user_action() method (see the example in Figure 8.23). Various possible widgets and each of their respective widget_user classes (as each defined widget recognizes specific user actions) can be represented in a schema called toolkit. The widget_user class represents the widget as seen by the application, whereas the widget represents the visual part (the window).

Interface class technique

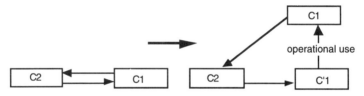

Figure 8.24 Reducing mutual dependency by using the interface class C'1.

The interface class technique can always be used as a last resort (Figure 8.24). Its principle is straightforward: if mutual use exists between C1 and C2, class C'1 is defined to provide the same services to C2 as C1 and is based entirely on C1 when performing these services. In this way, C2→C'1 dependency replaces C2→C1 dependency and the mutual dependency is removed. A loop does still exist, but the type of dependency between C'1 and C1 is not as serious (operational use).

8.4.2 Encapsulating

Encapsulation control is a significant part of the **design** phase when the model is divided up into independent self-contained parts. This enables the software to be developed in separate parts, tests to be conducted independently and software modules to be reused in other products. It also avoids having to control a complex application in one single unit.

Using visibility

Class member visibility must be minimized (private or protected visibilities), in order to guarantee maximum encapsulation. Both the public elements in a model and the number of public classes in each schema must therefore be minimized.

Design rules 163

Using events

Events are a powerful way of enabling two software elements to communicate, even if they are not aware of each other's existence. The only shared knowledge is the complete definition of the classes representing these events.

For example, a model can contain ship and fish classes (Figure 8.25). These two classes have no apparent mutual awareness of each other, even though any interaction between instances will require one of the two classes to use the other. In this manner, if a fish has to move out of the way of an oncoming ship, a traditional program would require the ship to send a move message to each fish present. The event technique, on the other hand, enables the ship class to send an «enter_area» event each time it enters a new area, thereby giving any occupant sufficient time to leave the area.

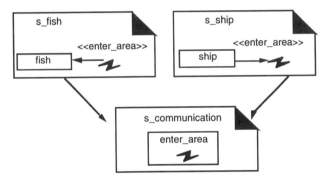

Figure 8.25 Events allowing communication without mutual awareness.

This in fact corresponds to reality, as fish move out of the way of a ship, when they detect the corresponding vibrations (events).

Masking derived classes

In a compiler, the role of a lexical and syntax analyser is to analyse a piece of source code, build the appropriate objects and determine a syntactical-semantic network for them. The objects created are elements defined in the syntax, such as *variables* or *types*. Once the object network has been built, these objects are used to generate code in a programming language.

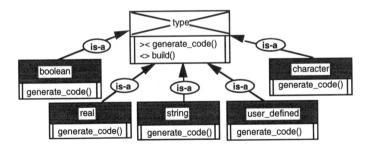

Figure 8.26 Creating a schema to mask all derived classes.

Many different types exist in this syntax, such as *boolean, integer, real, character, string*, and so on. When handling these types, the rest of the application is concerned only with its ability to generate the appropriate type in the specified programming language. It is, therefore, worthwhile masking the different types from the class users that implement them, so that they only have access to an abstract class, usually called *type* (Figure 8.26).

Users of this `s_type` schema, therefore, have limited access to the `type` class via a single method called `generate_code()`, each instance reacting in compliance with its end class definitions.

An instantiation problem does, however, arise for these objects which are of different types. If, for example, an object of the boolean type is to be instantiated, an instruction of the `boolean create()` type must be executed and the end class for this object must be known and handled. However, this is precisely the type of information being masked.

This conflict can be resolved by defining a class method `build()` in the `type` class. When the analyser encounters a boolean occurrence as recognized by the boolean character string in the source program, it then activates this class method: `type build("boolean")`, with the following code:

```
build (occurence : in string) return type ...
   processing
      DEPENDING ON occurence
         CASE "boolean" : boolean create ()
         CASE "integer" : integer create () ...
```

There is an operational use from the `type` class to its derived classes (use in the class body to implement instance creation); this is the most benign form of mutual usage. By applying this technique, users of the `s_type` schema are unaware of the classes derived from `type`. Only the criterion characterizing how an object is built is known to them.

8.5 General modelling approach

8.5.1 Determining classes

The problem to be solved must be modelled using the techniques described in Section 8.3.3:

- Use a *dictionary*,

- Avoid any preconceived abstractions,

- *Justify* class and method definitions in terms of needs, by applying the class determination approach taken from the **user** point of view (Chapter 9),

- Use system or architecture models, if required (to determine classes by decomposing *flow diagrams*).

By respecting method, relation and attribute definition rules (Section 8.3.2), these techniques enable the application *structure model* to be built. *Elementary classes* must be identified to determine which elements should become attributes or relations. The *structure* (schemas and domains) can be created *immediately*, in particular by using domains, or *later in the lifecycle*. This is particularly true in the case of schemas. *Invariants* must be specified, in order to give as precise a definition as possible of each class.

8.5.2 Finalizing method definition

For each class, try to determine which new services may be of use. The structure model has been set up to a large extent at this stage.

Describe the main *scenarios* used to check the validity of the classes in the system and the way in which they cooperate.

For each class, define the *operating model*:

- If the methods in the class cannot be invoked in any order, define a control automaton,
- Define the pre- and post-conditions for each method.

8.5.3 Defining how the system operates

Determine which objects have systematic behaviour patterns and which react in given conditions. Object reactivity must be described in class-level *trigger automata*.

Describe how the key methods operate, using the *object flow* model.

Events may be brought to light when modelling the reactive objects in the system, defining scenarios or when specific communication requirements are highlighted (exceptions, asynchronous mode, and so on).

8.5.4 Handling encapsulation and inter-dependencies during the design phase

Structure all classes into schemas. Specify the visibility for each class and each of its members, taking care to minimize public access. Avoid mutual dependency between classes and, more importantly, between schemas. If necessary, apply the principles described in this chapter (interface classes, and so on).

9 Methodology: SOFTWARE development phases

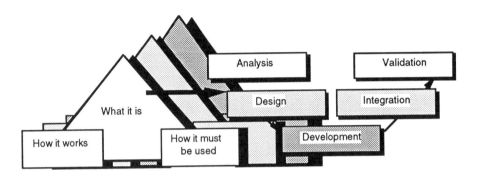

Note: *The previous chapters explained the class relation model (the way a problem is formally represented) and aspects of the method (the way the model is used). This chapter will now study the methodology, which defines how the model is applied during the various software development phases.*

9.1 Software lifecycle basics

9.1.1 General lifecycle and phase description

Overview

Software development corresponds to the production of a 'made to measure' product which meets a specific goal. The production process is divided into several **phases** (Figure 9.1). These phases can be applied to any technical domain, such as during construction or mechanical manufacturing projects.

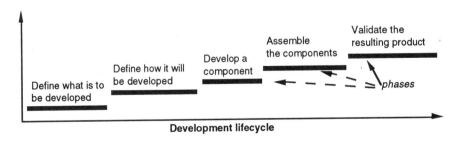

Figure 9.1 Project management approach.

The **lifecycle** notion formalizes these phases and measures project team progress from the customer requirement specification through to development of the final code and submission of the finished product.

The lifecycle notion has evolved at the same rhythm as the computing industry. This chapter discusses several forms of lifecycle, each of which is suited to different development structures.

In all lifecycles, the phases are linked together in sequence. A *phase* represents a development stage and is characterized by a particular purpose. For example:

- *Preparation phase* (or organization): its purpose is to define which development approach will be adopted and what hardware and software environment will be used for the product.

- *Analysis*: its purpose is to define the system to be developed, its inherent functions, and so on.

Traditional lifecycle forms

Waterfall or V lifecycle

One example of a traditional lifecycle is the *waterfall* lifecycle, an improved version of which is called the *V* lifecycle. Most of the phases in these two lifecycles are reused in nearly every lifecycle.

Rather than recommending a particular lifecycle form, this chapter describes how the *standard* phases can be applied to the class relation approach.

The following basic procedure (illustrated in Figure 9.1) must be used when developing a product or meeting a requirement:

- First describe what is to be developed (*analysis*).
- Then explain how it will be developed (*design*), placing particular importance on how:
  - The total product is decomposed into intermediary components (preliminary design) by describing the overall operating principles,
  - Each of the intermediary components will be developed (**detailed design**).
- Build the product by developing each component (**coding**).
- Validate each component developed (*unit tests*).
- Assemble the components and test the resulting product (*integration*).
- Validate the resulting product to ensure that it complies with requirements (**validation**).

Specific characteristics of the V lifecycle: upward and downward phases

The V lifecycle is illustrated in Figure 9.2. The downward phases correspond to definition and development phases, whereas the upward phases correspond to assembly and validation.

The class relation model is particularly concerned with the analysis and design phases, but also contributes to coding, testing, integration and validation.

Software lifecycle basics   169

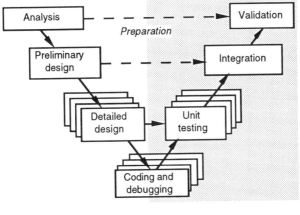

Figure 9.2 V lifecycle.

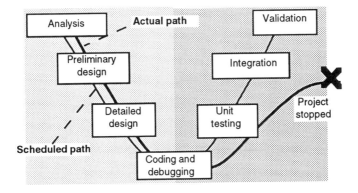

Figure 9.3 Typical software development failure.

The V lifecycle places particular importance on how the upward phases are prepared. The downward phases (analysis, and so on) work on theoretical models which may be incorrect, inconsistent or inapplicable. The decisive test takes place when these models are actually implemented. Often during the upward phases, when the model is applied to the 'real-life' operating environment, exceptions are detected in the modelling theory and consequently the implementation diverges from the model (Figure 9.3).

To avoid these stumbling-blocks:

- The validation and integration phases must be prepared as analysis and design progress:
    - At the end of the analysis phase, validation must be prepared,
    - At the end of the design phase, integration must be prepared.

170   Methodology : software development phases

- A strict methodology must be applied and a maximum number of consistency checks made on the model.
- Tests must be conducted as the phase progresses to analyse initial implementation results, or an *incremental development* approach can be adopted (see the description of the spiral lifecycle in Section 9.1.2).

General advantages of following a lifecycle

The impact of this lifecycle extends beyond the software development framework.

When a house is built, a client expresses requirements in terms of the number of rooms, their functions, the useful surface area, the number of floors and the style.

A plan is drawn to specify its general appearance, the rooms and the layout. This operation is analogous to the *software analysis* phase.

Studies are then conducted to determine how the house will be built: choice of materials, construction techniques and foundations. These studies correspond to the *preliminary design* phase.

Before requesting the work from various professionals, additional information may be provided for each room in the form of plumbing plans, electrical wiring diagrams and so on. This information is collected during the equivalent of the *detailed design* phase.

Once the whole project has been defined, the various professionals (plumber, mason, electrician) perform their jobs in compliance with the plans. For a software development project, this corresponds to the *coding* phase.

Finally, verifications and inspections are conducted during construction, before the end product is released to the client (*test, validation*).

9.1.2 Lifecycle adaptations

Code and test

Depending on the actual requirements stipulated for a given software project, the lifecycle presented here can be either shortened or lengthened. The most basic lifecycle form is called *code and test*, whereby the solution is coded directly and then checked to ensure its correct operation. Coding is then updated and the cycle repeated until a satisfactory solution is obtained. This lifecycle, frequently followed when prototyping, is useful in that it constantly checks that the implementation is operational. It is only suitable, however, for small-scale projects. Its advantage lies in the fact that it is pragmatic (implementation is tested immediately), but its disadvantage lies in the fact that it provides no overall view or strategy.

Backstepping

Linear phase sequencing is purely theoretical. When Phase1 is completed, Phase2 uses the results of Phase1 for its particular requirements. Loop holes and anomalies are always detected.

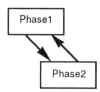

Figure 9.4 Phase2 → Phase1 backstepping.

A backstep must, therefore, be made to update the first phase in line with the comments generated during the second phase (Figure 9.4). This situation is usually represented by a backward arrow in the waterfall and V lifecycles.

Risk analysis, prototyping

V cycle limitations

The backstepping technique does not guarantee that the lifecycle will be followed correctly. If, for example, the analysis is too vague or incoherent in its expression of technical constraints or overall requirements, the design phase will fail; there will be too many backsteps and it will be impossible to control project schedules and end results. The V lifecycle is therefore over-simplified and cannot be applied *per se*.

One of the main problems is as follows. It is not always possible to provide a complete definition of the results expected from the development phase before the project team has obtained a more in-depth understanding of the software required, either by conducting development work prior to the actual coding phase, or by creating prototypes which constitute more solid foundations for decision-making.

The most popular solutions to this problem take the form of either functional tests highlighting functions and facilitating decision-making, or feasibility tests aimed at minimizing technical development risks.

Moreover, if the analysis and design phases are long and drawn out, the people concerned with the project start to lose confidence as their view of the software is highly fragmented and too far removed from the main overall functions. Intermediary results must, therefore, be presented to prove feasibility and demonstrate what the software actually does. This approach reassures all participants (management, developers, customers, and so on) that the project will actually be successful.

Risk analysis, spiral lifecycle

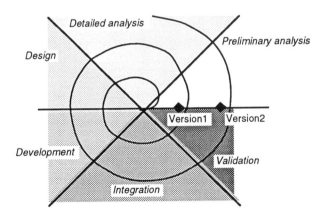

Figure 9.5 Spiral lifecycle.

The fundamental principles on which the V lifecycle is based are nevertheless valid. A strategy is therefore, adopted, whereby the software project is broken down into phases which are subsequently decomposed into into sub-parts:

- There are clearly identified sub-parts, to which a normal lifecycle can be applied locally,
- There are less evident sub-parts, on which clarification and risk analysis work must be conducted.

The work undertaken to develop the clearly identified sub-parts often clarifies the requirements for the other less evident parts. These less evident parts thus become clearly identified, and can be extracted and the cycle is repeated. This principle led to the definition of a *spiral lifecycle* by Boehm (1981), who introduced testing, prototyping and phase progress reporting in order to control inherent technical and functional risks (Figure 9.5).

The main conclusion to be drawn from this overview is that fundamental phases exist (analysis, design, and so on) and that a strategy must be adopted for each new project to define the appropriate development process.

Influence of the object model

Rule: *Lifecycle definition is not dependent on the software development techniques adopted. The use of an object-oriented language has no effect whatsoever on the lifecycle logic. The work required will, however, be modulated.*

Class relation model

The class relation method enables the project team to work on the same model from analysis through to coding. It provides automation features based on automatic code deduction and enhanced consistency management.

This approach demonstrates that the main difficulties arise during the analysis and design phases. The development and other upward lifecycle phases are easier to control. The initial lifecycle phases are, therefore, extended and the development and integration phases shortened.

Moreover, the greater emphasis placed on analysis is counterbalanced by simplified development, which means that staffing requirements are more evenly spread out over the project's lifetime. The sudden workload peaks previously experienced during the development phase are eliminated.

Hypergenericity

Hypergenericity is backed up by a language which expresses the implementation principles adopted. It forces the project team to conduct an in-depth study on the actual design, architecture and implementation principle formalization (H language).

Moreover, it enables the various software implementation strategies (for example, storage in files or databases, multi- versus mono-process architectures) to be quickly tested and adjusted. The software design phase is thus revolutionized since iterative testing can then be conducted as design decisions are made. It greatly simplifies the use of an incremental development strategy, which moves closer to the goal of a spiral lifecycle.

9.1.3 Computerizing a process: preliminary analysis

Example using a 'real' process

In this section, the term 'process' corresponds to predefined operations during which several active elements cooperate. Examples may be a *salary calculation* process, an *ore conveyor* process, a *manufacturing* process in a plant, a *CASE code production* process, and so on.

When a process is computerized, the initial lifecycle phases must be extended: firstly, the process to be automated must be represented, and secondly, the software being developed must be defined. To perform these tasks, the current process must be studied and improved upon, information flows and procedures must be rationalized and the sections that can be computerized must be highlighted.

In such cases, a **preliminary analysis** phase is required.

Preliminary analysis

The *scope* of the study must first be defined and the requirements understood. The *existing process* can then be modelled. *Development constraints* (hardware environment, performance, and so on) must be listed in order to determine what the limits and goals of the computer solution are. The process can then be remodelled to present the new structure. The sections to be computerized are deduced and the pre-analysis work conducted. At this stage, analysis *domains* must be established and the potential *users* of the system identified.

Preliminary analysis can, therefore, be defined as follows:

- Understanding of the requirements,
- Representation of the current process,
- Listing of all constraints,
- Representation of the new system,
- Definition of the software to be developed,
- Representation of the analysis domains,
- Definition of potential users.

9.2 Lifecycle definition

9.2.1 Generalized lifecycle

Overview

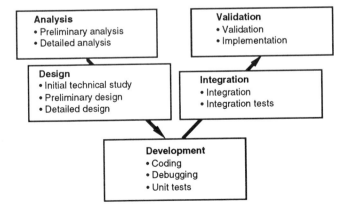

Figure 9.6 Generalized lifecycle.

174 Methodology : software development phases

This chapter adopts a generalized approach to the lifecycle (Figure 9.6) so that it can define how the model is used in each of the corresponding phases. The lifecycle can of course be adapted to the specific requirements of each individual development project. An incremental development strategy should however be adopted, whenever possible.

Purpose of each phase

The purpose of the *analysis* phase is to define which services are provided by the application. This phase is broken down into:

- *Preliminary analysis*, which defines the development framework by establishing the current situation, objectives and constraints applicable to the software. It ensures that the requirements have been correctly understood and determines the scope of the study (which parts are covered by the software).

- *Detailed analysis*, which gives an exhaustive definition of all services provided by the software.

The purpose of the *design* phase is to describe how the software will be implemented. This phase is broken down into:

- *An initial technical study*, in which the software *architecture* and implementation principles are defined. If *hypergenericity* is used, much of the design work can be systemized and thus eliminated.

- *Preliminary design*, during which the full software structure is described, together with its operating principles.

- *Detailed design*, which further extends preliminary design by preparing for the coding phase as far as possible.

The *development* phase includes system *coding* and *unit tests*. Detailed design is also sometimes considered to be part of this phase.

The purpose of the *integration* phase is to build fully operational software from the individual components developed during the previous phase. This phase includes integration testing, which checks that the components interact correctly.

The purpose of the final phase, *validation*, is to check that the software meets all requirements. *Implementation* must result in an operational software product, whixh can be made available to users.

9.2.2 Phase-specific issues

Models and lifecycle phases

Phase/model independence

Rule: *The use of a model does not characterize a lifecycle phase.*

The purpose of the analysis and design phases is to define and describe the problem to be solved. A formal representation of the problem must be given, using either a natural language or computer-based models.

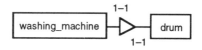

Figure 9.7 Describing a washing machine.

Current computer-based models are frequently based on notions similar to those used when programming, such as functional sequencing (SADT, SART, data Ffow) or modular coding (abstract machines).

There is no fundamental reason why the model should be changed when moving from analysis to design as, in both cases, the project team must specify which concepts are used, how they are interrelated and how the system operates. For example, a class relation model, which states that '*a washing machine is made up of a drum containing dirty washing*' (Figure 9.7), may be considered to be part of the analysis, whereas Figure 9.8, which illustrates how the washing machine operates by adding in the *ball bearing* notion, will become part of design.

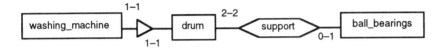

Figure 9.8 Drum rotation principle.

The fundamental differences lie in the issues considered during each lifecycle phase:

- *Analysis*: definition of the notions and services that meet the requirements and verification of overall consistency.
- *Design*: definition of how the application operates and how constraints are respected, and consideration of efficiency and software assembly issues.
- *Development*: conversion of the previously defined model into executable instructions suitable for both the computer and the development environment.

Encapsulation: a major exception

One major exception to the model-phase independency principle is encapsulation. This concept has a strong association with the design phase, as it determines which services are exported by a module (that is those required for other modules to operate).

During the analysis phase, all described classes are notions with which the user is familiar and can, therefore, be seen and accessed freely. The design phase, however, is concerned with stipulating how classes are accessed and setting visibility restrictions.

Rule: *The analysis phase is not concerned with modelling item visibility.*

9.2.3 Categories of issues

Several categories of issues must be considered during a software development project. They correspond to the conceptual, logical and physical levels of interest and are used to determine which domain is of particular interest to which phase and which phase requires which information:

- *Conceptual level*: this level expresses *what* the application is. Questions such as *Which elements make up the application's universe?* and *Which functions are performed by the application?*, reflect the main issues at this stage.

176   Methodology : software development phases

- *Logical level*: this level expresses *who*, *what* and *when* for the application. Access rights, timing and the localization of application elements are considered at this stage.
- *Physical level*: This is the lowest level. Once the higher-level issues have been solved, it is concerned with *how?* questions. For example, it will determine how an element is retrieved from a symbol table quickly, or which software tool on the market will be used to develop a given software function, and so on.

Table 9.1 illustrates the main categories taken into account during the various lifecycle phases.

Table 9.1 Categories of issues per phase.

Level/Phase	Analysis	Design	Development
Conceptual	✓		
Logical	✓	✓	
Physical		✓	✓

When validating analysis or design documents, the descriptions must be carefully examined to decide whether the appropriate issues have been taken into account. For example, to which levels do the following sentences correspond?

(1) Real-time monitor X will be used for this application.

(2) The compiler developed will include a dynamic array index control option.

(3) The car park entrance and exit barriers are the only access points to the car park and communicate with the control centre via a network.

(4) As the train travels at a maximum speed of 190 miles per hour, position information must be processed in less than 100 ms.

(5) Configuration data will be accessed in DMA mode (direct memory access).

(6) A dichotomic search will be used to determine network activities.

The category to which a specific sentence belongs may sometimes be subject to discussion, depending on the type of application. For example, the conceptual level of an operating system application may correspond to the physical level of a payroll application. This ambiguity highlights the difficulties met when writing software analysis or design documents and deciding on the level of detail to be provided.

It is obvious that sentences (1) (5) and (6) concern the physical level and should typically be included in the software specification documents. Sentence (2) addresses the functional level, despite its apparent technical nature, as the user both understands and makes use of compilation options; it concerns the conceptual level. Although Sentence (4) is more concerned with the logical level, it may be included either in the analysis documents (to express system constraints) or in the design documents (to expand on the technical constraints expressed in the analysis documents). Sentence (3) concerns all levels and is somewhat ambiguous. It is mainly concerned with the conceptual level, except that it refers to the use of a network which is covered on the physical level.

9.2.4 Role of the class relation model in each phase

The class relation model contributes to every phase, but is particularly important during the definition and construction phases (analysis, design and development). It will be seen later, however, that it is even of assistance during integration and validation. The definition phases use the model to formalize the application, whereas the integration and validation phases use it to control and organize work.

Table 9.2 describes how and to what extent each part of the model is used during each phase (••• mandatory, •• very useful, • sometimes useful).

Table 9.2 Contribution of each part of model to each phase.

Phase	Analysis	Design	Development	Integration	Validation
Structure model					
Domain	•••	•••	• (1)	••• (3)	•• (6)
Flow diagrams	•••	•••		•	•
Schema		•••	•••	••• (4)	
Class	•••	•••	•••	•••	•••
Method	•••	•••	•••	•••	•••
Relation	•••	•••	•••	••	•
Attribute	•••	•••	•••	•	•
Visibility		•••	•••	••	
Invariant	•••	••	•• (2)	••• (2)	••• (2)
Operating model					
Control automaton	•••	•••	•• (2)	••• (2)	••• (2)
Pre- and post-conditions	•••	•••	•• (2)	••• (2)	••• (2)
Dynamic model					
Trigger automaton	•	•••	••		
Events	••	•••	••	•	•
Object Flow	•••	•••	•••	• (5)	••• (5)
Scenarios	•••	•		•• (5)	••• (5)

(1) Domains are used to structure a code production environment.

(2) Invariants, pre- and post-conditions and control automata are used to control tests dynamically. They enable consistency to be checked automatically.

(3) Domains are used to define the application integration plan.

(4) The schema is the basic integration unit.

(5) These notions are used to define validation or integration sets.

(6) Domains are used to structure validation.

9.3 User-oriented approach: iterative analysis and design technique

9.3.1 What is a user?

Overview

This section assumes that the application environment is known and that the development project has been identified, that is, preliminary analysis has been more or less completed.

An application is always situated in relation to an external observer or agent called a *user*. The user represents the environment in which the application operates. The user interacts with the application by guiding it and sending it service requests, and the application returns the appropriate information.

Users may be *humans,* as in the case of application software products (for example, word processors, compilers or project management software tools). They may also be other *software products* in a given hardware or software context (a library, printer driver or network server for instance). The *user* is then no longer a human, but the element that activates and controls the software. Examples are a client process or the software using a generated library.

Example 1: Word processor

For a word processor application, the user is the human who operates it. The software handles *documents, paragraphs, styles, sentences, character fonts, characters, selections,* and so on. The human sends messages to representatives of these concepts, which must then perform the required function (`selectedWord set_to_bold()` or `stylesheet define()`, and so on). A multi-windowing interface clearly illustrates the representatives of the word processor notions on which the user acts.

Example 2: Defining the X-Window library

The principle is similar for a library, but the *user* is an external software product.

If the *X-Window* windowing library is analysed, three user categories are defined (as described in the X_Window documentation; see Figure 9.9):

- *Client*, or the application that uses the library to present an interactive graphic user interface,
- *WindowManager,* or a specific client which defines general screen ergonomics (for example, Motif) and has special privileges and prerogatives,
- *User,* or the human who handles the mouse and the keyboard.

When the X_Window system is specified, notions with which the user is familiar, such as *screen, window, event, graphic context* or *pixmap,* are defined.

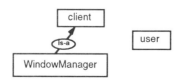

Figure 9.9 Various X-Window users.

9.3.2 Determining system notions: iterative approach

Discovering system notions

Discovery in user requirements

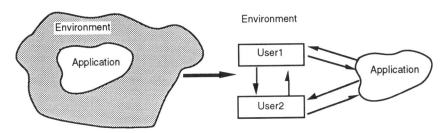

Figure 9.10 Defining users.

Once the development project has been identified, the first modelling task is to define the users with precision (Figure 9.10):
    Who is the application for?
To answer this question, *object classes* are defined to represent different user categories. This task enables the model start point to be defined. The actions that can be taken by these users must then be listed:
    What requirements do the end users have?
These *requirements* are described in terms of user-specific *methods*. The application itself is then defined:
    How do the users meet their requirements?
    How are the required services applied?

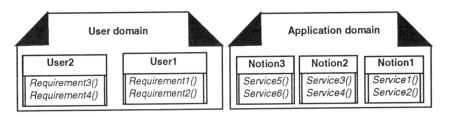

Figure 9.11 Defining requirements and then application services.

At this stage, an initial evaluation of requirements enables the necessary services to be listed. For each service identified (Figure 9.11), an application class must be defined with the corresponding method (*interface class*).

Using the model

The *structure model* (classes, methods, attributes) enables the *users*, their *requirements*, the *interface classes* and *services* to be represented.
    Scenarios can be set up to ensure that the identified procedures are correctly applied to the model. It is thus possible to represent how an invoice is processed

within a company or how selected text is put into bold characters using a word processor.

Individual *object flow* diagrams give a detailed indication of the operational sequence, enabling each user requirement to be met.

The diagrams representing the application are then consolidated and structured in the *structure model* (relations, inheritance, domains, schemas) and the normal form laws are applied.

Exhaustivity checks: *bottom-up* approach

When the model has been stabilized for the application classes (or *interface classes*), the analyst must check that all services have been defined by evaluating each interface class identified (*bottom-up* approach):

```
Which services can be provided by each class identified?
Which requirements are met by these services?
```

The actual purpose of each listed service must be identified.

Finalizing analysis

System analysis is complete when the *operating model* has been defined. The structure, operating and dynamic models are, therefore, set up for the *user classes*.

As far as the *interface classes* are concerned, the dynamic model is rarely used at this stage, except when defining *scenarios* and maybe the *events* handled by the system. The most frequently used diagrams are:

- Structure model: class and domain diagrams, flow diagrams,
- Operating model: control automata, pre- and post-conditions,
- Dynamic model: scenarios.

Process iteration

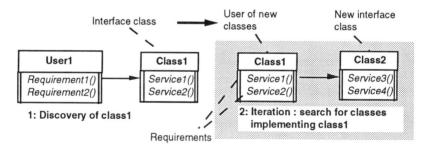

Figure 9.12 Interface classes become 'user' classes.

Once system analysis has been completed, the project team must determine how the system operates. In this case, new requirements made up of all methods in the interface classes are identified. The same approach is then reiterated and previous interface classes become *user* classes (Figure 9.12). This brings to light new interface classes and the whole process is repeated. If the analysis phase has already been completed, this new stage corresponds to the design phase.

This approach can be further extended and the dynamic model defined for the new *user* classes.

The iteration process is complete when the analyst is able to implement the interface classes directly in the development environment.

Analysing the existing situation

An application is often based on already existing initial elements, such as a clear idea of the model to be obtained, a database schema with which the application must comply, classes defined in other applications, and so on.

For example, if a system is modelled during preliminary analysis, some domains and informations flows are already known. As a result, the first classes can be created (see Section 7.5.4).

When describing the problem to be solved, already existing knowledge can be found in the text: *common names* may become classes, *proper names* may become objects and *verbs* may become methods. This technique is over-simplified, but it does provide an initial understanding (centralized in the *data dictionary*), which must be proven and validated by analysing requirements.

Apart from a few trivial cases (correct implementation of the *string* class for instance), the evaluation of an existing situation remains in step with the previously described approach. *User* classes and their requirements must still be defined. However, already known classes are immediately added to the application model as potential interface classes. The approach, whereby classes are brought to light and justified by analysing requirements, is still applicable and some of the pre-existing classes may then be adapted to the problem being studied and their usage justified.

9.3.3 Model reusability, 'genericity'

Reusability is not possible without a suitable methodology

In order to obtain a generic or reusable model, specific work methods must be adopted. The object model promotes reusability, but does not in itself guarantee success. Hypergenericity considerably increases reusability (see Chapter 12).

One common strategy is as follows:

- The most abstract notions possible are defined to increase the probability that they will meet future requirements.
- For each class defined by the application, all services that it may provide are listed.

Such a strategy very probably leads to the following results:

- The model contains very abstract notions which are of no apparent use,
- Development becomes significantly longer, because useless features have been added and the number of classes increased,
- The elements added with reusability in mind do not operate correctly and have not been tested (because they have no immediate use),

More importantly, there is no overall guarantee that they will be reusable.

Reusable modelling technique

It is commonly accepted that the first time software is to be reused to meet new requirements, it must be redeveloped. The second time around, however, it is more likely that it will be able to meet this third generation of requirements and so on.

To avoid initial failures, the following approach should be adopted :

- The types of potential requirements must be defined by adding :
  - New user classes,
  - New requirements to already existing user classes.
- The approach, whereby classes are determined in relation to requirements, must be applied systematically to all user classes.
- User classes must be completely modelled (dynamic model).
- A detailed model is only set up for the interface classes which are actually used immediately and the model for classes likely to be reused is kept.

The key aspect of this approach is simply *planning* for future reusability, given that as a result, even unexpected cases will be more likely to fit into the model.

Modelling quality has a direct impact on reusability. The development team must, therefore, check that :

- The components are sufficiently mutually independent: the classes or schemas are defined and operate in such a way that they are not highly dependent on other components.
- Components have been carefully delimited, particularly with respect to the conditions in which they can be used. It is important to have a detailed description of invariants and pre- and post-conditions.
- The model is clear and easily understood by any person not directly involved in the project.

10 Analysis

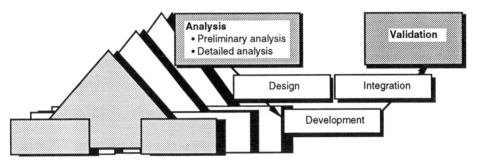

10.1 Purpose

The purpose of the analysis phase is to specify the development framework and system functions:

- To specify the development framework, the following questions must be asked:
    - What are the current requirement and what current issues must be resolved?
    - What is the existing situation?
    - What improvements can be made?
    - Which parts of the system require that software be developed?
    - What development constraints exist?
    - Who will use this software?
    - What will the future system be like, once the software has been developed and the reorganization implemented?
    - Has the software development project been fully thought through (development cost analysis, evaluation of the services provided by the software, return on investment and so on)?
- To specify the system functions, the following questions must be asked:
    - What services are provided by the software?
    - How will the users implement the software?
    - What are the specific constraints for each function?

Before considering the technical aspects of the software, analysts must first define the software development context, its objectives and functions.

10.2 Preliminary analysis

10.2.1 Purpose

The purpose of preliminary analysis is to determine the framework for the software to be developed without going into a detailed functional definition. The development framework appears in the following stage (detailed design) onwards.

The *requirements* must first be understood. During this stage, the analyst must detect any weak points and faults in the current system and list the objectives of the new enhancements. For example, when computerizing a company process, the analyst must first understand the deficiencies detected by current users, then assimilate the existing process and finally define the need for a new study and specify its objectives.

During this stage, constraints must be defined:

- Efficiency constraints: depending on the type of function, execution time constraints may be considered. For example, a user interface must react in compliance with normal reading, assimilation or input speeds, and a process control system must react more quickly than the elements it controls.

- Hardware environment constraints: there may be no choice about the execution environment, or the system may have to be ported to several different hardware environments.

- Budgetary or development schedule constraints: when faced with such constraints, software functions may often have to be limited in number.

- Constraints concerning compliance with company standards (quality, reuseability and so on).

One particular constraint concerns extensibility or adaptability. If the requirements may evolve over time, then the software must also be upgradable and its structure defined in consequence.

The analyst must attempt to define the ways in which the software can be extended, that is, the type of services that may be requested in the future and other potential environments.

10.2.2 Representing the current system

General system representation

Figure 10.1 General representation of a garage company.

The main entities from the current system, which are covered in the problem and which handle information or provide system functions, are initially represented as *domains* (Figure 10.1). For example, company divisions can become domains. A *domain diagram* can thus be created to represent the entire system.

Preliminary analysis

The information exchanged between the various entities must then be presented on one or more *flow diagrams* (Figure 10.2). The elements active in or handled by the system are identified and defined as classes.

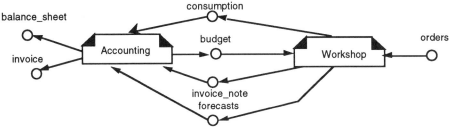

Figure 10.2 Flow diagram for major system entities.

Setting up the dictionary

All terms encountered when reading the requirements documents or talking with the experts in the field must be listed in a *dictionary*. The dictionary contains all terminology used to express the problem and the corresponding definitions. These terms express the concepts which may become classes, roles, relations and attributes (nouns) or methods (verbs) in the model. The links between each of these dictionary terms and the corresponding modellling item must be established in a matrix.

Identifying the initial classes

Inter-domain data flows are either class instances or messages sent to instances. The data flows must be defined in one of the domains.

Using the *dictionary* as the starting point, the key notions are initially represented as classes. All the other terms must then be presented as relations, roles, attributes or methods.

Key procedures are specified in *scenarios* containing examples of how the data flows are handled. This means that the active elements in the system must become representatives of new or already existing classes.

10.2.3 Representing the future system

The model set up for the existing system helps formalize the audit. Data flows, scenarios and method definitions are used to highlight both the automatable parts and the inefficient, expensive or redundant elements in the current system. The model may also identify obsolete parts resulting from environment changes. Finally, the existing system may not handle functions now considered to be essential. Once the existing system has been evaluated, the analyst can define the context for the future system by providing solutions to the highlighted problems.

Before automating part of an existing system, it is often necessary to rethink the way current human or material resources are organized. The overall future system is therefore represented, but the software is just one of its components. The modelling approach is identical to the one for the existing system. At this stage, the new system can be prototyped to focus on its advantages.

Both models must then be presented to the interested parties and reviewed by them.

10.2.4 Defining what is to be computerized

At this stage, the model does not express the actual *contents* of the software to be developed, as the model for the future system only shows the domains where the processing can be automated. The contents of these domains have not yet been modelled.

The domains requiring software development are identified. The current situation may, however, be reorganized to meet the new requirements without any software being developed. It may also be that the sub-systems to be computerized correspond to existing software and there is no need to develop new products.

The study must now go on to define the *users* of the software and describe in greater detail what is expected from the software:

- Definition of user *requirements*, by defining the methods specific to each user.
- Definition of the initial *interface classes*, by defining the concepts in the future system that must be handled by the software. The most obvious *services* provided by the software are represented as interface class methods.
- Preliminary definition of the software structure: the most obvious software decomposition is already represented in *domain* form, which enables the detailed analysis activities to be better prepared.
- *Scenario* reworking: some key scenarios in the future system can be described in greater detail to present the processing sequences followed by the software and its interaction with users.

Software development projects which do not handle real-world processes (for example, a compiler or a video game) do not need such a comprehensive requirements analysis phase; the analysts are not concerned with an existing system and requested improvements.

10.3 Detailed analysis

10.3.1 Purpose

The purpose of preliminary analysis was to determine the framework for the software to be developed. An initial functional description is drafted for the software. However, the actual functions have not yet been described in detail. The software entry points are known, specifically:

- Constraints,
- Users and their requirements,
- Environment,
- General functions required.

The purpose of detailed analysis is to provide an exhaustive overview of the:

- Concepts handled by the software,
- Services provided by these concepts,
- Conditions in which they are used,
- Actions the user must take with the software.

Detailed analysis takes full advantage of the class determination approach described in Section 9.3 to:
- Justify defined classes,
- Present concepts with which the user is familiar,
- Guarantee that all requirements are met,
- Set up a comprehensive model.

10.3.2 Defining requirements

The requirements, expressed in the user class methods, can be divided into *fundamental requirements* and *operational requirements*. Fundamental requirements are those which initially led to the system being developed and which must be met. For example:

- For a car:
    ```
    Move (StartPoint: in Position, ArrivalPoint: in Position)
    ```
- For a computer windowing system:
    ```
    InteractErgonomically (RequiredFunction: in action, InputParameters: in
    set_of_values, DisplayedResults: out set_of_values)
    ```
- For an elevator system:
    ```
    ChangeFloors (CurrentFloor: in FloorNumber, RequiredFloor: in FloorNumber)
    ```

Operational requirements are the set of actions taken by the user to meet a fundamental requirement in compliance with system-related constraints and interfaces. Using the same examples, operational requirements are:

- For a car:
    ```
    OpenDoor(), Start(), Accelerate(), ChangeGear(), and so on
    ```
- For a computer windowing system:
    ```
    MoveMouse(), Select(), Click(), and so on
    ```
- For an elevator system:
    ```
    GoToFloor(), CallElevator(), WaitForElevator(), and so on.
    ```

To deduce all operational requirements from the fundamental requirements correctly, the analyst must be familiar with the system's ability to meet the requirement. For example, someone who does not know what a car is cannot guess that the `ChangeGear()` operational requirement is needed to meet the `Move()` requirement.

In computing, systems are often being designed for the first time and the operational requirements must be discovered during the development process. One of the main criteria for proper analysis is that only the minimal number of operational

188 Analysis

requirements needed to meet the fundamental requirements (as simply as possible) are defined. Prototyping simplifies this work.

The advantage of specifying user requirements lies in the fact that it highlights the strengths or weaknesses of the future system.

10.3.3 Modelling the software

Modelling users

This activity has already been performed during preliminary analysis.

Reusing the information and the model

All existing modelling items are added to the interface classes identified during preliminary analysis:

- Classes, methods or domains that become obvious once the problem has been understood,
- Elements immediately brought to light when analysing the problem concepts (dictionary),
- Modelling items that already exist or have been brought out in previous studies (an existing database schema, for example).

Defining the classes and services required by the user

The requirement-oriented class determination approach is then applied to the part of the model that already exists. It is used to justify already selected classes, adapt them to requirements and add the newly identified classes. Each requirement for each user must be met by a set of services provided by several interface classes.

Structuring classes

Once the required classes have been identified, all relations between them are defined. The classes are then grouped together and any factorization of interest to the analysis phase is processed (inheritance).

At this stage, the model is standardized (see the normal forms laws in Chapter 8); this process helps group together or extract the concepts in the model.

Each group of classes or domains concerning a specific problem category then becomes a domain.

Checking consistency with the dictionary

All the terminology listed during preliminary analysis to describe the initial requirements, concepts and software functions is centralized in a dictionary.

Each dictionary term must correspond to a modelling element and all terms must be represented in the model. To a certain extent, the dictionary defines the language used in the software application domain. This is the very purpose of the model in that it gives a more formal, precise description.

Listing the services provided by each class

This stage is used to check that all system functions have been defined and that all requirements have been met. For each class defined, any new services that it may provide are evaluated. For each service identified in this way, the analyst must also decide on their importance and who will use them, to see whether they meet the requirements of other users, the aim being to obtain the most self-contained, comprehensive components possible.

Defining the interface class operating model

If necessary, the usage protocol is defined for each interface class in a control automaton. The conditions that must exist before a service is provided are defined for the methods in each interface class (pre-conditions). The conditions that must exist once the service has been provided (post-conditions) are also stipulated. The software services are thus completely specified.

Setting up the dynamic model for the appropriate interface classes

When the services provided by an interface class affect other interface classes, which in turn have an impact on users, a dynamic model must be created. More often than not, an object flow model is used, but trigger automata may also be used for *reactive* classes.

In the elevator system specifications, for example, it is important that the following sequence be defined. An elevator must be made available when a user wishes to change floors. To do so, the elevator is sent up or down and when it reaches the appropriate floor, the door opens. These notions are expressed in the object flow model for the appropriate services.

Setting up the dynamic model for users

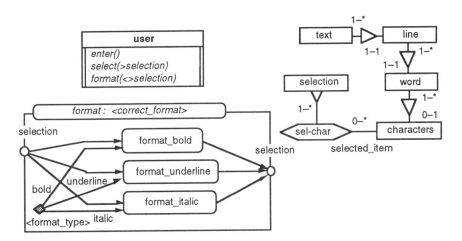

Figure 10.3 Object flow model for word processor user requirements.

When applying the requirement-oriented class determination approach, a preliminary dynamic model is created. The object flow model is then used to define software sequences for the user. In other words, the users are 'coded'. In object flow models, decision operators (if or case) are often used in a non-deterministic way. They indicate that a choice is expected of the user, but do not specify what that choice is. In Figure 10.3, the reasons behind the various formatting options are not defined, as it is left up to the users to decide which formats they want.

Events are also used to express exception conditions, which do not comply with usual processing sequences. They specify the actions taken by the user or the software if external events occur. Such events may be a power failure, a device failure, insufficient memory or the fact that a debtor goes into liquidation.

Specifying scenarios in the software

To present which software elements react when given procedures are triggered by users, the scenarios already defined during preliminary analysis are now expanded.

Prototyping internal system classes

It is easy to prototype a system. The dynamic model for users enables system activation to be simulated and determines the functions to be performed. A minimum number of interface classes are simply implemented to simulate system execution.

The purpose of prototyping may be to:

- Evaluate aspects that the specifications have not fully clarified or which require testing. For example:
  - System ergonomics,
  - Expected function efficiency,
  - Missing functions.
- Demonstrate the future system in order to convince managers or keep future users informed.
- Check and validate the model.

10.3.4 Using the class relation model

The aspects of the class relation model implemented during the analysis phase are reviewed in the Table 10.1.

During the analysis phase, the *visibility* concept is not taken into account and *schemas* are generally not used. Schemas are more closely related with design activities and are useful during coding, testing and maintenance.

scenarios are often used to give detailed information on key processing sequences and provide software implementation examples. They explain how and why the identified concepts are used.

Table 10.1 Use of the class relation components during analysis.

Modelling items	Interface classes	User classes
Structure model		
Domain	Functional sub-system	Usage domain
Flow diagram	Information exchanged within the system	Information exchanged between users and the system
Class	System concept	Users
Method	System service	User requirement
Attribute	Property	Property
Relation	Conceptual links between notions	Relations between the users and the concepts handled
Inheritance	Notion classification	User category
Invariant	Invariant	Invariant
Operating model		
Pre-condition	Usage context	Rarely used
Post-condition	System status once the service has been provided	
Control automaton	Usage protocol	User action sequencing protocol
Dynamic model		
Object flow	Interaction between interface classes visible to the user	Full definition of system usage
Scenario	Software operating sequences	Software usage examples
Trigger automaton	Description of how system concepts systematically react	Description of how users systematically react
Event	External or internal exception conditions	External or internal exception conditions

Events can be used as they reveal the flow of data between the external environment and the software. Events can be of the following types:

- Exceptions: any element which is not part of normal system procedures, such as anomalies or *ad hoc* requests that modify a current procedure, may be processed as an event. For example, the fact that a company employee is on sick leave may modify the procedures in which he or she normally participates.

- Priorities: the information received implies urgency and current processing must be interrupted. For example, a power failure received by a cassette recorder can be considered to be an event. This particular event will stop the current procedure (playing, recording, and so on).

- Asynchronous events: events must be used during asynchronous communication when the sender is not concerned with whether the event is received, when it is processed, or even whether it is processed at all. Events can, however, be synchronous.

192 Analysis

- Events aimed at unidentified objects: if the sender has little information on the receiver, as is the case between a *transducer* and a *software product*, or if it is not clear which instances and which classes will handle the information, an event can be used. It may be accepted informally within a company that any person available with a given level of responsibility can react to an unscheduled stimulus, such as an accident, the receipt of an unusual order, and so on. If the frequency of such events increases, then a specific procedure must be implemented and events can no longer be used.

10.3.5 Completing analysis: validation

Finalizing the model

The only classes that must be modelled are those with which the 'users' are familiar. The analysis phase is considered to be over when:

- All user requirements have been satisfied, that is, all user class methods have been implemented in the form of interface class services,
- All concepts known to the users and all services provided by these concepts have been defined,
- Structure and operating models have been created for the interface classes,
- Structure and dynamic models have been set up for user classes,
- The specification documents have been made clear to all those participating in the software project, by walking through the scenarios or by setting up a prototype.

Preparing validation

The level of precision attained in specifications is never perfect. To add the finishing touches to the software definition, once analysts have described the expected services, they must determine how they will ensure that the resulting product actually corresponds to the specifications. The advantages are two-fold: analysts prepare validation and define the specifications more precisely. A series of *scenarios* based on **elementary validation sets** are defined for validation purposes.

Elementary validation sets consist of processing sequences specifying input values and expected results (Figure 10.4). They are defined in terms of *requirements* (user class methods). Specific object flow models are set up based on those describing how each user requirement is met.

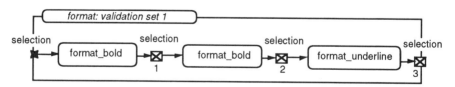

Figure 10.4 Example of an elementary validation set applied to the format() method.

The validation object flow models define:

- Specific input values,
- Suitable sequences (requiring choices),
- Check points, that is, locations in the processing sequence where certain conditions must be checked.

The ⊠ symbol is used to specify the expected result, whereas the ✖ symbol indicates input information. For example:

```
✖ :    The selection is a set of lines without any
       character formatting attributes
⊠ 1:   The selection is placed in bold characters
⊠ 2:   The bold attribute is removed
⊠ 3:   The selection is underlined
```

In this manner, all requirement-derived methods in the user classes are defined and become elementary validation sets. The validation process is made up of a series of elementary sets and can be expressed using scenario diagrams (Figure 10.5).

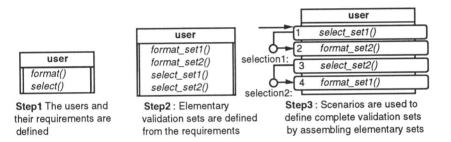

Step1 The users and their requirements are defined

Step2 : Elementary validation sets are defined from the requirements

Step3 : Scenarios are used to define complete validation sets by assembling elementary sets

Figure 10.5 Validation set development stages.

10.4 Example: elevator system

10.4.1 Requirements

The application to be computerized simulates a system controlling four elevators in a six-floor building. People can use any of the four elevators and the system must optimize elevator movements. Each elevator can stop at any floor. Given that the building has a ground floor and six other floors, there are seven floors in all.

Each floor has:

- A control unit to indicate that someone wishes to send an elevator up or down – the ground floor only has an Up button, whereas the top floor only has a Down button,
- A position display unit (0 to 6 floors) for each of the four elevators,
- One position detector per elevator.

Each elevator has:

194   Analysis

- A control unit with one button per floor, a stop button and an alarm button,
- A position indicator (0 to 6 floors),
- An overload detector,
- A detector at door level to detect when people get in or out of the elevator.

The elevator doors are opened and closed by a single motor. Each of the system detectors (floor position detector, elevator overload detector, user presence detector at door level) use a physical coupler to take the necessary samples.

The following operator actions are used to control the overall elevator system:

- Reset the system: all elevators are sent to the ground floor and the doors open,
- Stop the system: the whole system is blocked and no requests are accepted, at either floor or elevator level,
- Start the system: the stopped or reset system is restarted,
- Trace floor states: the actions taken at each floor level are displayed by the operator,
- Trace elevator states: the actions taken at elevator level are displayed by the operator.

10.4.2 Preliminary analysis

Representing the overall system

For the purposes of this example, the problem presented is limited in scope, and so the preliminary analysis phase is less crucial. The whole application and not just a subset of a larger system is to be computerized. Moreover, no existing system to be improved on, as the system is a simulation. This first stage has, therefore, been omitted.

Setting up the dictionary

All terms defined in the user requirement documents or met when analysing these requirements are listed. Each term is defined in the dictionary. Terms representing concepts are differentiated from those representing actions. The dictionary illustrated below simply lists the terms in the problem domain.

Concepts:

```
Alarm button, Building, Control unit (floor), Control unit (elevator),
Door, Down button, Elevator, Elevator overload detector, Elevator position
display unit for each floor, Elevator state, Floor, Floor button in
elevator, Floor position detector, Floor state, Ground floor, Motor,
Operator, Overload, Physical coupler, Position indicator (in elevator),
Stop button, System, Top floor, Up button, User presence detector in door.
```

Actions:

```
Block (system, elevator, floor), Control, Go down, Go up, Open, Reset
system, Start (system), Stop (elevator), Stop (system), Trace (floor
states), Trace (elevator states).
```

Example: elevator system

Some terms must be clarified, particularly with the aim of detecting synonyms or polysemes. For example, the difference between an `elevator` and a `system` or between a `position display unit` and an `indicator` must be clarified. A distinction is made between the terms `position display unit` and `indicator`. Finally, missing information or ambiguities may be detected. For example, the requirement talks about `elevator doors` but not about `floor doors`. Both notions may have to be retained.

Determining the initial classes

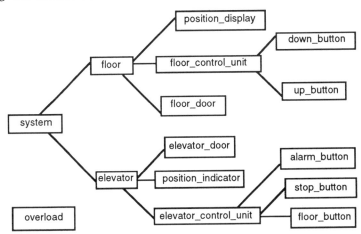

Figure 10.6 Initial classes and associated links (relations).

Using the dictionary as the starting point, the key notions in the requirements are expressed as classes (Figure 10.6). The links between these classes are then drawn to show relations and inheritance. No inheritance appears in this example.

An effort must be made to remain as close as possible to the terms used in the dictionary and not to attempt to attain ideal factorization or modelling in this first draft. The aim is to reflect 'reality' with as much objectivity and exhaustivity as possible.

Representing the future system

The analyst determines that the main software entities are the `system`, the `elevator` and the `floor`. They are represented as *domains*. A *flow diagram* is used to represent a future system and to highlight the information exchanged (Figure 10.7). External information (`users`, `detectors`, and so on) is also identified.

196 Analysis

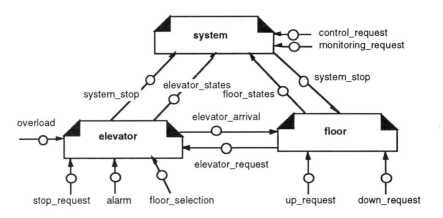

Figure 10.7 Flow diagram for the future system.

Defining what is to be computerized

The purpose of this exercise is to create a simulation of an elevator control system. The application, therefore, comprises a man/machine interface representing the elevator system and an internal system, controlling elevator behaviour.

Defining users

Two types of users are defined for this application (Figure 10.8): the user who wishes to change floors and the operator who supervises the system. User requirements are simply to change floors, whereas operator requirements are to control and monitor the system.

Figure 10.8 Presenting user classes and associated requirements.

Presenting initial scenarios

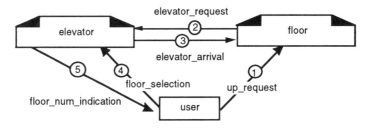

Figure 10.9 General 'change floors' scenario.

In Figure 10.9, a general scenario is presented to provide an overview of the key elevator system procedure: change floors.

10.4.3 Detailed analysis

Defining requirements

First, the initial requirements identified during preliminary analysis are further specified in order to provide a detailed description of the *operational requirements*, that is, the actions taken by the user on the system. Methods are also added to the users (Figure 10.10).

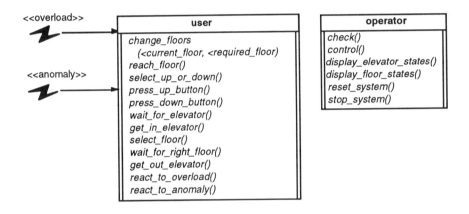

Figure 10.10 Details of user classes and associated requirements.

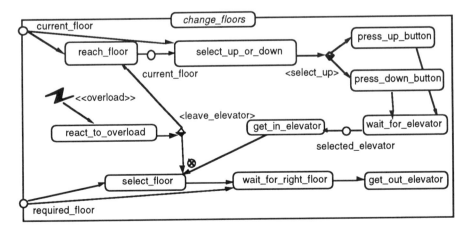

Figure 10.11 Object flow diagram for the change_floors requirement.

To determine operational requirements, the dynamics between the initial requirements must be defined and the corresponding system services identified. The *object flow* model is used to define the operations that the user must perform, as illustrated in Figure 10.11 for the key user requirement (change_floors()).

Defining the classes and services required by the user

When user requirements have been described in detail, each service corresponding to a system concept must be identified to ensure that each requirement is met. For example, users require that the door be opened so that they can get into the elevator and they must then press a button to select the appropriate floor. This approach is based on the *classes initially determined* during preliminary analysis (Figure 10.12).

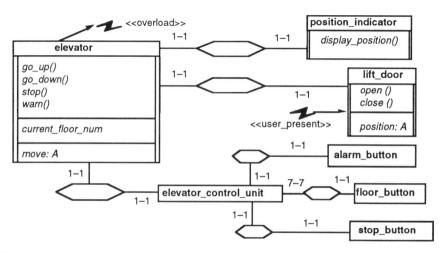

Figure 10.12 Example of user-required classes and services.

Structuring classes

In this example, the domain-based structure defined during preliminary analysis still meets the detailed requirements (provided that an initial domain is added for users). However, this is not usually the case. Often some classes are of no interest to the user or of no particular importance. The previous stage ensured that all notions in the specification had been defined, but they must now be grouped together and given a specific structure.

The elevator_control_unit class is of no particular use (no specific services, no requirements met). It is, therefore, deleted from the model (Figure 10.13). The buttons, regardless of their functions, are all of the same type. They are, therefore, grouped together in the same class and specific relations with the elevator are used to distinguish between the different button functions. The position_display_unit and position_ indicator classes are also of the same type (they both display a number to indicate the position of an elevator). They are, therefore, merged together into the same class called `display_unit`. The `elevator_door` and `floor_door` classes are also identical and are grouped together in the same class called `door`.

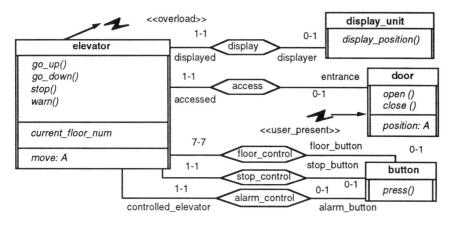

Figure 10.13 Reworking the interface class definition after structuring the model.

Checking consistency with the dictionary

Table 10.2 Correspondences between dictionary terms and model elements.

Dictionary term	Translated into	Internal name	Dictionary term	Translated into	Internal name
Building	XX		Position indicator	Class	display_unit
Control unit	XX		Stop button	Class/Role	button/stop_button
Door	Class	door	System	Class	system
Down button	Class/Role	button/down_button	Top floor	Constant	top_floor
Elevator	Class	elevator	Up button	Class/Role	button/up_button
Elevator state	Automaton	move	User presence detector	Event	user_present
Floor	Class	floor	Block (system, elevator)	Method	block (*)
Floor	Integer	floor	Check	Requirement	check
Floor button	Class/Role	button/floor_button	Control	Requirement	control
Floor state	Automaton	floor_status	Go down	Method	go_down
Ground floor	Constant	ground_floor	Go up	Method	go_up
Link	Class/Role	button/alarm_button	Open	Method	open
Motor	XX		Reset system	Method	reset
Operator	User class	operator	Start (system)	Method	start
Overload detector	XX		Stop (elevator)	Method	stop
Physical coupler	XX		Stop (system)	Method	stop
Position detector	XX		Trace (floor)	Method	trace (*)
Position display unit	Class	display_unit	Trace (elevator)	Method	trace (*)

Table 10.2 specifies how the notions in the dictionary are represented in the model. Each dictionary term not represented in the model must be justified individually. Some terms may be external to the object to be computerized (for example, building), or may concern the design phase rather than analysis (for example, motor or detector).

New terms identified during application analysis and of significance to the requirements must be added to the dictionary.

When reading the dictionary, 'missing' notions may be detected in the model. They are indicated by an '*' in Table 10.2 and imply that the model must be reworked.

Listing the services provided by each class

This activity brings to light missing information and gives an initial idea of how the interface classes cooperate. As a result, several methods can be defined for the elevator class to enable it to cooperate with the system class or handle requests. The dynamic model will provide further information. The fact that new trace methods are defined for the elevator class implies that a second control automaton called trace_mode must be created.

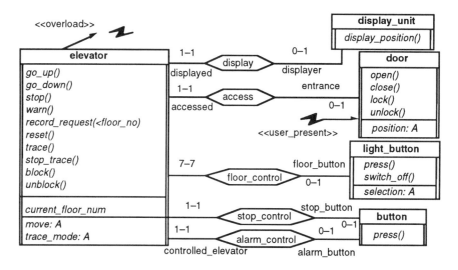

Figure 10.14 Adapting the model for interface classes.

It can be seen that some buttons light up when they are pressed to inform the user that the request has been received but not yet been answered. This is particularly the case when the user selects the required floor in an elevator. Some buttons do not have this requirement; this is the case of the alarm_button which takes immediate effect. The button class is, therefore, decomposed into two classes, light_button and button. It seems logical for these two classes to inherit from the same base class, but the need to handle a button abstractly does not apply to this application. No base class is, therefore, defined. Figure 10.14 presents the new version of the same model after the dictionary has been consulted and the services provided by each class listed.

Defining the interface class operating model

The `elevator` class is used as an example. It has two control automata, one describing how the elevator moves, and the other describing the trace mode (Figure 10.15). Each of the services provided by its classes are then defined in detail by specifying the pre- and post-conditions.

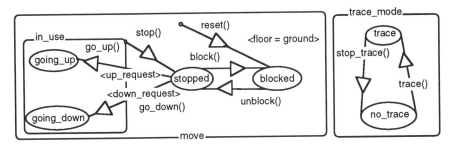

Figure 10.15 Control automata for the `elevator` class.

Defining the dynamic model for the appropriate interface classes

The manner in which interface classes visible to the user cooperate is then defined. For example, it must be remembered that the `go_up()` method in the `elevator` class closes the elevator door. In the same way, in Figure 10.16, the processing performed by the elevator when it stops at a floor is not specified. It is however important for the user and must be defined in the application. A `reach_floor` event can be defined, its sole purpose being to specify the appropriate processing.

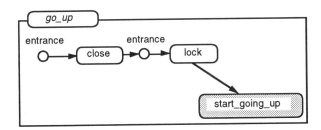

Figure 10.16 Object flow model for the `go_up` method in the `elevator` class.

Updating the dynamic model for users

The dynamic model initially created for users must be reworked and updated to reflect changes made to the interface classes.

Updating key scenarios

The same applies to the scenarios, which were too general in the initial approaches. They must be defined in greater detail and structured so that each concerns a specific analysis domain. In this manner, the scenario representing how a user changes floors can be decomposed into a part concerning the floor and a part concerning the elevator.

Defining the man/machine interface

This activity is not covered at this stage. The graphic aspect of the man/machine interface and the appropriate dialog boxes are defined in the class relation structure model (see Section 12.5.11).

Preparing validation

The `user` and `operator` classes and their requirements are used to define validation scenarios, each containing the necessary validation sequences (see Section 10.3.3).

11 Design

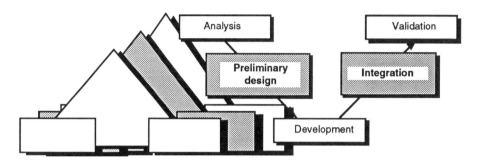

11.1 Preliminary design

11.1.1 Overview

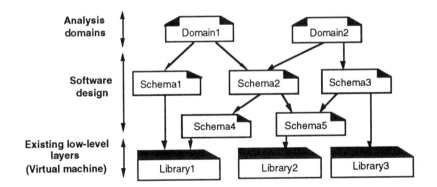

Figure 11.1 Design defines the intermediary layers required to apply analysis to the virtual machine.

During analysis, the problem domain is modelled, without taking into account physical implementation constraints or the machine on which the software is executed. The preliminary design phase is used to determine how the specifications will actually be implemented to respect all constraints in the final execution environment (efficiency, and so on).

Definition: *Design defines the application hardware and software environment (virtual machine) and the way the specification is implemented on the virtual machine (Figure 11.1).*

11.1.2 Defining the architecture

Architecture concept

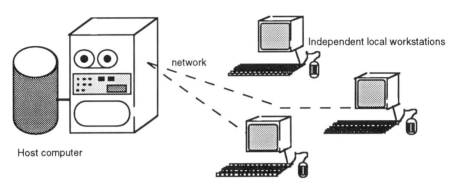

Figure 11.2 Centralized architecture.

The *architecture* defines the physical configuration of the software in its run-time environment. Diagrams are used to represent the:

- Physical processing media (*process*, *task*, *thread*, *machine*, and so on),
- Data storage media (*file*, *database*, and so on),
- Communication vectors between physical processing units (*network*, *message queues*, *interrupts*, and so on),
- Devices accessed (*printer*, *monitor*, *detectors*, *hardware card*, and so on).

Architecture also defines the *virtual machine* (execution machine, libraries used).

Data and processing can be distributed for technical reasons, such as the need to work on several networked machines or to use multi-tasking applications. A correspondence must therefore be defined between the analysis model and this artificial separation between data and processing. For example, some software systems use the architecture illustrated in Figure 11.2. This architecture enables a large volume of information to be centralized in one place and processed intensively by a powerful machine, while the final user has a standalone, user-friendly workstation able to handle other types of tools (spreadsheets, word processors, and so on).

This type of architecture may be considered to be a constraint during the analysis phase, but its actual implementation concerns the design phase. The following typical questions must then be answered: *What type of network will be implemented? What protocols will be used between the server and the clients?*
During analysis, a model is created for the problem domain, irrespective of the architecture, and network or database specific problems which are not covered; rather this phase merely concerns the services provided by the application.

The system *architecture* must consider the virtual machine when distributing processing, data storage and inter-process communication facilities. It defines physical system coupling and is concerned with such concepts as the *network*, *files*, *database*, *tasks*, *processes*, *interrupts* and *mail system*, as they are the basis for the implementation techniques.

At the end of the analysis phase, a *preliminary technical study* must be conducted to specify the architecture in terms of the model created during analysis, the virtual machine and any other implementation constraints. Its purpose is also to decide on the implementation guidelines which define the starting point for the actual design phase (Figure 11.3).

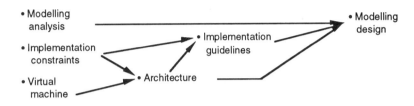

Figure 11.3 Steps leading to preliminary design.

Deducing technical domains and schemas

When defining an architecture, an *architecture diagram* must be created to present the physical elements in the system, their interconnections and the data exchanged (Figure 11.4).

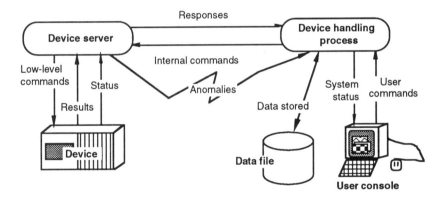

Figure 11.4 Example of an architecture diagram.

Several *active elements* (*processes*, *tasks*, *threads*, and so on) are highlighted in the architecture diagram. An *active element* is a physical unit in the virtual machine used to execute code. The architecture diagram can also present *libraries* or *shared code* used by several active elements.

The active elements and shared code systematically become *domains* or *schemas*. The architecture diagram can thus be immediately transformed into a domain or flow diagram.

206 Design

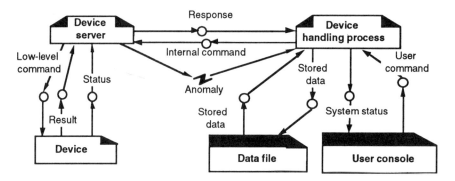

Figure 11.5 Transforming an architecture diagram into a flow diagram.

In Figure 11.5, the `data file` and `user console` elements have been represented as *'library' schemas*, whereas `device` has become a *schema*. This is because no specific development is required to access a file or a console as the operating system provides the necessary primitives, whereas low-level code provided in a schema is required to access a device.

Applying the analysis model to the architecture

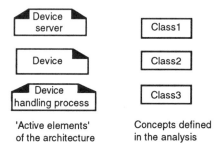

Figure 11.6 Preliminary design starting point.

An active element in the architecture corresponds to the context in which the modelling concepts are executed. All system concepts identified during analysis must be represented in one or more execution contexts (Figure 11.6).

The application must then be decomposed once again so that each concept can be represented in one or more contexts and its implementation defined specifically in the appropriate contexts. New concepts concerning the technical environment for an execution context therefore need to be added (*processes, message queues, files, windows*, and so on).

Concepts appearing in several active elements are generally represented together in the same class relation schema. Table 11.1, based on the elements in Figure 11.6, is therefore created to determine which active elements implement a given concept. This table shows that Class1 must be implemented for Process C and so will be called *ClassC1*. It must also be implemented for Process B; in this case, it will be called *ClassB1*. It is highly probable that *ClassC1* and *ClassB1* have points in common, which can be factorized in a class called *Class1*, belonging to a schema shared by both processes (joint schema). A schema/domain diagram is then set up, as illustrated in Figure 11.7.

Table 11.1 Active elements that implement analysis concepts.

Architecture / analysis	Class1	Class2	Class3
Process C	✔	✔	✔
Process B	✔		✔
Device			

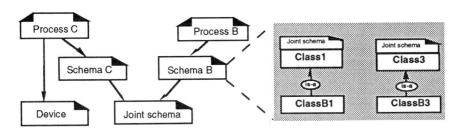

Figure 11.7 Extending the analysis structure during design.

To conclude, the following tasks are performed during preliminary design:

- The classes (or schemas) highlighted during analysis are distributed between the active elements in the architecture,
- Technical classes (or schemas) are added in order to implement those highlighted during analysis.

11.1.3 Converting a model for design purposes

Adding technical classes to analysis classes

Technical classes are defined during the design phase. These classes are not visible to end users who are unaware of their existence. `File`, `message` and `buffer` are classes which can be identified when designing an accounting application, even though the user is only familiar with the `invoice` and `customer` concepts, and so on. These classes are used to implement analysis.

During the design phase, *technical* domains are also used to support the functional domains specified. The design approach may be:

- Bottom-up: starting from the virtual machine, new domains are gradually created until those defined during analysis are reached.
- Top-down: the analysis domains are expanded to include implementation features, until the virtual machine is reached.

208 Design

In practice, given the start point (virtual machine) and end point (analysis), the designer adopts the most efficient approach to join the two points together (design schemas). Therefore, both approaches are often combined.

Along with defining new classes (to implement analysis classes), a more technical aspect of design must be considered; operating principles must be determined for the analysis classes. The addition of *technical* classes is the simplest case. It enables specific schemas, independent of analysis schemas, to be created during the design phase (Figure 11.8).

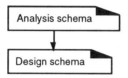

Figure 11.8 Analysis schemas are based on design schemas.

Generalizing analysis classes

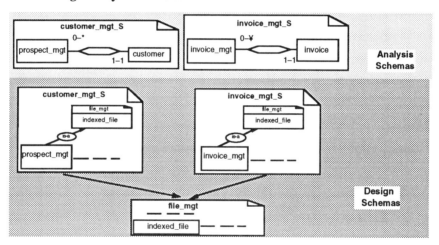

Figure 11.9 Design generalizes operating principles.

Design is concerned with how analysis classes operate. For example, if two classes defined during analysis apply a similar operating mechanism, the designer should generalize this mechanism, so that the two classes inherit from a joint class created during design.

In Figure 11.9, it was not clear before the design phase that prospect_management and invoice_management were implemented by means of an indexed_file. Any other implementation choice, such as a database table, could also have been made.

Adapting analysis classes

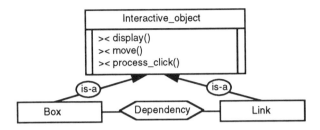

Figure 11.10 Interactive_object class.

The design phase is not just adding the extra classes required by the analysis classes, via inheritance or usage. Although the definition of an analysis class cannot actually be changed, the class can be adapted:

- By adding properties, such as *technical* attributes required to implement the class
- By transferring class properties in new base classes

In practice, one of the purposes of the design phase is to generalize operating principles. Technical problems are therefore decomposed into separate classes and schemas. This naturally highlights factorization possibilities, whereby specific classes are decomposed into several other classes and the corresponding base classes are created.

In the following example, a *box-link* schema is used to handle all types of interlinked boxes graphically. The schema has been defined as a utility library and the user is only concerned with concepts such as *box* or *link*, both of which inherit from the interactive_object class, defined in Figure 11.10.

```
class abstract interactive_object
  description
    text : analysis
    This class represents all interactive graphic objects,
    that is, those objects that have a graphic form and
    react to user requests (mouse click). The 'display()'
    message causes the graphic object to appear, whereas
    the 'move()' message causes it to move in accordance
    with the argument supplied. The 'process_click()'
    message indicates that the end user has clicked on the
    graphic object. This class must be redefined to define
    application-specific graphic objects.
    end text
  public ...
    method
      display();
      process_click();
      move (move: in length);
      ...
```

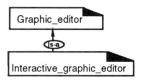

Figure 11.11 Decomposing technical problems into schemas.

This class definition was not essential during analysis, however, it is of interest at this stage. It factorizes many behaviour patterns so that they need only be specified once.

During design, it is noticed that two types of technical problems exist when handling interactive objects:

- Graphic management (display and printing, image refreshing, scrolling),
- Interaction management (assignment of mouse clicks to graphic elements, element display levels, and so on).

Given the scope of each problem, two schemas must be defined, one for graphic object management and the other for interactive graphic object management (Figure 11.11).

The `interactive_object` class is thus divided into two classes (Figure 11.12), a `graphic_object` class and a new derived class, called `interactive_object`. Each class concerns a different type of problem and belongs to a different schema. The *display()* and *move()* methods are included in the `graphic_object` class, whereas the *process_click()* method remains in the `interactive_object` class.

Properties are redistributed between the `interactive_object` class and the `graphic_object` base class. The actual definition of the `interactive_object` class remains unchanged, as each representative combines the properties in `graphic_object` and `interactive_object`, as defined during analysis.

Rule: *Design does not attempt to change the way in which analysis classes have been defined.*

Normally, the definition is extended by adding new classes or by adding new properties to analysis classes. Properties may sometimes have to be redistributed, however, by adding new intermediary classes to the analysis class inheritance diagram.

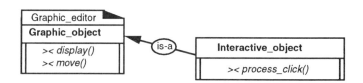

Figure 11.12 Decomposing the `interactive_object` class.

Preliminary design   211

Denormalizing

Overview

Analysis is not concerned with the implementation of the model. Classes are defined in terms of known domain concepts and the model must comply with the normal form laws (see Section 8.2).

On the other hand, design must take into account implementation cost restrictions (size, efficiency) and, as a result, may need to *denormalize* the analysis. Thus, the design must meet physical requirements.

Definition: *Denormalization is a deliberate action whereby a model is changed, so that it no longer complies with normal form laws but does take into account implementation constraints (performance, implementation impossibilities, and so on).*

Denormalization must be a deliberate decision provoked by specific constraints. A model must never be denormalized without good reason. It is merely an emergency loophole and not the primary role of preliminary design.

Programming languages

Regardless of the programming language, compromises will have to be made during implementation. Designers who are aware of the weak points in the implementation language should adapt the analysis model so that it can be implemented as easily as possible. They should consider the way programming languages convert certain concepts in the class relation model so as to avoid potential problems.

Removing multiple inheritance

Multiple inheritance may seem perfectly justified during analysis, but may be difficult to implement. This is particularly the case in C++, as illustrated in Figure 11.13.

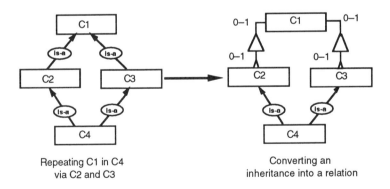

Figure 11.13 Example whereby multiple inheritance is removed.

In C++, unless the programmer is particularly careful, C1 is repeated in C4 (repeated inheritance). To avoid this repetition, the C++ compiler uses an implementation mechanism called *virtual inheritance* (*virtual* keyword). C++ virtual inheritance is difficult to code and implement when moving around the inheritance

212 Design

diagram. These problems can be avoided by removing multiple inheritance from the model.

Figure 11.13 illustrates one possible way of removing multiple inheritance. In absolute terms, this is not necessarily a satisfactory solution. The position of these classes within the application and the context in which they are used will help designers choose the best compromise.

Optimizing frequent accesses via a composed relation

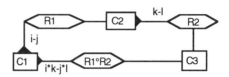

Figure 11.14 Optimization by adding a redundant relation.

The need to access data may require the application of several optimization techniques, as illustrated in Figure 11.14, where a shortcut is utilized to enable specific information to be accessed immediately.

In this manner, an instance of C1 that wishes to access an instance of C3 will do so in one step, via redundant relation R1°R2. More memory is required (duplicate links between data), however execution times are reduced.

Coupling between two linked classes

When two classes C1 and C2 are linked and an instance of C2 is accessed, an instance of C1 is almost always accessed as well. If C1 and C2 are merged into the same class (violation of normal forms 2 and 3), access times can be reduced and the relation between C1 and C2 removed (less memory) (Figure 11.15).

Figure 11.15 Merging two interlinked classes.

Defining a linked class as an attribute

In Figure 11.16, the first normal form is violated. This structure can only be considered correct if no classes inherit from C2.

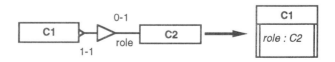

Figure 11.16 Converting a relation into an attribute.

Implementation inheritance

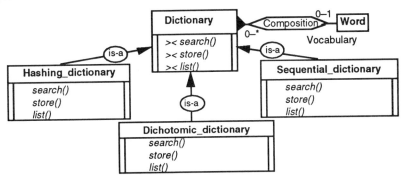

Figure 11.17 Implementation inheritance.

For the example in Figure 11.17, analysis defined a *dictionary* as being a set of words. A *dictionary* can be used to search() for a word, to store() a word, to list() words in a given range, and so on.

Design may, however, focus on the need to implement the same dictionary in several different ways, for example:

- The first version must be efficient in terms of processing, while being able to retrieve one *word* quickly out of many. The 'hashing' technique must be used to implement this *dictionary*.

- The second one is more concerned with space rather than processing times. A simple sequential storage technique is therefore used.

- The last one must compromise between processing efficiency and the memory used by the *dictionary*. The 'dichotomic search' technique is then used.

All three versions correspond to the same analysis as each instance of the *dictionary* can be implemented differently, depending on its specific requirements. Design, therefore, adds to the analysis, as illustrated in Figure 11.17.

11.2 Case study: databases

Database requirements are determined when selecting the system architecture. Database management systems (DBMS) are frequently used to handle data storage problems and are then part of the virtual machine. In such cases, designers must take specific precautions when creating the model and apply the appropriate model transformation techniques, as discussed in the following paragraphs.

11.2.1 Basic definitions

A *database* is used to store *consistent* data, the service life of which is not dependent on application execution or system shut down. Usually, a *DBMS* is used to store, retrieve and manage data. In addition, it stores definitions and the most stable consistency rules.

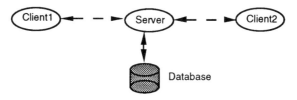

Figure 11.18 Typical DBMS architecture.

A DBMS normally allows several different applications to access the same information simultaneously. It guarantees data integrity, by preventing the same data from being updated at the same time by several distinct entities. The architecture (simplified in Figure 11.18) is always based on a *client/server* principle, whereby the server centralizes data management, integrity control and consistency checking for several *clients*.

A database *schema* is a description of the type of information stored and the links between this information. Schemas are defined in a data definition language (*DDL*), which is interpreted by the DBMS. Data is accessed by sending queries via a data management language (*DML*), also interpreted by the DBMS. SQL, used particularly on relational databases, combines both the DDL and the DML (see Figure 11.19).

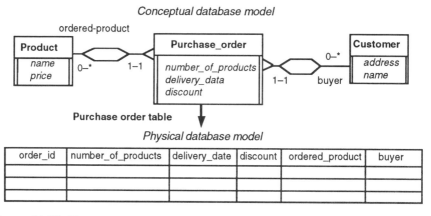

Figure 11.19 Example of a relational database schema.

Each client sends *transactions* to the database. A *transaction* is a logical processing unit, made up of one or more DML or DDL instructions that are executed either completely or not at all. Transactions are terminated by a:

- *commit*, in which case all modifications requested by the transaction are confirmed,

- *rollback*, in which case the modifications requested since the start of the transaction are cancelled, that is, the transactions are ignored.

There are two key types of DBMSs:

- *Server*, whereby the same database is accessed from several applications which may be located on different machines. This type corresponds to almost all DBMS systems.
- *Distributed*, whereby data in one database is distributed between several different machines. This technique is difficult to implement, and thus is still rare.

Characteristics of database applications

A database application stores and uses *persistent* data. Typical examples are management applications (personnel, pay roll, accounting, inventory, banking, insurance, and so on) where large volumes of information are handled. CAD applications use databases to store complex graphic data. Other examples are medical imaging applications, cartography or software engineering applications in which models are stored.

Database technology

A universal DBMS does not yet exist, however, techniques for data storage have been developed over a period of time and all are geared to meet specific requirements, specifically:

- *Sequential files*: this technique is used often. It has the advantage of being available immediately (supplied with all operating systems). It is often used by applications that simultaneously store and load 'raw' data packets, but do not share the stored data. This is the case of many office automation software products (word processors, spreadsheets, and so on), and software engineering tools (compilers, link editors).
- *Hierarchical databases*: these were the first database systems to exist and are based on a hierarchical data storage model. This model can be compared with a geography database made up of *countries*, in turn made up of *regions*, then *towns*, *sectors*, *roads*, and so on. This technique is no longer practical.
- *Network databases*: these databases were developed to fill in the gaps left by the hierarchical model. Data is represented as entities interconnected by direct links which enable the user to navigate through an information network. The CODASYL model is the reference in this domain. Even if many of them have suffered from the appearance of relational databases, they are still used frequently.
- *Relational databases*: one disadvantage of the network model is that any user navigating through the database has to use predefined links and thus must be familiar with them. The model must therefore be implementation-oriented, which makes it difficult to query variables. Codd (1970) defined the relational model, which is a purely mathematical model based on *relation*, *selection* and *union* notions. Relational databases are based on this model and all use the standard

query language SQL. They are very popular, particularly for management applications, and have to a large extent supplanted network databases.

- *Object-oriented databases*: this last generation, based on the object model, uses the inheritance concept in an enhanced model. Some databases provide query facilities similar to the ones in relational databases (selection, joining, and so on), however they also always provide a direct inter-element link mechanism, which result in faster navigation techniques. They often provide a direct correspondence between the dynamic objects handled by the program and the static objects stored in the database. They are used to store complex data (images, sound, and so on) and their champions hope to supplant relational databases, as relational databases themselves supplanted network databases. Currently, this is far from being the case. Often, object databases are used by applications for which relational databases are considered to be unsatisfactory (Hypertext, CAD, and so on).

Problems specific to database applications

Particular care must be taken when modelling data

Data modelling becomes a key factor for applications storing and handling data.

Retaining stored data

The model for an application that does not use databases may be completely revised when a new version is developed, even though the actual effect on current users may be negligable.

Upward compatibility is extremely difficult to guarantee when an application stores data. If the format of stored data changes, the new software version will not be able to handle the data stored with the previous version. Developers may have to code a data conversion program which users often find both tedious and unpractical to use.

Adding and upgrading software

Frequently, once a database application has been completed, other requirements appear; as a result, the stored data must be processed or enhanced. Examples of such situations are statistical analysis applications developed for already existing data, or an interface between an inventory management application and an accounting application.

In an ideal world, the database schema remains unchanged. The existing data schema is therefore used as a baseline for the developers creating new applications. Since a change made to the database schema has a significant impact on all applications using that database, it is even more difficult to upgrade it.

Multiple applications handling the same database

During development, a large-scale application is often broken down into several sub-applications, all of which handle the same data. For example, a management system may handle a database for personnel management, accounting or inventory management applications. The applications each have their own specific model, a common core of which resides in the database schema (Figure 11.20).

During software development, this structure is controlled by appointing a single person to be responsible for database schema modelling.

Case study: databases

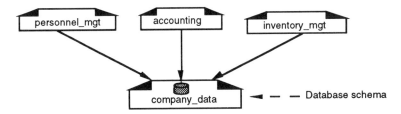

Figure 11.20 The database schema is shared by several applications.

Data security

Storage system reliability
Reliability problems must be solved by the database management system. The main aspects of data security are:

- Lock management to prevent any concurrent access to the same data
- Error recovery mechanisms to ensure that the database remains consistent after a system failure and that no information is lost.

Stored data consistency
No information in the database must be duplicated. Any duplicate information is likely to generate inconsistencies after updating. This aspect must be taken into account when modelling and the resulting model must respect the normal form laws.

Data confidentiality
The data stored for management applications may be highly confidential. To maintain this confidentiality, databases use a sophisticated access rights mechanism, often specified during the analysis phase.

Access efficiency (physical model)

For a given DBMS, access efficiency may vary significantly depending on the physical database model, that is, the way in which the schema is implemented. Efficiency is a critical factor when designing database applications.

To optimize results, the physical schema is based on application access and navigation requirements. For example, the physical schema may:

- Group together entities that are accessed simultaneously from the same physical location (cluster),
- Define indexes or adopt a database search strategy (B-tree, hashing, and so on).

The physical schema may be deliberately denormalized in order to optimize implementation.

Transaction management

The DBMS provides lock management and consistency controls. The applications (clients) must, however, follow a carefully defined transaction management strategy. If a client requires intensive processing to modify a large volume of data and does so in one single transaction, the database is locked for all other potential clients. On the other hand, if it divides its processing up into a series of short transactions, it will have little impact on the others. A transaction management strategy must therefore be adopted by each application.

Moreover, if a commit is refused by the database, the application has an incorrect snapshot (as the modified data objects have not been saved). If the application wishes to continue processing, it must be able to rollback to the previous state before the objects were modified, and reload any data that may have been modified in the meantime by someone else.

There is no single solution to all these problems. It depends on the type of application.

Methodological approach well suited to persistent data

Handling persistent data

Object database myth

Object databases simplify data management via an object-oriented language. They frequently provide high coupling and thus data access transparency for the programmer: a given data item in a database is accessed in the same way as it would be accessed in RAM memory. This means that the storage space for persistent data is considered simply to be an extension of RAM.

Some database management systems go much further along these lines by using the programming language itself as the DDL (C++, Smalltalk). This approach, although apparently very practical on paper, is only suitable for simple applications which work independently and exclusively on the database. This is particularly useful for prototyping applications.

On the other hand, it is dangerous for heavy-duty applications:

- Concurrent data access management requires specific care when handling persistent data (transaction management). This data is shared by several processes, unlike RAM memory, which is specific to each process.

- The database schema is closely linked with the application code, which prevents the application from being updated easily, and independently of the data model. Any change made to the code may have a serious impact on the database schema, which could mean that previously stored data can no longer be used.

- The fact that the same data is shared by several applications means that a totally different methodological approach must be adopted. Database objects must be analyzed as if they were self-contained components, to be kept as separate as possible from user applications.

Rule: *Object databases simplify object-oriented application programming, but not database modelling. The database schema must be defined separately.*

The advantage of object databases lies, however, in the significantly more direct link between the object model and the object database, which simplifies transformation activities.

Specific modelling characteristics

The persistent nature of data is actually not considered until the preliminary design phase. The main purpose of the analysis phase is to determine which concepts are

Case study: databases   219

handled by the user and consequently, which information must be made available. Preliminary design attempts to determine all persistent classes.

During the design phase, persistent classes must be grouped together into specific schemas and domains. The role of the design phase is to differentiate between the persistent classes and the dynamic classes in the application. Technical attributes may be added to the analysis classes, but they are not necessarily stored in the database (see Figure 11.21). In this example, the persistent class called Permanent_a/c (persistent attributes, integrity constraints) is a projection of the application class, Bank_account.

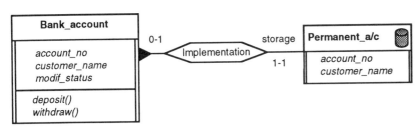

Figure 11.21 Representing persistent and dynamic classes.

Special care must be taken with persistent classes (respect of normal form laws, access modes and specific queries, and so on).

Case study: Already existing databases

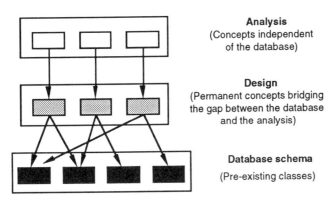

Figure 11.22 Design establishes the link between the functional model and the existing schema.

Often, the database has been defined before the application is developed and so the database schema is part of the information which must be considered during analysis. However, the resulting specifications do not necessarily comply with the pre-existing schema. The role of the design phase is to determine classes in such a way that the permanent concepts identified during analysis are adapted to the database schema (Figure 11.22). The pre-existing database is then part of the virtual machine. The design must be adapted accordingly and great care taken when specifying any changes to the database itself.

Methodological approach

The fact that an application uses databases has no impact on analysis, only on the design which must take into account specific constraints. Persistent classes must be grouped together in specific schemas for a given domain.

The pooling of permanent data enables the complete database schema to be normalized.

Adapting to the DBMS

The conceptual database schema is therefore defined locally for the whole database, the aim being to maintain the view that the rest of the application has of the data (persistent classes), regardless of the underlying storage mechanism.

It is not certain that the resulting persistent classes can be stored directly in the selected DBMS. Moreover, both the DBMS's performance and the data access programming interface must be considered. Depending on optimization constraints and data access modes, lower-level classes may be required for the *physical* database level (Figure 11.23). They are the body classes in class relation schemas.

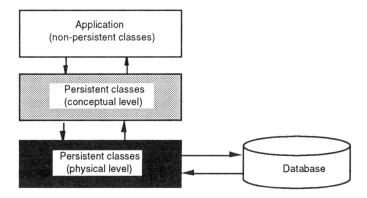

Figure 11.23 Encapsulating the physical level for the application.

For example, changes may be required because inheritance is used with relational databases. Many object databases do not have the class attribute notion. To implement these attributes, specialized tables must be defined.

Finally, depending on the access strategy adopted, the type of application and the way in which the database is used, an object/data correspondence is not necessarily required within the database.

11.3 Case study: multi-tasking applications

11.3.1 Problems specific to multi-tasking applications

Defining self-contained processing units

When analysing an application, decomposition into processing units is often problematic. Objects are considered to be self-contained active elements, which do not take into account synchronization problems or the physical location of the processing units.

The *task* or *process* notion comes into play during the design phase. This notion is not part of the object model and corresponds to a physical processing unit defined by the virtual machine. For operating systems such as Unix, Windows NT, VMS, and so on, the *process* notion defines a specific run of an executable binary file. In the case of real-time monitors, a *task* notion exists; it is similar to the process notion but applies more sophisticated priority management and synchronization mechanisms. Finally, some operating systems provide a *thread* notion, which decomposes the same process down into several parallel runs.

For given architecture requirements, independent, parallel processing units may have to be defined. This division is generally not closely correlated with the model developed during analysis; the classes must therefore be divided up specifically between the processing units.

Communication problems

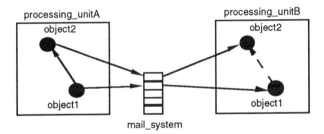

Figure 11.24 Object transmission and environment rebuilding for two processing units.

Generally speaking, processing units correspond to independent runs of executable binary files with no shared information. Object-oriented languages only control the objects and messages within the same processing unit, inter-unit communication being outside their control. A virtual machine mechanism must then be used to communicate with other processing units. Examples of these mechanisms are *mail systems*, *semaphores*, *shared memory* or *interrupts*.

One inherent difficulty in these mechanisms is the fact that communication often takes place on a very low level using character strings and the object structure is no longer apparent. Moreover, objects in one processing unit are used in a specific context (particularly in the case of related objects) and when they are transmitted to another processing unit, the context must be rebuilt in the target unit (Figure 11.24). (The links are rebuilt with other objects.) It will however be seen later that all 'client/server' features or object transmission requirements can be automated using hypergenericity.

Synchronization problems

Processing units must intercommunicate, react to specific external events and share resources. There are therefore, moments in time when two processing units meet, when one unit is waiting for another or when processing is interrupted by an urgent event.

These problems exist in most multi-tasking software, but are crucial in real-time applications, where their reactivity and ability to process events in a given period of time are decisive. Unlike sequential systems, multi-tasking applications are non-deterministic: their behaviour is not known at a given moment in time. Cooperation must be modelled to avoid all synchronization errors, such as *deadlocks*, where several processing units block each other as each is waiting for the other.

Finally, some tasks must process exception events by interrupting current processing and taking specific actions. Frequently, segments which cannot be interrupted safely must be declared *uninterruptable*. For example, if a short dialogue session is established with a device, it is not possible to interrupt it and then restart it. This dialog must therefore be *uninterruptable*.

11.3.2 Division into domains

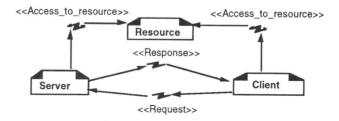

Figure 11.25 Flow diagram modelling multi-tasking communication.

Once the various types of processing units have been defined, generally in the form of individual executable binary files, specialized *domains* must be created for each type.

Flow diagrams are then used to model the processing units and specify how they communicate.

A client/server application is illustrated in Figure 11.25. One specific aspect of this application is that a resource (such as a device) is shared by both the client and the server. As this resource can only be accessed by one user at a time, a synchronization problem may arise between the client(s) and the server. The *flow diagram* focuses on this communication constraint and indicates the synchronous or asynchronous nature of the events. It does not, however, solve synchronization problems. *Object flows* are used instead of *events* if processing units communicate via messages rather than interrupts.

11.3.3 Defining reactive classes

When defining inter-processing cooperation, only those classes taking part in the dialogue will be presented. All internal classes are ignored as their sole purpose is to execute the tasks required by each processing unit.

In very general terms, each processing unit is itself a class, the instance of which represents its execution (for example, a process or a task). These classes are then represented in the same diagram (Figure 11.26). *Scenario* diagrams can also be used to illustrate a typical dialogue sequence between processing units.

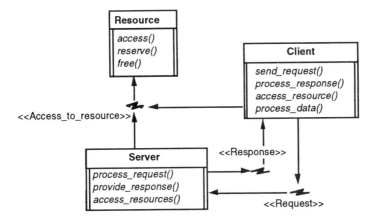

Figure 11.26 Representing reactive classes taking part in inter-processing communication and synchronization.

11.3.4 Using the event model and trigger automata

Modelling synchronization

Trigger automata can be used to model system dynamics. All automata can then be presented together on the same diagram, in what will be called an *automaton overview*, to provide an overall view of inter-process cooperation and synchronization.

The automata in each class are represented as expanded abstract states. Output events are sent to the appropriate classes. Figure 11.27 shows that no deadlock exists when the client or the server accesses the resource, as they are not in a state in which they must communicate with each other; this state is maintained until the problem disappears.

224 Design

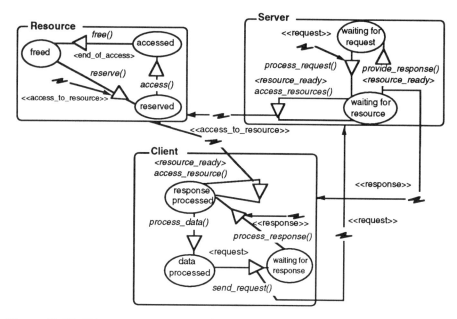

Figure 11.27 Trigger automaton overview used to validate synchronization.

Controlling uninterruptable segments

Transition semantics are used to declare uninterruptable segments; an event is only taken into account when the current transition has taken place. A transition is therefore an *uninterruptable* processing unit. If a class is highly reactive, simpler transitions must be declared, so that more elementary methods are invoked.

11.4 Using genericity

Genericity is a useful complement to inheritance, in that it enables coding segments to be factorized. It is particularly useful during design and coding activities.

Definition

If a program is to provide a function called swap_salary(), the purpose of which is to exchange two instances of salary, the function will be coded as follows:

```
swap_salary (P1 : inout salary, P2 : inout salary)
   processing
       text: C++
           salary buffer;
           buffer = P1;
           P1 = P2;
           P2 = buffer;
       end text ...
```

In the next example, the `swap_employee()` function is developed to invert two instances of `employee`:

```
swap_employee (P1 : inout employee, P2 : inout employee)
    processing
        text: C++
            employee buffer;
            buffer = P1;
            P1 = P2;
            P2 = buffer;
        end text ...
```

When coding this second example, the programmer gets a feeling of *déjà vu* as the two routines are very similar, except for the type of items handled. If a word processor were used and all occurrences of `salary` were replaced by `employee`, the `swap_employee()` function would be obtained automatically.

In more general terms, a *generic* function called `swap_<type>()` can be coded to build a function model as a basis for all functions inverting representatives of a given type. The following code would be developed:

```
swap_<type> (P1 : inout <type>, P2 : inout <type>)
    processing
        text: C++
            <type> buffer;
            buffer = P1;
            P1 = P2;
            P2 = buffer;
        end text
```

A function such as `swap_salary()` can then be built automatically using a simple instruction of the `instantiate (swap_<type>, type = salary)` form.

Thus, by defining the generic element in a parameterized model, other elements can be created automatically, simply by setting certain parameters.

In the previous example, the `swap_<type>()` function is generic and the `swap_salary()` function is a *genericity instance* of `swap_<type>()`, with a *genericity parameter* called `salary`.

Genericity is a feature provided in several programming languages, such as Ada, Eiffel and C++. In languages such as C, a pre-processor can be used to develop generic code.

Genericity and inheritance

B. Meyer (1986) wrote a well-known article on the links between genericity and inheritance. Using the same example as above, the `swap()` function could have been factorized for the `salary` and `employee` classes. A class called `swapable_element` could simply have been defined, such that `employee` and `salary` inherit from it. Parameters for the `swapable_element` class could then be set for the general `swap()` function and instances of `employee` or `salary` inverted indifferently via this function.

With genericity, as many different functions as required are developed. The final result is equivalent to coding all of them manually. In contrast, with inheritance, one single function exists for all types concerned. Inheritance is dynamic; the function behaves differently depending on the instances for which it is executed. Genericity is static; all functions corresponding to genericity instances are developed before compilation, using an automatic coding process. They are therefore implemented for each kind of usage before being invoked.

Definition: *Genericity consists in defining a program model to be used as a basis when automatically coding program parts.*

For the `swap()` function, the use of inheritance to factorize processing is not recommended, as unrelated derived classes would inherit from the same base class. Inheritance diagrams would become complex and unrealistic, even going as far as having an adverse impact on the application. Moreover, the fact that classes are generalized (in this case, the `swapable_element` class) may generate meaningless operations on end instances. For example, an instance of `salary` may be inverted with an instance of `employee`. A pre-condition stipulating that *parameters must be members of the same end class* must be set for the `swap()` function. Genericity is therefore only useful for a very specific type of problem.

Generic classes

If part of a class is generic (typically, a class method), then the whole class must be generic. A method can never be instantiated individually, as this action can only be applied on class level. To declare *generic* classes with the class relation method, the following directive is used: `@generic (instantiation parameters)`.

Applications of genericity

If genericity is applied, it is no longer necessary constantly to recode forward and backward link management algorithms, and so on. The main advantage of genericity appears when handling different types of sets, such as *containers*, *stacks*, *queues* and *lists*. The advantages of genericity are however limited to this type of low-level class.

Including genericity in a model

Generic classes or schemas can be represented in the class relation model. The final application model only contains non-generic classes representing real application notions. Regardless of whether these classes are coded automatically as genericity instances or programmed manually, the model is exactly the same.

11.5 Preparing integration

11.5.1 What is integration?

Definition: *Integration is an activity whereby the software components identified during preliminary design and checked during unit testing are gradually assembled.*

Integration must comply with the strategy adopted during preliminary design. Preliminary design defined the components required to obtain the final product and must determine how and in which order the elements are assembled.

Preparing integration

The following problems must be considered for an integration strategy:

- *Feasibility*: elements are sometimes simply too complex to be assembled directly and require intermediary assembly and test stages.
- *Testability*: two complex elements cannot be assembled directly, without first having tested them. Final testing would be complex, difficult to implement and many software errors would be enmeshed.
- *Scheduling*: the implementation of one component may require the availability of another, which implies that some components are put on hold and the schedule therefore must be extended.
- *Costs*: in an ideal situation, integration occurs after testing all the components. To conduct the necessary tests, the execution environment may have to be emulated for some components. This may require the development of specific tools, which impacts the overall budget. If the budget does not extend this far, some components may have to be assembled without being tested individually.

11.5.2 Figurative example

In Figure 11.28, the basic decision criteria are feasibility and ease of assembly. In the first strategy, the uprights and scaffolding are built for each part, and then the two parts are brought together, which is technically out of the question. In the second strategy, there are no assembly problems.

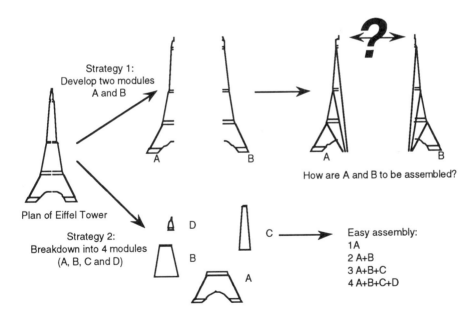

Figure 11.28 Two integration strategies.

11.5.3 Integration levels

Preparing the integration plan

Integration is based on inter-domain and inter-schema dependency diagrams and uses a bottom-up approach to determine which sub-parts can be tested independently (leaves on the diagram). It then specifies the order in which the other sub-parts must be assembled to simplify testing, until all parts have been integrated.

Figure 11.29 shows an example of an integration plan created from an inter-schema dependency diagram. Given that one of the components (schema S4) is developed after the others, it must be emulated so that integration is not interrupted.

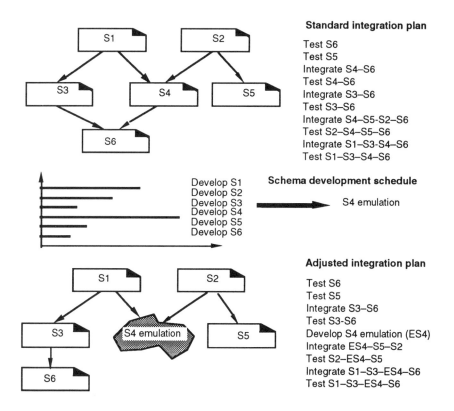

Figure 11.29 Defining an integration plan in line with schedules.

The *architecture diagram* (Figure 11.4 and 11.5) represents the integration summit and is probably the key diagram for integration purposes. The most difficult task is often to integrate several active elements (processes, tasks, and so on) which interact together.

Modelling the integration plan: Integration domains

Domains are used to represent each integration stage. They contain system components grouped together specifically for integration purposes (*IS1*, *IS4* for example). The integration stages in Figure 11.29 are represented as domains in Figure 11.30.

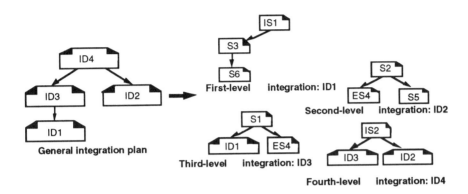

Figure 11.30 Integration plan divided into domains.

A self-contained mini-application must be produced at each stage and the necessary test code developed. Schemas s1 and s2, which are at the top of the dependency diagrams, apparently enable a self-contained application to be built. On the other hand, during the previous stages leading up to integration, a specific integration schema (IS1) may have to be produced to enable the assembled schemas to interact. In the same way, a specific integration schema IS2 may be required to devise integration tests for the s1-s2 interaction.

To help develop integration test sets and implement the assembled classes, special classes can be created using the formal unit test representation rules discussed in section 13.3.

11.5.4 Integration principles

Integration is always a key phase in software development. It is at this stage that many projects fail, fall behind schedule or have to regress to earlier stages. Integration must be carefully prepared by:

- Defining the interfaces between separate parts,
- Describing the order in which the parts are integrated,
- Adopting an integration test strategy.

For object-oriented programming, particular care must be taken with inheritance which indicates stronger coupling between software parts than does ordinary usage.

230 Design

Inheritance-related problems

If class c2 inherits from class c1, c1 must be developed before c2. c2 can only be developed once c1 is stable and fully tested. Any correction or change made to c1 has a significant impact on c2. This constraint is not particularly important if the same person is responsible for developing both c1 and c2, but may be difficult to control if this is not the case. c1 and c2 can only be developed one after the other in that order.

Applications containing inheritance links between two software parts are not infrequent: a significant change to one part often requires that the other one be completely reworked.

Although several different test strategies may be adopted, only one is really possible. c1 is developed and tested before c2 which is based on c1. The definition of an interface between the two main parts enables a traditional safe approach to be adopted, as illustrated in Figure 11.31.

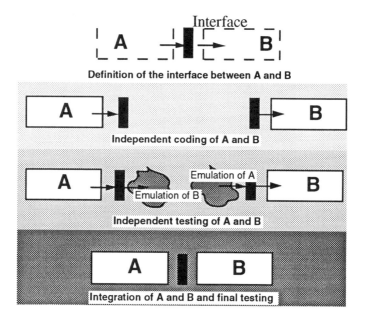

Figure 11.31 Stages used to build two interlinked modules.

The most secure development approach possible must be determined during the design phase. It is very dangerous to integrate a large volume of code at the same time if it has been developed by different people and has not been tested prior to integration.

It is recommended that external classes be used in schemas instead of inheritance in schemas whenever possible. Of course, it is also better to use inter-schema usage rather than inheritance. Inter-class inheritance indicates a strong dependency for the derived class and limited encapsulation for the base class.

A complex inheritance diagram with many class levels often reflects poor design. Rather than reducing the amount of code to be tested as intended, excessive factorization simply complicates integration.

Removing mutual dependencies: using interface classes

Section 8.4 discussed the various techniques used to remove mutual dependencies. The design phase must always result in a schema diagram containing only acyclic dependencies. Different techniques are available for this, including the use of *interface classes*. It must also be noted that the use of *events* not only simplifies dependency diagrams, but also facilitates integration.

11.5.5 Defining integration tests

The purpose of integration tests is to show that the components that have just been assembled work together correctly. These tests must be determined at the end of the design phase, once the integration plan has been drawn up.

A test sequence must, therefore, be provided for each integration stage (for example: S3-S6 test or S2-ES4-S5 test).

When part of the software was emulated (ES4, for example), the software parts based on the emulation (S1 or S2) must be tested again separately.

If unit tests were not conducted on one software component because another was not yet available (for example, S3 with respect to S6), the unit tests can be considered to be an initial integration check.

The tests defined for each class in the integrated parts do not usually guarantee that the classes work correctly together. External classes must often be defined to perform more comprehensive testing.

In the iterative user-oriented class determination approach, classes using the system serve as a basis for integration tests. The test definition technique is then the same as the one used during validation (see Section 10.3.3).

11.6 Class relation design approach (review)

Taking into account architecture constraints

Input for the design phase comes from the model developed during analysis, *technical constraints* highlighted during preliminary analysis and the *virtual machine* providing all elementary instructions required to develop the code.

Once these elements are known, an *architecture diagram* (Figure 11.5) can be drawn to focus on initial design schemas and domains.

At this stage, the analysis model is restructured to divide all modelling items up between the domains in the architecture.

Determining systematic implementation principles

It is very important to be able to determine the general implementation principles and rules applicable to the project. At this stage, *hypergenericity* (Chapter 12) is used to describe the principles and automate development.

Iterating the 'user' principle

Final implementation has not yet been defined. To do so, the requirement-oriented class determination technique (Chapter 9) is used on all classes defined during analysis and grouped into architecture domains and schemas. This iteration continues until the classes can be developed directly on the virtual machine.

Applying design-specific rules

The rules described in Section 8.4 must then be applied. The model is modified to remove mutual dependencies, ensure maximum encapsulation, present software layers, and so on. The schema diagrams show that these rules have been correctly applied.

Ending preliminary design

One question must be asked at all times: at what stage does preliminary design end and *detailed design* begin? This transition can take place once the application structure has been fully defined and the operating principles established.

To do so, all *schemas* must have been determined, which implies that most classes have also been identified. Some classes, however, may only be brought to light during detailed design, when an *operational use* of a new class emerges.

At the end of preliminary design:

- Implementation principles must have been established,
- Each class must have been assigned to a schema,
- There must be no mutual use between schemas,
- Class and class member visibilities must be minimized.

Preparing integration

At the end of preliminary design, the following activities must have been performed:

- The way in which each schema is tested must have been determined,
- The way in which the schemas are integrated must have been defined,
- Any work required to develop integration tests must have been specified.

These activities consolidate design by preparing the work ahead.

11.7 Example: designing the elevator application

Architecture constraints

The purpose of this application is to simulate an elevator system on a multi-windowing workstation. The development environment selected is a Unix workstation with X-Window and Motif ergonomics.

Few architecture constraints have been brought to light at this stage (no server, distribution or real-time constraints, and so on). The simplest architecture in this situation is a mono-process application, based on a Unix system and X-Window-Motif libraries (Figure 11.32).

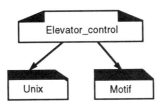

Figure 11.32 Application architecture.

Determining systematic implementation principles

This process will not be discussed at this stage (see Chapter 12). For the elevator application, the following principles can be implemented automatically by *hypergenericity*:

- Graphic user interface: a systematic device must be implemented to handle communications between the graphic user interface (Motif *widgets*) and the application, so that the widgets correspond to application classes and the callbacks generated by them can be handled to trigger internal software actions.
- Event management: the class relation event mechanism is implemented by hypergenericity in line with systematic implementation principles.
- Reactive element management: it will be shown in the following paragraphs that the *reactive element* concept will be required to handle certain types of communication in accordance with design rules.

Systematic implementation principles are determined by solving general technical problems such as:

- How will the relations be created and deleted by each class?
- How will a floor be informed that one of its buttons has been pressed?
- How will an elevator know that it is on the same level as the floor?
- Which technique will be used to assign elevator requests to the appropriate elevator?
- How will the floor be informed that the elevator has arrived, so that the call buttons can be switched off?

In order to answer each of these questions, a general communication and sequencing strategy must be adopted. Three solutions are then possible:

- Each class (`elevator`, `floor`, and so on) is aware of the other classes and can easily send them messages. This solution, often selected in poorly-designed software, must be rejected. There is no class encapsulation and software integration becomes very difficult. This has a negative impact on software quality with respect to maintainability, upgradability and reliability.

234 Design

- The elevator system is aware of all its components. It is used as a sequencer to query the elevators and floors on a regular basis and then send messages to each class to indicate the general situation. It therefore centralizes information and distributes it to the appropriate elements. This solution is more satisfactory than the first one, but does however have two disadvantages: on the one hand, it only works for the simulation and on the other, a large amount of information must be brought together at system class level, which makes this class difficult to manage.

- The operating principle is based on the real-life situation. A series of detectors inform each component of the events to which it must react. For example, each elevator has a detector which informs it that it has gone past a floor. In principle, this last solution is more realistic, in that each component is only given the information it requires (good encapsulation). It will be chosen for this example and the *event* concept will be used to solve communication problems between the outside world and the elevator or the floor.

Applying design-specific rules

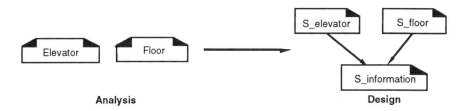

Figure 11.33 Dividing classes up into new schemas.

Based on the analysis models, all mutual inter-class dependency must be removed and the model divided up into the most appropriate schemas. The elevator and floor domains, therefore, become schemas (s_elevator and s_floor). The button and display_unit classes were divided up between these domains. They must now be included in a separate schema called s_information (Figure 11.33).

The classes in the s_information schema cannot use classes in the s_elevator and s_floor schemas. Moreover, it would not be acceptable for an elementary component such as button to base its operations on a complex component such as elevator. The mechanisms used to inform an elevator or a floor that one of its buttons has been pressed must therefore be designed in such a way that the elevator/button relation is not mutually oriented.

The following paragraphs describe a solution which complies with the one recommended in Section 8.4.1, in which the operating mechanism is generalized and all mutual usage is avoided. The general problem concerning coupling between an information receiver and a component in the elevator system is modelled in a more abstract schema called s_interaction.

This new schema contains two classes (Figure 11.34). The interactive_element class receives information from the outside world (such as the button or detector classes), whereas the reactive_element class represents a system component which is linked with several `interactive_elements` (`elevator` or `floor`) and which reacts to the information received by `interactive_element`. An `interactive_element` receives information in event form, which corresponds to the way the `buttons` are actually used.

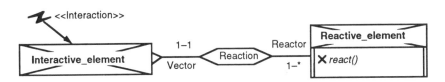

Figure 11.34 Representing the `s_interaction` schema.

In this manner, the `elevator/button` relation remains oriented in a single direction, while the `button` is still used to get the `elevator` to react (Figure 11.35).

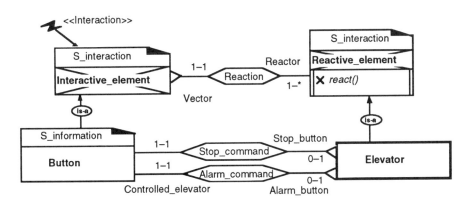

Figure 11.35 Applying this principle to the `button` and `elevator` (`s_elevator` schema).

Structuring the software

The general software structure is illustrated with the graphic user interface in Figure 11.36. The classes corresponding to communication *events* have been grouped together either in `s_information` (`overload`, `floor_reached`) or `s_interaction` (`interaction`). The flow diagram in Figure 11.37 shows the information exchanged between each high-level schema, as reviewed during the design phase.

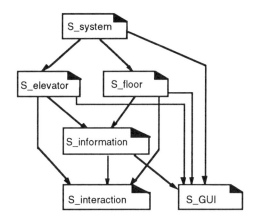

Figure 11.36 Application schema diagram.

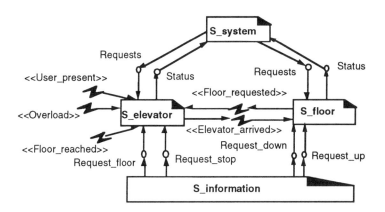

Figure 11.37 Inter-schema flow diagram.

Detailed view of the `s_elevator` schema

The design phase highlights the need for a `request` class to provide the highly complex processing required for elevator movement requests. The `request` notion therefore becomes a key issue. In fact, each time a `user` requests that the elevator go up or down from inside the `elevator`, the `elevator` must execute this command. To do so, it must store it in the list of any other current commands so that an execution priority can be established. For example, if the `elevator` is moving from the fourth floor to the sixth, the request to go back down to the first floor will be executed after a request to move to the fifth floor.

Moreover, if the `elevator` is called from a `floor`, the system must select which `elevator` is in the best position to meet this request. For this reason, the `evaluate_request()` method in the `evaluate` class provides an integer value representing the degree of difficulty in reaching the requested floor. The `record_request()` method defined for the `elevator` class reacts to the `floor_requested` event and selects the appropriate instance of `elevator` to execute the request at minimum expense.

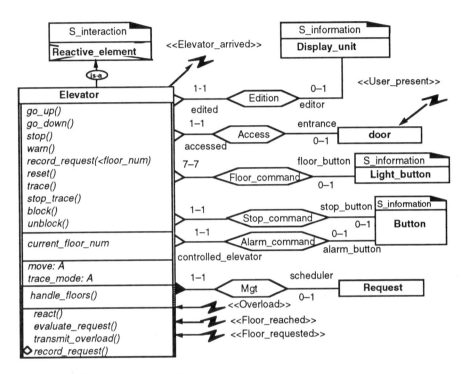

Figure 11.38 `S_elevator` schema.

Figure 11.38 does not give a detailed view of the `s_elevator` schema. It does, however, highlight the key issues: the appearance of the `request` class, the change in `door` class visibility (body class), relation visibilities and the communication mechanisms between the `elevator` and the `floor`. The `elevator` transmits a general `elevator_arrival` event when it reaches a floor and reacts to a `floor_requested` event from a `user` on a `floor`. It is informed of the actions taken by the `user` via its `buttons` because it inherits from the `reactive_element` class and redefines the `react()` method in line with its own specific requirements. This method is activated by one of its `buttons` (derived from `interactive_element`).

Preliminary design defines the visibility for each modelled item.

Preparing integration

The integration domain diagram in Figure 11.39 illustrates the integration plan:

- Stage 1: `I_GUI` including `s_GUI` + `Motif`.

238 Design

- Stage 2: I_information including s_information + s_interaction + I_GUI.
- Stage 3: I_elevator including s_elevator + I_GUI + I_information, or I_floor including s_floor + I_GUI + I_information.
- Stage 4: I_system including s_system + I_elevator + I_floor.

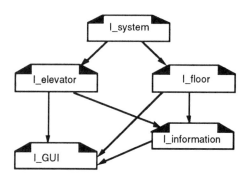

Figure 11.39 Integration domain diagram.

12 Carrying through a model: hypergenericity

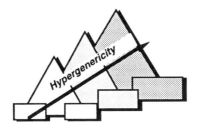

12.1 Introduction

12.1.1 Advantages

Reducing development complexity

During both the design phase and model implementation, many technical details are added to the model in the form of classes, attributes, methods, and so on (Figure 12.1). The resulting application model is, therefore, quite complex. Consequently, the end user or author of the user requirements can review the analysis phase but no longer understands design and implementation documents.

Systematic principles imposed by technical environment choices (virtual machine) and the implementation strategy adopted are, however, frequently used as a basis for implementing the model. For example, a graphic user interface in the X-Window environment must always handle the same callback mechanism and this always has a disruptive effect on the initial model. The ideal solution is therefore to represent known implementation principles separately, so that they can be applied automatically to the model when it is implemented (Figure 12.2).

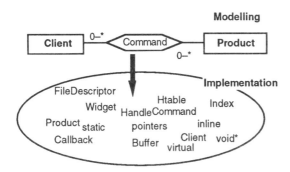

Figure 12.1 The initial model is swamped in technical details.

240 Carrying through a model: hypergenericity

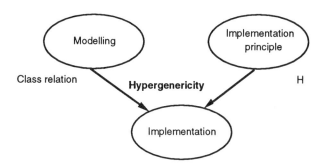

Figure 12.2 Hypergenericity separates the model and implementation principles into two distinct models.

As a result, the model remains clear and is not swamped in highly specific technical details concerning implementation decisions.

Favouring reuse

The possibility of reusing an implementation is limited, as a particular technical solution has been combined with the model for a specific domain (Figure 12.3). It is possible to reuse a *Unix payroll* product, based on *X-Window* and a *relational database* or *VMS-based payroll software* using a *character mode screen* and a *network database*, but not just a *payroll* system.

If the implementation principles can be kept separate from the model, then the same model can be reused with different implementation principles, or the same implementation principles can be reused on different models.

A *payroll program* can therefore be reused, regardless of how it is implemented, or the *Unix-based X-Window relational database application implementation principles* can be reused on different models.

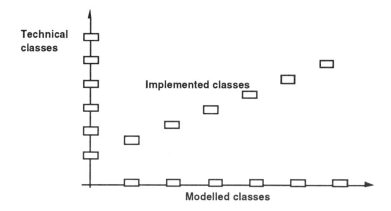

Figure 12.3 Implemented classes are a combination of technical and analysis classes.

Introduction

Finally, the task of modelling an application can be efficiently differentiated from the tasks required to implement it in a specific environment. Implementation expertise is therefore centralized in a set of implementation rules.

Using model information to develop software

It has been seen that computer models enable an application to be described in detail. Their features can be extended to transform them into fully-fledged application description languages on a higher level than programming languages. Their advantage lies in the fact that they can specify what must be done without taking into account the way it will be done. They are particularly useful during the analysis phase.

Nevertheless, a model reflects a great deal of hard work, which should be reused during the following development phases, and constitutes a valuable source of information for the future application. The model should be integrated as systematically as possible.

Moreover, in a great many software projects, the same implementation rules are applied throughout the system, thus generating repetitive development work. If the final code for a product is analyzed in detail, it can be seen that a large proportion of it is 'run of the mill' code and only a small part (10% to 20%) is actually specific to the corresponding problem. Even if powerful features such as *inheritance* and *genericity* are used to factorize the code, this ratio remains the same.

Hypergenericity (Desfray, 1993) is a paradigm which carries forward both the *model* describing the current problem and the *implementation principles* selected, and converts the model automatically into its actual implementation. This new technique reinforces and automates the *iterative model fine-tuning approach* applied from analysis through to coding.

Finally, it is used to express model implementation principles formally and develop a truly design-oriented language called *H* (Figure 12.4).

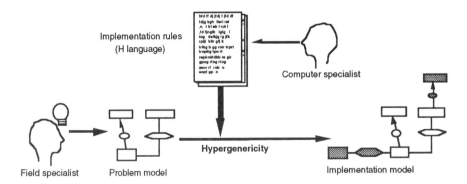

Figure 12.4 Hypergenericity separates the model from implementation principles and automates implementation.

12.1.2 Definition

Definition: *Hypergenericity is a mechanism whereby a model is automatically transformed by applying external rules.*

Although one of the main uses of hypergenericity is to apply design principles automatically, it actually has a much broader scope. The *H* language supports hypergenericity by providing a way to:

- Handle models,
- Generate code or documentation,
- Define specific controls for a model.

Hypergenericity can be applied in all cases where it is possible to stipulate rules to:

- Produce a new modelling item from already existing modelling items,
- Transform existing items.

For example, the following rule can be expressed using hypergenericity:
All public attributes for a class (A : ClassA) *must be read-only.*

In most programming languages, this rule takes the following form (Figure 12.5):
All public attributes for a class (A : ClassA) *will be implemented as a public method accessing* A (GetA() : in return ClassA) *and a private attribute* A.

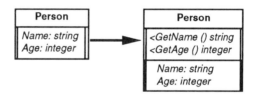

Figure 12.5 Hypergenericity is used to automatically apply the above transformation.

12.1.3 Principle

Hypergenericity is a model transformation mechanism that expresses rules in a dedicated language called *H*. Section 12.3 discusses the structure of the *H* language in greater detail.

The following principle is used to lay down hypergenericity rules. Modelling items are carried forward to reflect their definitions in the actual model. Neither hypergenericity nor the *H* language are specific to the class relation model. They both have a much broader scope.

For example, a print() method may have to be defined for each class in order to print its contents. The hypergenericity rule for a current class called C will be as follows:

Add the print() *method to* C;
Assign the in *passing mode to* print();

Assign the following code to `print()` :
```
Code name := C++ ;
```
For any attribute A *of* C
  Insert the —name of A—*.Print()* ; *instruction* ;

In the `person` class example, this rule can be applied to produce the following method:

```
Print : in ()
   Processing
      text: C++
         Name.Print() ;
         Age.Print() ;
      end text
```

This example illustrates the power of hypergenericity which provides a level of automation impossible to achieve up to now via genericity and inheritance alone. A model is in fact extended or adapted, each element being specifically transformed in line with its own definition.

12.2 Implementation directives

Definition

Implementation directives are a means to add more information to a model to specify how it is implemented in a given environment. They are used to extend or adapt a class relation model in line with specific requirements.

Example

In the example using the `print()` method, some classes may be 'printable', whereas others are not, or a given attribute within a 'printable' class may be 'printable', whereas others are not. The `@Print` directive is therefore added to the printable classes, and the `@NoPrint` directive is added to the non-printable attributes within the printable class. In the example below, the `person` class is 'printable', whereas its `name` attribute is not.

```
class person ...
text : directive
   : @Print
   name : @NoPrint
end text ...
attribute
   name : string (*) ;
   age : integer ; ...
```

Hypergenericity rules defining the `print()` method use these directives to transform the model.

IF C *contains the* `@Print` *directive*
  Add the `print()` *method to* C ;
  Assign the in*passing mode to* `print()` ;
  Assign the following code to `print()`:
```
Code name := C++ ;
```

For any attribute A *of* C *without the* @NoPrint *directive insert the* —name of A—.Print() ; *code ;*

Applying this technique

The directive approach enables notions in the class relation model to be defined exclusively in terms of their semantic importance, rather than because a great many mechanisms may prove useful. For example, the *interface class*, ***transmutable class***, *persistent class* and *generic class* notions can (and should) be handled exclusively via directives and hypergenericity.

Moreover, the class relation model can be applied to any computer language, without becoming dependent on it, as it uses directives. For C++, a set of very specific notions exist, and they are expressed by directives:

- 'Virtual' methods or inheritance (@virtual directive),
- 'Inline' methods (@inline directive),
- Passing of parameters by pointer (@* directive).

These directives are then handled by hypergenericity rules, which highlight the specific characteristics of the implementation environment (languages, tools, libraries, and so on).

They enable the class relation model to be extended by the programmer who annotates each specific modelling item. As they are defined in a separate section within the class relation description, model independence is guaranteed; the rules can be modified without changing the model.

12.3 The H language

12.3.1 H and the meta-model

Overview

H is the model handling language that processes the definitions in the model. *H* is therefore based on the **meta-model** for a given model (the class relation model in the following examples). The *H* language is used to access and modify each item accessible from a given modelled item (such as a *class*). These items may be the class name (Name) or its related classes, and so on. *H* is an object-oriented language, but not a programming language. The objects handled are modelled items (person class, eat() method, age attribute).

Modelling items

Each item in the model can be accessed and handled via the *H* language, using the **MIt** (modelling item) concept. An MIt is a symbol representing a specific type of information within the model. For example, a *state*, *transition*, *event* or *class* is represented in the *H* language and handled via MIts. Each MIt is identified by name (for example, in the class context, ComponentAttribute indicates its attributes and Name its name).

The H language

All *H* rules are applied to an item in the model (such as the `person` class), a specific value being assigned to the appropriate MIts.

The following *H* rule:

```
"This is the class called" + name
```

generates the following result when applied to the `person` class:

```
This is the class called person
```

Note: *The following convention has been adopted in* H *syntax examples: keywords are in bold and MIts are underlined.*

Simple and complex MIts

In Figure 12.6, the `Name` MIt is a *simple MIt*, as its occurrence is expressed by a simple value. The `ParentClass` MIt however is not considered to be a simple MIt, as it refers to all classes related to the current class, each related class being itself a complex structure. This is also the case of `ComponentAttribute` or `ComponentMethod` for a class, and `ComponentParameter` for a method, which are all complex MIts. A simple MIt is a single object (such as the current class *name*), whereas a complex MIt represents a series of objects (such as the *methods* in the current class).

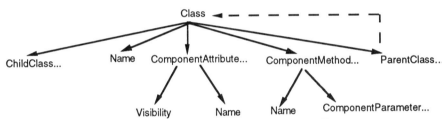

Figure 12.6 Dependency diagram for simple and complex MIts.

MIts and the meta-model

Definition: *A meta-model is the model of the model itself.*

All MIts predefined by the model are determined by the *meta-model*. For example, Figure 12.7 illustrates a small part of the meta-model for the class relation model. MIt definition rules are used to express which MIts can be accessed from a class:

- Simple MIts:
    - Name
    - IsAbstract
    - IsElementary
- Complex MIts:
    - ComponentAttribute
    - ParentClass
    - ChildClass

246 Carrying through a model: hypergenericity

Complex MIts are created by concatenating the role and the name of the related class:

role name→Parent Class ←class name.

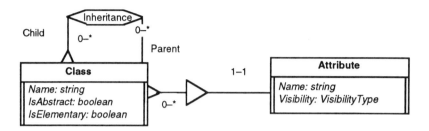

Figure 12.7 Partial view of the class relation meta-model.

An MIt such as `Visibility` cannot be accessed directly from the class. The *context* for the corresponding attribute must be established before accessing its visibility. It will be seen that the *H* language is used to navigate through the modelling items and to change contexts by following the links defined by the meta-model (for example, from `Class` to `Attribute`).

MIts are objects

H classes

Each type of information that can be accessed in the model becomes an *H* class (`Method`, `Attribute`, `Schema`, `Class`, and so on). Inheritance links may of course exist between these classes; `Method` and `Attribute` for example both inherit from `Member`. All *H* classes inherit from the *MIt* class (equivalent to the 'object' class in object-oriented languages). Five classes have been predefined in the *H* language:

- `MIt` class,
- `string` class,
- `boolean` class,
- `integer` class,
- `SetOfMIt` class.

H therefore enables the classes defined by the meta-model to be managed. The meta-model defines the classes, attributes, relations and inheritance links that represent the information supported by a model. The *H* language specifies how the instances are used, by defining methods. It is a transformation rule declaration language.

It is assumed that the meta-model has been predefined, and so the *H* language programmer simply writes *H* methods for meta-model classes. These methods express transformation rules for instances representing a given model.

MIt overview

H MIts are a means of expressing one or more class representatives (parts of a model). They are objects, the class of which may be:

- An MIt class (`Integer`, `Method`, `Schema`, and so on),
- A set of MIt class instances, called `SetOfMIt`.

For example, the `ComponentMethod` MIt used in the `Class` context refers to all instances of the `Method` class, that is all methods in the current class. The `ParentClass` MIt indicates all representatives of the `Class` class, that are base classes for the current class.

Sets

Sets (`SetOfMIt`) can reply to messages:

- `Card()` returns the number of instances included,
- `Add(element or set)` is used to add new element(s) to a set.

Sets include a *broadcast* mechanism. If a message is sent to a set but does not correspond to a particular method in that set (`Card()`, `Add()`, and so on), the message will be broadcast to all set instances.

For example, in a class context, `ComponentMethod.delete_pre_condition()` generates the `delete_pre_condition()` message for each method in the class.

H methods

Description

An *H* program is made up of *H* methods applied to the current meta-model. As seen earlier in this chapter, *H* does not enable new classes to be created (it is limited to the model to which it is applied). New methods can, however, be defined and instances created, deleted and modified.

Each *H method*, containing a set of *H* rules, is defined in a specific context for a given class relation item, such as a `Class`, `Domain`, `Attribute`. The *context* contains the current instance, for which the method is invoked.

A *message* is activated for a specific MIt, to which it applies the rules in the corresponding method.

Example

The `person` class is a modelled item. The *H* method defined for its *H* class (in this case `Class`) can therefore be applied. The '.' operator is used to invoke an *H* method for the item accessed. The following example illustrates how the rules in the `Example()` method are invoked for classes inheriting from the current class:

    ChildClass.Example()

An *H* method is declared in the meta-model via the class relation model.

```
class Class ...
Example ()
processing
```

```
        text : H
          Result : string
          ComponentMethod
             begin
                Result := Result + Name
             end
        end text
```

Parameters

As in the class relation model, methods may have *parameters*, for which the following information is defined:

- Name,
- Passing mode (*in*, *out*, *inout*),
- H class,
- Return value.

```
        class Class ...
        Compare (operand : in Class, result : out boolean)
        processing
          text : H
            result := false
            ComponentAttribute
               begin ...
            end text
```

Unnamed methods

Rules may be written for a specific MIt without defining an actual method for the MIt class. To do so, the required rules are placed after the MIt between the **begin** and **end** keywords.

```
    ParentClass
    begin
       Result := Result + Name + " : " + ComposedSchema.Name + ", "
    end
```

This example is the same as defining a method

```
    class Class ...
    NoName ()
    processing
      text : H
        Result := Result + Name + " : " + ComposedSchema.Name + ", "
      end text
```

and then sending a message:

```
       ParentClass.NoName()
```

Variables

Variables can be declared and initialized in the *H* language. Their types are determined by the name of the corresponding class:

```
          V1 : MIt := "Hello World"
          V2 : Class := V
```

```
V3 : string := "Bye"
```
When the variable concerns a complex class (such as an `Attribute` or `Method`), it is initialized by referencing an already existing MIt or by using the `Create()` instruction illustrated below.
```
V1 : Attribute.Create ()
```

Context

Overview

These initial examples have demonstrated that all information is not necessarily accessed on the same level. A model navigation system is used, as illustrated in Figure 12.7. When instructions concern a specific MIt, they can handle any information related to its environment or *context*. For example, the context for an *H* method is the MIt to which it refers.

When a specific MIt is referenced, the **begin** and **end** keywords delimit its context. The following example includes a series of nested contexts (unnamed methods) within an instruction. It returns the names of all schemas in a domain, all classes in each schema and finally all methods in each class.

```
Schema
begin       -- Schema context
   Result := Result + Name + " :"
   ComposedClass
     begin -- Context for a class in the schema
       Result := Result + Name + " :"
       ComposedMethod
         begin      -- Context for a method in the class
           Result := Result + Name
         end
     end -- Return to schema context
     Result := Result + ","
end
```

The execution context for a rule not only represents the object to which it refers, but also the *path* required to access it. The path can be handled using specific context management operators.

Context management

Contexts can be handled by *predefined variables* or *scope operators*. The following predefined variables exist:

- `Self` or the current MIt to which the rules apply,
- `Previous` or the previous MIt in the path which led to the current context,
- `Root` or the entry-point MIt used to initiate hypergenericity rule execution.

The *scope operator* (:) is used to specify the context corresponding to the required element out of all contexts used to access the current one. For example, if the current context concerns a *method* accessed via its class, the name of its class can be accessed in two different ways: `Previous.Name` or `Class:Name`.

The *invocation operator* (.) is used to access information in the appropriate context for the MIt.

12.3.2 H language instructions

Control structures

H contains control structures similar to those used in procedural languages. They are adapted to navigation around a model and are based primarily on the *context* and *message broadcast* concepts.

An *H* method is a group of *H* instructions, which either handle modelling items (MIts), constants and variables or declare variables.

Operators

Several types of values can be handled:

- *Character strings*, which are used the most frequently,
- Modelling item values (*Class*, *ParentClass*, and so on), which are complex values that must be further decomposed,
- *Integer* values,
- *Boolean* values used in conditional expressions.

H provides the necessary operators for each type. For example, the assign (:=) and compare (=) operators can be applied to modelling item values. The concatenation operator (+) can be used on character strings.

A *condition* is a boolean expression placed in brackets, the purpose of which is to handle a boolean result (comparison or return value). It is used in language control structures. The traditional *and* and *or* operators can be used in boolean expressions.

Create, delete and assign instructions

The `Create()`, `Delete()` and assign instructions are used to provide the model transformation capability in hypergenericity. They are used to modify modelling values, create new modelling items and delete existing ones, thus performing design work automatically on an analysis model.

An element can be created in two ways:

- A variable is defined and initialized,
- The `Create` instruction is executed on a set of elements.

The `Create` instruction creates new representatives in a set. It activates the constructor (specific method in the called class) and sets the context for the created element; each property can then be assigned. For example, a `Print()` method can be created in the current class (see the example in Section 12.1.3):

```
class Class ...
MakePrintable()
processing
 text : H
   CodeMethod : string
```

```
ComponentMethod.Create ()         -- Create a method
    begin
      Name := "Print"
      PassingMode := "in"
      ProcessingText.Create()
 -- Create C++ code for the method
        begin
          Name := "C++"
          -- Define C++ code to execute "Attributes.print();"
          Class:ComponentAttribute
            begin
              CodeMethod := codeMethod + Name + ".Print() ;"
            end
          Content := CodeMethod
        end
    end
  end text
```

The `Print()` method is automatically added to a class to which the `MakePrintable()` *H* method is applied.

Assignments are also used to modify an existing element. For example, `Visibility := "Private"` transforms a public attribute into a private attribute. Finally, the `Delete()` instruction concerns the element itself. For example, the following instruction deletes all public methods in a class. The `Self` predefined variable and `Select` instruction are also used.

```
class Class …
ExampleDelete()
processing
  text : H
    ComponentMethod.Select (Visibility = "Public")
    begin
        Self.Delete()
    end
  end text
```

Loops

Principle

Only some of the data is in set form; this is typically the case of complex MIts. For example, `ComponentMethod` refers to all methods in a current class. Loops are key structures in the *H* language; they enable each set element to be processed in turn. A loop is expressed by referencing the set name, followed by the **begin** and **end** keywords.

```
Set
   begin
   --Instructions for the current set element
   end
```

It is similar to the *broadcast* principle used with unnamed methods to send messages to all occurrences in a set.

252 Carrying through a model: hypergenericity

For example, the following program lists all the methods in a class, with their respective parameters. Each parameter is followed by a comma.

```
Method
  begin
    Result := Result + Name + ":"
    ComponentParameter
      begin
        Result := Result + Name + ","
      end
  end
  Result.print()
```

When applied to the class in Figure 12.8, this program generates the following output:

```
m1 : p1, p2
m2 : p3, p4
```

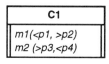

Figure 12.8 Example class.

Select instruction

The `Select` instruction is used to select set elements that meet a given condition. It is similar to the SQL instruction. The general syntax is shown below:

```
Set.Select (condition)
```

It also produces a set, to which the following programming instructions can be applied:

```
-- Assign result set to another one
E := Set.Select (condition)
-- Execute the 'method()' message on all selected elements
Set.Select (condition).method()
-- Nested selects
Set.Select (condition).Select (condition2)
-- Loop on selected set
Set.Select (condition)
  begin
-- Instruction for current element
  end
```

For example, the following instructions are used to display the names of only the public methods in a class:

```
ComponentMethod.Select (Visibility = "Public")
  begin
```

```
Result := Result + Name + ", "
   end
```

Conditions

Conditions use the traditional *if* structure on boolean expressions:

```
if (Name = "Arthur")
   Result := "Element found"
else
   Result := "Element not found"
end
```

12.4 Temporary or persistent hypergenericity

12.4.1 Temporary hypergenericity

Hypergenericity rules are used to transform a model automatically. The purpose of this transformation may be, for example, to meet specific implementation requirements. These rules may add new classes, methods or attributes, and so on. If the resulting model, or *transformed model*, can be implemented immediately (executable code can be deduced), the transformed classes can be released (Figure 12.9).

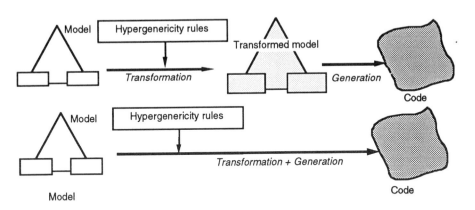

Figure 12.9 A model can only be changed temporarily for implementation purposes.

The view does not therefore become overly complex, as implementation-related elements are masked. For example, a rule states that:

All oriented relations with 1–1 or 0–1 cardinalities are implemented as a C++ pointer attribute in the source class, pointing to the target class.

This attribute does not need to be included in the model; it only needs to be considered during implementation. Any changes made to the model may be reported in the implementation by executing the hypergenericity rules again, which is not the case if the transformed model is being updated.

12.4.2 Persistent hypergenericity

The advantage of persistent hypergenericity becomes apparent when the transformed model can be used as a starting point and enhanced prior to final implementation. This is the case when hypergenericity:

- Did not produce a model that could be implemented immediately,
- Has produced a transformed model, the new elements of which are important to the model itself and can be reused.

For example, hypergenericity can transform a class relation schema into a logical RDBMS schema of interest to the implementation team (as it creates relational tables immediately). Additional modelling work can then be performed on the transformed model, for example, to take into account physical optimization requirements (Figure 12.10).

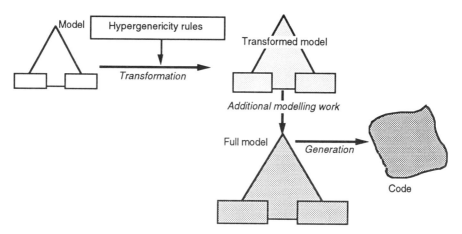

Figure 12.10 Modelling work continues on the transformed models produced by hypergenericity.

12.5 Examples using hypergenericity

Note: *The following pages contain a series of examples that illustrate the advantages of hypergenericity. Novice users may find some technical implementation principles difficult to understand, but they should not consider it to be a stumbling block as the main point is to understand the potential of hypergenericity. All examples are for C++.*

The examples are not necessarily complete, their purpose being to present the primary principles of hypergenericity.

12.5.1 Attribute encapsulation rules

Description

To prevent one instance from being modified by another, a specific C++ implementation technique must be used. To do this, all public attributes (AttributeName) in a class are transformed into protected attributes and the attribute value can only be accessed via a specific public method called GetAttributeName() (See Figure 12.5.). As a result, an attribute cannot be modified directly from outside the current instance and encapsulation is maintained. The rule described in Section 4.3.1, whereby any attribute can be transformed into a method, is applicable here.

Implementation principles

> The following rule is applied:
> *For any public attribute of a class*
>   *Assign protected visibility*
>   *Create a public method called* getAttributeName()
>   *Implement C++ code to return its value*
> This corresponds to the following H code:

```
class Class …
AttributeEncapsulation ()
processing
text : H
CurrentAttribute : Attribute
-- Select public attributes
     ComponentAttribute.Select (Visibility = "public")
       begin
            Visibility := "protected"  -- Protected attribute
            CurrentAttribute := Self
-- Add a method to the class
--(here Previous corresponds to the attribute's class)
          Previous.ComponentMethod.create ()
            begin
-- Method name = 'Get attribute name'
               Name := "Get" + CurrentAttribute.Name
               Visibility := "public"
-- ModelClass is the class typing the attribute
               ReturnClass := CurrentAttribute.ModelClass
               ProcessingText.Create ()
                begin
                    Name := "C++"
                end
-- Defining the return value during processing
               Processing.Return := CurrentAttribute.Name
            end
       end
end text
```

Example

The `person` class is defined as follows:

```
class person
 public
  attribute
    Name : string (*);
    Age  : integer ; …
```

When the H `AttributeEncapsulation()` message is received, the class is transformed as follows:

```
class Person
 public
  method
    GetName () return string (*);
    GetAge  () return integer;
 protected
  Attribute
    Name : string (*);
    Age  : integer ;
body person

GetAge () return integer
end method GetAge return Age;

GetName return string (*)
end method GetName return Name ; …
```

12.5.2 Storing and retrieving objects in files

Description

Some class instances must be stored in files during program execution and retrieved later. The implementation difficulty lies in handling inter-instance links. These links are lost when instances are stored in a file. The value of each attribute must also be converted into a value in the file.

Implementation principles

The principle is systematic: all attributes and related instances are stored for each instance and then reloaded with appropriate link management. A directive called `@storable` is used to specify that class instances can be stored in and retrieved from a file. For any 'storable' class, a `save()` method is created automatically to save the instance, and a `load()` class method is used to reload it from the file (Figure 12.11).

When an instance is saved, it is no longer identified by a memory address, but by a file index. To handle memory address/file index equivalence, the `save()` method returns the file index and the `load()` method uses it to reload an instance.

Examples using hypergenericity

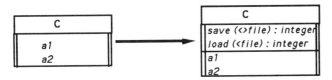

Figure 12.11 Automatic transformation using hypergenericity.

These two methods can be called several times with the same values. A duplicate save or load simply returns the instance with the file index specified, or the index corresponding to the specified instance, respectively.

A simplified version of this algorithm is presented below. It shows that the save() and load() processing implements any existing base classes, in order to combine all processing specific to the derived class with that of the base class. The following principle is applied:

>   *For each 'storable' class* C
>   *Add the* save() *method to* C
>   *Define its processing:*
>   *Start*
>   *For each base class* C' *of* C
>   *Invoke* save() *for class* C'
>   *For each attribute* A *of* C
>   A.save()
>   *Record the* '/' *separator*
>
>   *For each relation* R
>   *For each instance* I *linked to* C *by* R
>   *Save* I *and link to* I *(index of* I*)*
>   *Record index returned by* I.save()
>   *Record the* '/' *separator*
>   *End*
>   *Add the* Load() *method to* C ...

The corresponding *H* code is as follows:

```
class Class ...
Storable ()
processing
text : H
  MethodCode : string
  if (directive ("@storable") )
     -- Add the 'save' method
     ComponentMethod.Create ()
     begin
        Name := "save"
        -- The return value is the storage index
        ReturnClass := "integer"
        -- Add a parameter to the "save" method
        ComponentParameter.Create ()
        begin
```

258 Carrying through a model: hypergenericity

```
            Name := "file"
            Passing mode := "inout"
            ModelClass := "ostream"
         end
         -- Assign the method code.
         ProcessingText.Create ()
          begin
            Name := "C++"
            MethodCode := "int i;" + "int return_value = 0;"
            -- Invoke the 'save' method for all base classes
            --    of the current class
              if (Previous.Previous.ParentClass.Card() = 0)
                --There are no base classes
                begin
                  MethodCode := MethodCode +
                             "return_value = file.getIndex();"
               end
             else
               Previous.Previous.ParentClass
                 begin
                    MethodCode := MethodCode + "return_value =" 
                                  + Name + "::save();"
                 end
               -- Save each attribute in the current class,
               --    using the '<<' operator
               Previous.ComponentAttribute
               begin
                  MethodCode := MethodCode + "file <<" + Name +";"
                   "file << '/' ;"
               end
-- Save the storage index for each instance linked with the
--    current instance via all class relations
               Previous.ComponentRelation
                  begin           -- C++ loop on linked instances
                    MethodCode := MethodCode + "for (i = 0; i < Card"
                           + RoleName + "(); i++)
                           {
                            file << Get" + RoleName + " (i)->save();
                            file << '/' ;
                           }"
    -- RoleName is the name of the target class role. GetRoleName
    -- in the C++ implementation corresponds to the name of the
    -- method used to access the linked instances
                 end -- END of relation usage
             Content := MethodCode
          end -- END of code description
          Processing.Return := "return_value"
       end -- END of 'save()' description
    end -- END of IF
```

```
...
end text
```

Example

The `storable()` message is now applied to the example of a 'storable' class c (Figure 12.12).

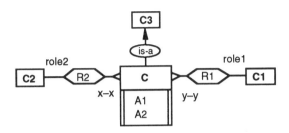

Figure 12.12 Example of a 'storable' class.

This *H* method will automatically add a new method (`save()`) to the c class. It has the following class relation description:

```
save (file : inout ostream) return integer
processing
text : C++
   int i;
   int return_value = 0;
   return_value = C3::save();
   file << A1 ;
   file << '/' ;
   file << A2 ;
   file << '/' ;
   for (i = 0; i < Cardrole1(); i++)
      {
      file << Getrole1 (i)->save();
      file << '/' ;
      }
   for (i = 0; i < Cardrole2(); i++)
      {
      file << Getrole2 (i)->save();
      file << '/' ;
      }
end text
end method save return return_value ;
```
Twenty-two lines are therefore automatically deduced from 55 lines of *H* rules. Only two simple classes or one more complex class need to be implemented, or several changes made to the class definition for the operation to be worthwhile.

260 Carrying through a model: hypergenericity

12.5.3 Displayable objects

Description

Each object in an application is to be handled by creating an individual window. Each method is represented by a button and each attribute by a button used to display or enter its value. Moreover, each relation provides access to related instances.

Implementation principles

The above example, although relatively complex, can be implemented automatically for any class.

Need for a specific library
A library must first be created, the purpose being to define the following actions in such a manner that facilitates implementation. A button must be displayed, the application must be informed that the button has been activated and a window such as the one illustrated in Figure 12.13 must be created.

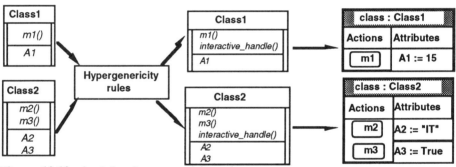

Figure 12.13 Applying hypergenericity rules.

Using a special-purpose directive
The classes for which instances can be displayed use the @InteractiveHandled directive. The implementation principle is described below:

> *For each class* C *with the* InteractiveHandled *directive*
> *Add the* InteractiveHandle *method to* C
> *Define processing :*
> *Start*
> *Create an instance of the handling window HW for* C *(use of the library)*
> *For each base class* C' *of* C
> *execute H message* handleProperties()
> *-- NB:* 'C'.handleProperties()' *is simply executed*
>
> *execute H message* handleProperties() *on* C
> *End*
> ...
> handleProperties()

Start
  For each attribute A *in the current class*
    Create an attribute button on HW for A
  For each method M *in the current class*
    Create an invoke button on HW for M
  For each relation R *in the current class*
    Create a relation button on HW for R
End

12.5.4 Relation management rules

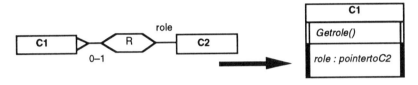

Figure 12.14 Systematic transformation implementing a relation.

Description

When a relation is oriented from class c1 to class c2, and c2 plays the role role, then class c1 will have the following method:

- Getrole() providing all instances of c2 linked with the activated instance of c1.

See Figures 12.14 and 12.15.

Figure 12.15 All wives of instance 'Smith' of the Man class are returned by sending the 'Smith.Getwife()' message.

Implementation principles

All modelled relations are transformed by adding the methods required to access related instances. The way in which access methods are implemented depends on the principle adopted. When dynamic objects are handled, the relation is implemented in C++ pointer form, whereas database objects are accessed via a search for related elements.

Required rules

There are no class members called Getrole(). In the following example, the *H* language is used to perform consistency checks rather than transform a model:

```
CheckRelations()
processing
text : H
    ComponentRelation
    begin
        Class:ComponentMember.Select
                    (Name = 'Get' + Previous.Previous.Name)
        begin
            Error handling
        end
    end
end text
```

12.5.5 Logical and physical database schemas

Description

A model must be systematically reworked before it can be implemented on a database. Depending on the type of database, class relation schemas must be transformed to:

- Implement inheritance if the database is not an object database (for example, a relational database),
- Implement the links for the relations,
- Apply physical database optimization rules (indexes, storage, and so on).

The conceptual model is thus transformed into a logical model which is in turn transformed into a physical model. Whereas conceptual to logical model translations are well-known and can be applied systematically, logical to physical model translations must be specified individually for each component.

Finally, it must be possible to code the classes represented in the class relation model in compliance with the conceptual model, the logical and physical transformations performed being masked. In this case, hypergenericity enables the whole development process to be automated, by making data storage completely transparent for the application.

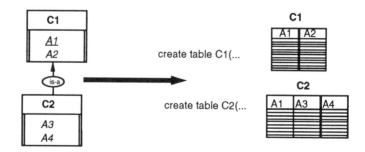

Figure 12.16 Example whereby a structure model is transformed into a logical database schema.

Implementation principles

The implementation principles are not described here because they are complex and depend on the database used. The technique used does, however, respect the following principle.

For each type of optimization allowed by the DBMS (hashing, BTree, cluster, and so on) suitable directives must be defined. Examples are `@hash (attribute1, attribute2)`, `@BTree (attribute1, attribute2)`, `@cluster(class2)`. The `@persistent` directive specifies that only some of the attributes are to be stored.

The conceptual schema is transformed into a logical schema by applying systematic rules on:

- Relation cardinality,
- Relation orientation,
- The existence of inheritance links.

Specific routines to save or retrieve attributes in the database must be developed to make the necessary assignments and conversions.

Required rules

```
-- Classes related with persistent classes are themselves
-- persistent
-- A class derived from a persistent class must also be
-- persistent
    PersistencyControl ()
    processing
    text : H
      RelatedClass.Select (not Directive ("@Persistent"))
        begin
          Error handling
        end
      ChildClass.Select (not Directive ("@Persistent"))
        begin
          Error handling
        end
    end text
```

12.5.6 Client/server applications

Description

In client/server applications, the same class is often present in both the client and the server parts, with each process implementing its own specific viewpoint of the concept. In many cases, a service is made available by the client. If it is selected, the client sends a request to the server which performs the actual service.

The following tasks must therefore be performed systematically:

- The identities of the client and server instances must be handled. This often takes the form of identifier management.

264 Carrying through a model: hypergenericity

- The inter-process messaging protocol must be handled to indicate the identity of the instance that is to process the message and the type of processing to be performed.
- An identical protocol must be implemented for each method invoked on the client. Thus:
    - A message must be prepared,
    - A message must be sent to the server,
    - It must wait for the response,
    - The response must be interpreted and the results analyzed,
    - Errors must be processed, if necessary.

See Figure 12.17 and 12.18.

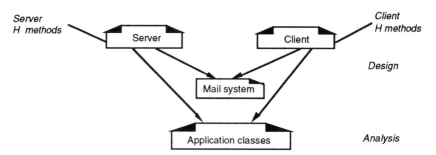

Figure 12.17 The client/server application is broken down by applying hypergenericity rules to analysis classes.

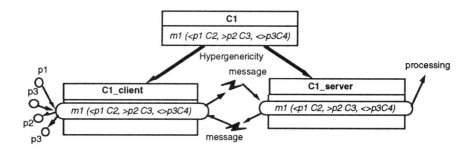

Figure 12.18 The service is requested by the client and executed by the server.

Implementation principles

Once the principles have been determined, the classes shared by both the client and the server must be defined (Application classes domain in Figure 12.17). Their implementation, however, will be distinct since hypergenericity rules will be applied.

Within these shared classes, however, the services provided exclusively by the client must be distinguished from those performed exclusively by the server, and from those corresponding to client/server communications. To do so, two directives are defined on method level: @client and @server.

A library for messages transmission between a client and the server is therefore required. This type of processing is lengthy to code and relatively complex. It can, however, be fully automated via hypergenericity.

12.5.7 Dynamic typing

Description

One important aspect of object-oriented programming is the ability to determine dynamically the type of an object, as illustrated in the following example.

A number of people are walking along a road. One of them is taken ill and faints. One of the other people must therefore be asked to look after the person. As it is not known which of them is a doctor, it is not possible to pick one of them to look after() the patient. It must first be determined whether one of them is a doctor. A doctor then comes forward. This person, considered up to now on the more general level of human being is now considered to be a doctor, which enables the take care of (patient) message to be sent.

It can be seen here that amongst all instances handled on a general level for a class (apparent class human), it is possible to determine whether one of them is an instance of a specific class (doctor). It may also be necessary to determine to which class an object actually belongs before deciding 'what it is'.

The *H* language provides such services, as do some object-oriented programming languages (Eiffel); others, however, do not (earlier versions of C++). To compensate for these differences, hypergenericity can systematically implement the required methods (Figure 12.19):

- GetClass () return string to return the class name of an instance,
- BelongTo Class (p : in object) return boolean to determine whether an instance belongs to a class.

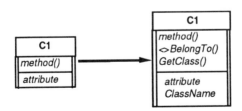

Figure 12.19 Transformation made by hypergenericity.

Implementation principles

A @DynType directive is used to specify that a class provides dynamic typing services. The following principle is applied in C++ for these classes:
   Create a class attribute:

266 Carrying through a model: hypergenericity

```
ClassName Class : string := NameofClass ;
```
Implement a public virtual method `GetClass()`, *the code for which is simply* `return ClassName`.

Implement a public class method `BelongTo()`, *the code for which is as follows:*

> *If the name of the class for instance p is equal to the current class name,*
> *Then the result is true*
> *Else the* `BelongTo()` *message is executed on the base classes of the current class.*

Required rules

The base classes for a class with dynamic typing must also have dynamic typing.

```
DynTypeControl()
processing
text : H
    if (Directive ("@DynType") )
        BaseClass.Select (not Directive ("@DynType") )
        begin
            Error handling
        end
    end
end text
```

12.5.8 Class handling its instances

Description

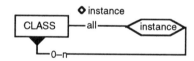

Figure 12.20 Representing a class that handles its instances.

This principle was described in Section 8.1.3. A relation is used to declare that a class 'handles' its instances (Figure 12.20); it is thus aware that they exist and knows how to access them. An implementation mechanism must be provided to access all instances of a class, when that class is known.

Implementation principles

A means of accessing instances is provided by implementing the modelled relation, as described in Section 12.5.4. The following link update principle is added to the hypergenericity rules:

> *If the class has constructors, then*

> For each constructor, add code to create a new link to the instance
for the instance relation
>> Else
>>> Create a constructor to set up the new link.
>> If the class has a destructor, then
>>> Add code to delete the link to the deleted instance in the instance relation
>> Else
>>> Create a destructor and add the same code.

12.5.9 Transmutation

Description

Transmutation is the ability of an instance to change owner classes. It is included in the formal representation of some methods. Transmutation is used to model situations where the same instance can be assigned very different irreversible states during its lifetime. For example, a *baby* becomes a *child* who then becomes an *adult* (Figure 12.21). These various stages correspond to very different faculties and can then be represented as transmutable classes. The same can be said for a *car*, which has a very serious accident and therefore becomes a *write-off*, or for *electrons* which, when they collide, change completely to become *protons* and *neutrons*.

This type of model does not comply with basic class relation principles, which stipulate that a class is a *stable* category of instances (Section 3.2.3). Transmutation is therefore more frequently represented by different *states* within the same class, but the following disadvantages exist:

- Transmutation is difficult to control in a model, as the stable and invariant parts are no longer known.

- The *invariant* principle is inadequate in this case, as at a given moment in time an instance changes invariant rules.

- This feature provides little security as it is not possible to guarantee that all users of a transmuted instance are not still using it as if it had not been transmuted (for example, the driver of a *car* is not driving a *write-off* without knowing it!).

Hypergenericity does however enable this feature to be handled automatically.

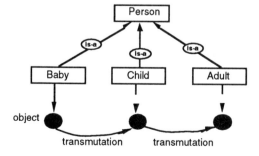

Figure 12.21 Transmuting an object between classes.

268 Carrying through a model: hypergenericity

Implementation principles

An instance of class `c1` may be transmuted into an instance of `c2`, using the `@transmute (C2)` directive in the `c1` definition.

The problem with transmutation is that computer languages can only create two different instances for two different classes(see Figure 12.22):

- A `c2` constructor must be created to build an instance of `c2` from an instance of `c1`. To do so, *persistent hypergenericity* must be applied as the developer must define the code required to convert the specific properties of `c1` into specific properties of `c2`.

- A class handling a *logical reference* to the instance must be created so that the parts handling the instance of `c1` always handle the same instance once it has been transmuted.

- It must be guaranteed that any relation oriented to an instance of `c1` uses this logical reference.

- A `transmute()` method must be created for `c1`, its role being to convert the instance by calling the constructor specific to `c2` and performing the appropriate operations on the logical pointers of `c1`.

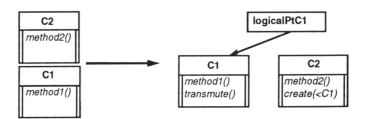

Figure 12.22 Systematic transformation handling transmutation.

12.5.10 Interface classes

Description

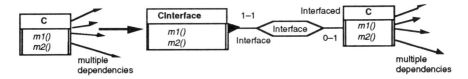

Figure 12.23 Systematic transformation handling interface classes.

The principles applicable to interface classes were described in Section 8.4.1. Interface classes are used as a last resort during design to avoid mutual inter-class dependencies. Given class `c` with many dependencies (related classes, derived classes, and so on), an interface class `CInterface` is a class with all public methods of C and similar definitions, but which, when implemented, simply sends any received messages on to the related instance of C. The advantage of this technique is that C dependencies are not passed on to users of CInterface (see Figure 12.23).

Implementation principles

The @Interface directive is defined to specify which classes must have interface classes.

    CreateInterface()
    For each class C *for which an associated interface class must be created*
      Create a class called CInterface
      Add an interface relation
      For any public method of C
        Create an equivalent method in CInterface
        Define a method body to transmit the invocation to the related instance of C

This principle can be extended, by passing the name of the schema for the interface class as a parameter of the CreateInterface() method. The interface class is then created within the schema. As a result, interface schemas can be created automatically, in order to set up actual software layers.

12.5.11 Specifying and implementing a graphic user interface

This more complex example will not be developed here in detail. It simply shows the scope of hypergenericity. A graphic user interface is often developed using specific tools to paint windows and screens and generate the corresponding code. Several questions must however be asked when building a graphic user interface:

- How is a graphic user interface specified?
- What relation exists between the graphic user interface and the application model?
- How is the graphic user interface linked with an object-oriented application?

Graphic user interface generators are useful when painting windows and screens, as they guarantee good ergonomics, but they are not good analysis tools. Two concerns should be distinguished and addressed when creating a graphic user interface:

- A distinction must be made between the information entered by the user and the information displayed by the software,
- Ergonomics, that is the way this information is presented, must be considered.

It is recommended that the information exchanged with the user be specified within a class relation structure model, which enables data consistency and exhaustivity to be checked. This approach enables:

- The link between the graphic user interface and the software to be automatically implemented,
- An initial graphic user interface to be generated, which can then be reworked via interactive editors.

270   Carrying through a model: hypergenericity

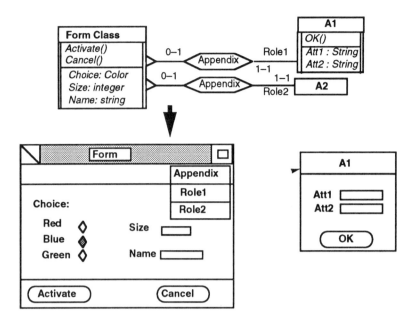

Figure 12.24 Example illustrating the possible correspondence between a model and a graphic user interface.

Rules stipulating the correspondence between a class relation model and display screens exist, and can be defined using directives (Figure 12.24).

12.6 Structuring hypergenericity rules

12.6.1 Defining H messages for an element

Several temporary hypergenericity rules can be applied to the same modelling item, in which case they are always applied consecutively. Thus, the second uses, as input, the output generated by the first, and so on. Execution sequencing is therefore of great importance, as the input information varies according to the order.

The following example combines rules for printable classes with those for persistent classes. The sequencing determines whether attributes in the persistence definition are to be declared printable or whether some printable class attributes are to be made persistent.

For each item, the rules to be applied and their order must therefore be defined. This information is provided in the same location using directives. The following example specifies that the *PersistentRules* hypergenericity rules must be applied before the *PrintRules*:

```
class person ...
text : H_rules
    PersistentRules ()
    PrintRules ()
```

```
end text ...
attribute
    name : string ;
    age  : integer ; ...
```

A specific text area can be used to indicate which *H* messages are applicable to all key structuring entities in the class relation model:

- Domains,
- Schemas,
- Classes.

Other class relation items can be processed via specific *H* methods, invoked systematically from methods declared in the *domain* or *schema* classes.

12.6.2 Hypergenericity and domains

Advantage of domains

Implementation domains

Domains are particularly interesting, as they enable other domains, schemas and classes to be grouped together and allow a specific set of rules to be applied to them. A domain can thus be used to access all associated classes and apply general implementation hypergenericity rules.

In this manner, domains are used to structure an application and define the modelling parts which must comply with a given implementation principle. For example, a domain can be defined for *storable* items or for *InteractiveHandled* items.

Some classes may comply with specific implementation requirements and are not necessarily part of the general structure. For example, *transmutable classes* can be shown in separate areas. In this case, the directives defining applicable hypergenericity messages are specified on terminal class level.

Multiple implementations of the same model

For client/server applications (see Section 12.5.5), two domains can be used to define the compositions of the client and the server. These domains refer to common classes, each of which is implemented differently by applying specific implementation rules.

Domains can be used to define decompositions imposed by the architecture and apply specific implementation principles to the same elements. The advantage of this feature is that the analysis model remains unchanged and independent of implementation principles. The same analysis model can be implemented several times in different ways, thus increasing reusability. If hypergenericity rules are applied to all classes referenced by a domain, methods of the following type will be obtained:

```
class Class ...
ExampleRule ()
processing
    text : H ...
```

```
class Domain …
ExampleRule ()
processing
text : H
   ReferedDomain.ExampleRule ()
   ReferedClass.ExampleRule()
   ReferedSchema
   begin
      ComponentClass.ExampleRule()
   end
end text
```

12.7 Hypergenericity methodology

12.7.1 Determining implementation principles

When developing an application, and more importantly when considering a *virtual machine*, all systematic aspects of model implementation must first be listed. The applicable principles are then defined. Once this is done, it is then possible to use hypergenericity to express implementation principles in the *H* language.

The advantages of using hypergenericity to systemize principles must, however, be weighed against the following factors: how difficult is it to write these principles in the *H* language (number of potential lines), in how many cases is systemization of interest, and what reuseability requirements have been specified?

12.7.2 Determining consistency rules and directives

If implementation principles can be systemized, the associated directives almost always have to be defined. The implementation team must provide control mechanisms to check that these directives are applied correctly by users. These mechanisms are also based on *H* language rules.

12.7.3 Writing hypergenericity rules

Before specifying the rules, an implementation example should be written in the programming language, using code similar to what is expected from generation.

Once the example has been reviewed, it is easy to write hypergenericity rules. These rules are applied for the first time on the same example, to ensure that the generated results actually comply with those obtained manually.

12.7.4 Testing rules

Once the rules have been defined, they are used repetitively. The code produced by hypergenericity must be put through exhaustive testing, so that future users do not have to conduct unit tests on it. The code must also be optimized to ensure that the resulting software will be of a very high quality. It should also be noted that hypergenericity can be used for prototypes, as it gives very quick results. In such situations, rule implementation can be simplified.

12.8 Impact of hypergenericity on the lifecycle

12.8.1 Design phase

Hypergenericity has a significant impact, particularly on the design, development, and test phases. During *preliminary design*, the implementation principles to be systemized for an application are determined. These principles are expressed in *H*, a fully-fledged design language. Once these principles have been defined, the attributes, methods or classes required to implement the analysis model no longer need to be deduced manually from the adopted principles.

The design phase is therefore more formal as the appropriate rules must be written. At the end of preliminary design, the implementation principles are defined and grouped together by *topic* (for example, persistence, graphic user interface generation, transmutation, interface classes), each of these topics being made up of a set of *H* rules (methods defined on a meta-model). Documentation is written for the methods to define their purpose and function, but the methods themselves are not necessarily written.

All *H* rules will be written during *detailed design*, at which stage they are also tested on examples, the resulting output being also tested.

12.8.2 Coding and test phases

The coding and test phases are simplified and shortened (see Chapter 13). The coding phase annotates the model by adding the appropriate directives (such as @persistent), and defines the hypergenericity rules applicable to classes, schemas or domains (by creating **text** : H_rules sections). It adds code that has not already been defined and applies hypergenericity to deduce code. *Unit testing* is not required on the parts generated automatically, as they have already been tested during preliminary design.

12.8.3 Incremental development

Hypergenericity greatly facilitates incremental development. Sections of the model can be developed and rapidly implemented by this means. Different implementation principles can be tested on the same model by applying different hypergenericity rules in turn and determining which ones are the most suitable. An initial solution can also be implemented quickly using simplified rules which do not optimize or only partially implement the architecture; only the 'functional' part of the code is developed to highlight software features. Finally, implementation modes are transformed to reflect the final architecture. (This process can also take place in parallel with the others.) For example, a client/server application can be implemented initially as a single process, in order to enable work to be undertaken on the main software features, while the separation between processing, communication and exchange protocols is implemented in parallel.

12.8.4 Improving reusability

As seen in Section 12.1.1, hypergenericity is used to separate *implementation principles* from *application modelling*. The application model can therefore be reused independently. The same implementation rules are applied to different applications, or different implementation rules are applied to the same model. For example, the persistent objects in an application can be stored in a file, a relational database or an object database using different H rules. The way printable objects are handled can also be changed to display them in different ways (without the methods, on a character-mode terminal or on a graphic workstation, and so on).

13 Development

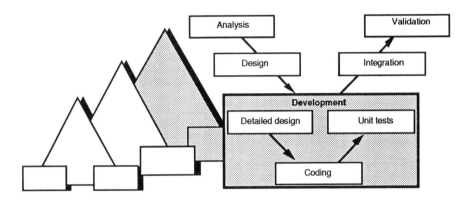

13.1 Detailed design

13.1.1 Overview

The preliminary design phase has enabled the following elements to be determined:

- Software functions,
- Overall software architecture,
- General software structure, particularly its domains and schemas,
- Implementation principles used to code each class.

The software has been decomposed, but all classes have not necessarily been defined or described in detail. Once preliminary design has decomposed the software system, the development strategy has been established and the software integration plan and general software operating principle have been defined, development activities can start.

Definition: *The main purpose of detailed design is to prepare for coding by smoothing over obstacles inherent in this phase.*

Preliminary design finalizes the software structure by identifying the domains, schemas and classes. Detailed design then further specifies each class using the operating and dynamic models. New classes may be highlighted but new schemas cannot be created at this stage.

13.1.2 Detailed design work

Finalizing the description of all components to be implemented

At this stage, the application model must be finalized using the features of the class relation model. The structure model descriptions must first be completed (classes, relations, inheritance, invariants, and so on), and then the methods and attributes specified for each class should be defined.

Control automata must be created systematically for each class, if its methods cannot be used in any order. *Scenarios* use key examples to validate how the classes work. The *dynamic model* indicates how the reactive objects behave (*trigger automata*) by describing the most important methods in the *object flow model*.

Giving a detailed description of pre- and post-conditions for each method

During preliminary design, pre- and post-conditions were not necessarily described in detail for each method; this is the role of detailed design with the help of a programming language. This provides solid foundations for implementation, as the programmer can use automatic consistency checks for each processing unit to be implemented.

```
        take_off (runway_number : in integer, flight_altitude : in
   altitude)
        pre
        text : Preliminary_design
        The plane is on the ground. The landing gear is out.
        end text
        text : C++                    -- Transformation during detailed
   design
        ==> altitude == 0
        ==> landing_gear_position == out
        end text ...
```

Describing how each method performs its tasks

Detailed design must solve complex algorithmic problems using suitable models (trigger automata, object flows) or *pseudo-code*.

Pseudo-code can be a useful complement to the object flow model, as it provides a detailed description of the tasks undertaken by certain processes, while keeping the actual processes at a higher level of detail. Pseudo-code may also be useful to describe algorithms quickly; moreover, this technique is adopted in operational research manuals when describing the principles behind specific algorithms, even though the actual code is not generated. An 'object-oriented' pseudo-syntax provides a precise and powerful mechanism for expressing pseudo-code.

```
        -- Minimum tree algorithm
        Sort peaks of {G} in ascending order
        {V} = Ø
        WHILE peaks remain
            IF first one does not form a cycle with {V}
                THEN add it to {V}
```

In this example, the general principle behind the algorithm is given and so does not duplicate final code. It is expressed in terms of objectives, rather than instructions. For instance, the *IF first one does not form a cycle with {V}* condition is no doubt converted into a complex coding sequence; it is nevertheless possible.

Operational uses ('use' syntax in methods; see Section 4.4) are determined at this stage, as the way each method is implemented has now been defined.

Implementing development-related hypergenericity mechanisms

Preliminary design highlights all systematic implementation principles that can be automated via hypergenericity. Detailed design then implements these principles with the *H* language.

It also implements the corresponding model consistency checks. Once the principles have been automated, they are tested on modelling examples. The generated code is also tested thoroughly. This saves time later when coding and testing the parts generated automatically.

Preparing unit tests

Detailed design specifies the tests to be conducted for each class and method. As a result, each method not only has pre- and post-conditions but also the corresponding test definitions used to check that sample behaviour patterns are followed correctly (see Section 13.3).

13.2 Coding

13.2.1 Overview

Objectives of the coding phase

All the activities during the previous phases defined what the software should do and how it should do it. Software structures, objectives and operating principles were established. The purpose of coding is then to write the actual instructions executed by the computer and develop the final product.

Definition: *During coding, the description of the model entities is adapted and all elements not yet described in the model are developed.*

The processing required by the methods or non-decomposed object flow processes must be defined in the programming language selected, using the modelling structure as the base. Moreover, any associated implementation mechanisms are described by adding *directives* to the elements.

The fact that the programmer can deduce a large proportion of the code from a class relation model indicates that the actual coding activity has changed in comparison with the traditional software lifecycle.

Programming languages

Programming and modelling languages

The purpose of a modelling language is to describe a problem, without having to consider the execution environment. To do so, it may use descriptive techniques, such as functional sequencing, data flows and data structure descriptions. It is able to express requirements irrespective of machine constraints, and therefore represents the problem rather than a potential implementation solution to the problem.

On the other hand, all programming languages impose implementation-related constraints and force the programmer to provide a great level of detail. Concepts can be expressed, both in programming languages and in modelling languages (class concept, functional sequencing). During programming, however, the modelling part is submerged in a sea of detailed implementation decisions. Coding-specific sections must therefore be kept separate from analysis information.

Programming languages are more or less close to implementation. For instance, Ada requires that the programmer specify a passing mode for parameters (in, out or inout), without indicating how they are actually passed. On the other hand, C++ does not have the parameter passing mode concept. It forces the programmer to describe how parameter passing is implemented (by pointer, value or reference).

C++ is very close to the actual machine. Its syntax tends to describe how an element is implemented, rather than its actual semantics. For example, the 'static' keyword does not actually indicate that a property is of the class type, but rather that it is implemented as if it were a 'static' object (that is, an object that exists throughout the application execution lifetime).

The use of a model in addition to a programming language is always justified, particularly for languages such as C++, which includes all the necessary programming features, but does not recommend an overall standard approach or guidelines as to how each feature is to be implemented.

Examples of object-oriented programming language

Smalltalk

After its predecessor, *Simula*, (introduced as early as 1967), Smalltalk is considered to be the reference for all other object-oriented languages. It was developed in the 1970s by Alan Kay, in collaboration with Adele Goldberg and Daniel H. Ingals, initially at the Rank Xerox laboratories.

Smalltalk is an interpreted or semi-interpreted language which reuses Simula concepts, while placing additional emphasis on dynamic binding features and including weak typing inspired by Lisp. In Smalltalk, anything can be an object (there are no types like in Eiffel or C++). The 'meta-class' concept was introduced to try to merge together the class and object concepts. Smalltalk does not allow multiple inheritance.

The Smalltalk development environment is accompanied by a whole programming universe; so it is more appropriate to talk of the 'Smalltalk system' rather than the Smalltalk language. Smalltalk is frequently used in modelling and prototyping applications.

ObjvLisp

This language is part of the 'Lisp-based' family, that is, object-oriented languages based on *Lisp* (such as *Loops*, *Flavors*, *Clos*). As a result, it takes full advantage of the power of objects, while maintaining Lisp flexibility. This interpreted language is used in artificial intelligence or modelling/prototyping applications. It allows multiple inheritance, uses dynamic binding and, above all, includes a more advanced 'meta-class' concept (Cointe, 1987) than the one in Smalltalk.

Eiffel

It is widely accepted that Eiffel is the most precise compiled object-oriented language. Its author, B. Meyer, intended it for use with software engineering applications. It includes strong type checking and the *inheritance* (single and multiple) and *genericity* notions. Some of its more original features are the *invariant, pre-* and *post-condition* concepts, unique in programming languages.

Objective C

Brad J. Cox was the first to define a compiled object-oriented language above C. Objective C is a cross between Smalltalk, of which it reuses the concepts and part of the syntax, and C. Like Smalltalk, it provides dynamic binding. It has loose type checking, due to dynamic binding, and only supports single inheritance.

C++

C++ was originally designed by B. Stroustrup at the Bell laboratories to be a simulation language based on Simula concepts. It was then decided that C++ should replace C. C++ has changed considerably over the various versions released (1.1, 1.2, 2.0, 2.1, 3.0, 3.1, 4.0, 4.1). C++ has gradually included *multiple inheritance, genericity* and an *exception* handling mechanism. It will soon become an ANSI standard, once its definition has been finalized and clarified by the Institute. C++ had to respect two major constraints:

- Upward compatibility with C,
- High execution efficiency.

As a result, B. Stroustrup had to make a series of compromises rejected by many object-oriented language purists. Not all elements in the C++ language are objects, and programmers can continue to work in the same way as with C. Moreover, C++ (like C) is very close to the implementation and supports keywords, such as 'virtual' or 'static', which are more concerned with how the final code is implemented rather than actual semantics.

Its two strong points are extensive typing (less so, however, than in Ada or Eiffel) and sophisticated encapsulation management, using the 'protected' visibility, 'friend' class and 'private inheritance' notions. Its success in industry is undeniable and it will probably be the most common language in the later half of the 1990s.

Ada

Ada was created for the US Department of Defense (DOD). Its aims were to put a stop to the multiplication of largely incompatible languages and adopt a language enabling the real-time aspect to be handled ('rendez vous' concept), with extensive typing for optimized source control and high software security. However, it was not originally an object-oriented language (having no inheritance). A recent upgrade (Ada 9X) introduced the inheritance concept and has since become a fully-fledged object-oriented language.

Ada failed in its ambition to become a universal language, but it is still used extensively for applications where security is a key factor (aeronautics, military, transport, and so on).

H

The *H* language presented in this work is not a programming language. It is a model processing language, a function of which is to generate code in one of the above languages. It is however based on the same concepts and also includes notions specific to the domain in which it is used. Its main purpose is to navigate through a model (*context, unnamed method* and *broadcasting* concepts). It uses the interpreted *dynamic binding* mechanism (see the following paragraphs). This choice was made with the aim of maintaining flexibility, by not imposing any efficiency constraints as to how it is used.

H was created in 1992 by Softeam and came into application in 1993. General distribution started in 1994. Its main purpose is to process the hypergenericity paradigm.

Two language families

Two concurrent technologies underlie object-oriented languages: *dynamic binding* and *static binding* (see Table 13.1).

Table 13.1 Type of binding used by object-oriented programming languages.

Language	Linking
Smalltalk	Dynamic
ObjVLisp	Dynamic
Objective C	Dynamic
Eiffel	Static
C++	Static
Ada 9X	Static
H	Dynamic

Two philosophies exist in this field. Object o in class c2 inheriting from class c1 is activated and is considered to be an instance of c1 (apparent class). In the first philosophy (static binding), if message m() is sent to o, c1 or its base classes must have a method m(), the signature of which corresponds to the passing parameters. If, for example, o is considered to be an instance of a boolean class, the o cry() instruction will be rejected during compilation (booleans do not cry). In the second philosophy, the object receives the cry() message and reacts in accordance with its actual class. The error will then only be detected during program execution. When an o cry() message is invoked, object o will not find the cry() method in its base classes.

The advantage of the first approach (static binding) is that the corresponding languages can provide a high level of typing control (Eiffel, C++), which is not the case for the other language families. Moreover, an efficient message transmission mechanism can be provided (C++ owes its efficiency to this approach).

The advantage of the second approach (dynamic binding) is that it provides greater handling flexibility and advanced polymorphism. To enable such varied objects as a bicycle, banana, animal or stone to recognize the fall() message, it is not necessary to create a fallable_object class from which this strange set of classes inherits. The fall() method simply exists in the corresponding inheritance diagrams for each object. Multiple inheritance is therefore not as essential in languages such as Smalltalk or Objective C.

Its disadvantage lies in the fact that the fall character string can have significant semantic variations which may generate bugs: stock_exchange_rates can fall, a pressure can fall, and so on. The increase in flexibility is therefore counterbalanced by a fall-off in security. Many errors detected statically by compilers when the static binding approach is used (message arguments, typing) become bugs that need correcting in the second approach. Table 13.1 summarizes the binding type used by various languages.

13.2.2 Maximizing automatic code generation

A necessary step forward

Coding has always been a complex activity, the results of which are difficult to control, particularly for a large-scale project. Applications containing several millions of lines of code are not unusual and are generally major headaches when it comes to maintainability, reliability and upgradability. Object-oriented programming helps control large-scale software products, but is not a panacea.

Code developed manually is likely to contain errors. The greater the number of instructions, the greater the probability of having such errors. Moreover, in almost all cases, the final code does not comply with its model, as it is developed and upgraded separately.

Finally, updates are necessary when applications are used for a long period of time (change in the virtual machine or software functions). Any change, however, to a large volume of code is particularly difficult to handle as it can have unexpected repercussions on the rest of the application. Of course, encapsulation management and the definition of invariants and pre- and post-conditions make upgrading easier, but what guarantee is there that a team of more than fifty people all respect ideal programming rules?

The solution to this problem necessarily lies in automatic code generation and more importantly in the *hypergenericity* principle. H code rules must be defined with great care for each principle selected and then applied to the model, so that it can be implemented automatically, regardless of its volume. Changes to the virtual machine only affect the H rules, whereas functional changes only affect the model (see Figure 12.2).

The class relation model has been defined so as to facilitate automatic code deduction. Relations, events, control automata, trigger automata and object flows are all elements for which implementation can be easily deduced.

An iterative model fine-tuning approach is therefore recommended when deducing final code. Moreover, it guarantees careful, precise modelling.

Code deduction examples (using C++)

Inter-class dependency management

Three types of use

There are three types of inter-class uses:

- *Conceptual use* when inheritance or relation links exist between classes,
- *Contextual use* when other classes are used as parameters for methods in the current class,
- *Operational use* when classes are used to process a method.

In C++ (unlike Eiffel or Ada), the notion of inter-module usage does not exist. The only means of handling usage is via the C++ *pre-processor* which works exclusively on the text in C++ sources. It includes text elements (`#include` instruction), performs substitutions within the text (`#define` macro instruction) or deletes parts of the text in given conditions (`#ifdef` conditional compilation instruction). The pre-processor is not an integral part of C++. It does, however, serve to transform the text in the C++ source before it is compiled. This is a very specific feature of C and thus, C++.

The programmer must therefore handle inter-module dependency manually using the C++ file include mechanism. Each of the three types of uses corresponds to an `#include` instruction for the interface corresponding to the used class. Operational use is, however, different from the other two types, given its position in the C++ source for the class.

Rule: *Any class using class* C *contains an instruction of the* `#include` *'C.hxx' type.*

In the case of *conceptual* and *contextual* uses, the includes for the used classes are part of the user class interface, whereas, for *operational* uses, they are part of the body. For example, the following class relation definition requires the includes shown in Figure 13.1.

```
class C1
      is_a C2;                               -- conceptual use
      interface schema S1; ...
      relationship
          R : (i-j) to C3 (k-l) as role;-- conceptual use ...
      method
            m1 (P1 : in C4);                 -- contextual use ...
end interface class C1
...
      m1 (P1 : in C4)
         use C5;                             -- operational use
         processing ...
end class C1
```

The number of includes in class interfaces must, however, be minimized to prevent include 'snowballing' between C++ interfaces, due to transitivity.

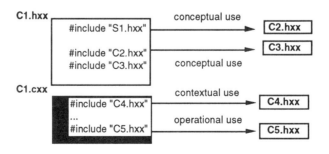

Figure 13.1 Implementing different types of uses.

Whenever possible (such as pointers or references to used class), the includes must be placed in the class body, using the C++ forward declaration mechanism:

```
class C3;    -- Forward declaration

class C1
  ...
    C3* role; ...
;
```

- In this case, the 'C3.hxx' include appears in the class body

Methods

Class relation methods simply become C++ methods. Their names remain unchanged and parameter passing mode conversion rules are applied. The *class method* concept also exists in C++ ('static' keyword) so this type of conversion is problem-free.

With respect to parameter passing, C++ does not include the 'input', 'output' or 'input-output' passing notions, but it does provide a way of developing the passing modes by transmitting pointers or values.

The *elementary class* concept is essential in C++, as it is used to determine whether objects can be transmitted by value. Passing modes can be translated in the manner shown in Table 13.2.

Table 13.2 Translation of passing modes.

Class relation syntax	C++ syntax Elementary class		C++ cyntax Non-elementary class
P1 : in	class_name	class_name P1	const class_name& P1
P1 : out	class_name	class_name& P1	class_name& P1
P1 : inout	class_name	class_name& P1	class_name& P1

Attributes

A class relation attribute generally corresponds to a C++ attribute. Specific C++ code sequences must, however, be generated to process public attributes and default values.

Public attributes

A class user must never be allowed to modify class contents directly. More importantly, a public attribute must only be accessed in read-only mode. This concept does not, however, exist in C++ (unlike Eiffel). As a result, a method must be defined to return the attribute value. An 'inline' definition can be used to avoid any access time problems:

```
class article ...
   public
      attribute
         Price : dollars; ...
```

The above example corresponds to:

```
class article
    {
    public :
        dollars& GetPrice () {return (Price);} …
    protected :
        dollars Price; …
```
In line with the principle explained in Section 4.3.1, the user only processes an instance of *example* via methods, whether to obtain attributes, relations or class relation methods. This provides the following advantages:

- Class *upgradability* is reinforced (when an attribute becomes a method, as illustrated in the example concerning the net_salary attribute in Section 4.3.1, the interface remains unchanged for external users).
- Instance *reliability* is increased (only an instance can modify its data).
- The *invariant control* principle is guaranteed (the only possible invariant transgression points are in the actual methods within the class).

Attribute default values

In the class relation model, default values can be assigned to class attributes. This is not possible in C++. The only way to implement this feature is to assign the default value via all class constructors.

C++ enables the value of a *class attribute* to be initialized statically, by adding an initialization declaration outside the class definition.

This class relation definition:

```
class article …
    private
        attribute
            margin                    : real := 0.3;
            sales_tax_rate class      : real := 0.18; …
```
corresponds to the following C++ instructions in the class body:
```
float article::sales_tax_rate = 0.18;
…
article::article (…)
: margin (0.3)            // This operation must be performed
  { … }                   // for all class constructors
```

Handling invariants and pre- and post--conditions

The invariant for a class relation class is transformed into a method that checks that all invariant conditions are true for a given instance. This invariant must only be active when the developer wishes to run dynamic controls on a given class. The situation can be parameterized in C++ using conditional compilations (#ifdef instruction). The invariant control mechanism is transparent for the programmer when it is generated automatically.

Pre- and post-conditions also correspond to dynamic controls. The same technique is used to add controls to the start and end of the method.

In this manner, the class relation syntax:

```
    class adult_woman
        is-a woman;
        interface schema society
        invariant
            code
                ==>age ≥ 18
            end code ...
```
generates the following C++ instructions:
```
#include "woman.hxx"   // Imposed by inheritance from the
                       // 'woman' class
class adult_woman:woman // Inheritance expressed in C++
    {
      public : ...
      private : ...
#ifndef CHECK          //Conditional compilation used to set
                       // the invariant if required
        void _invariant ();// The invariant is only accessed
                       // by the instances of the class
                       // and is therefore private
#endif
    };
//-------CLASS BODY---------------------------

#ifndef CHECK //conditional compilation
  adult_woman::invariant()
      {
        woman::_invariant();   // The class invariant must
                               // comply with the base class
                               // invariant
        society::_invariant();// The class invariant must
                               // comply with its schema
                               // invariant
        if (!(age>=18))        // Invariant not respected =>
                               // Abort application
              error ("Invariant not respected : age >= 18");
      }                        // END adult_woman::invariant
#endif
```
All pre-conditions in methods other than class constructors must comply with the class invariant, as must all post-conditions in methods other than the class destructor.

Handling relations

Accessing objects related to a current object

Relations correspond to an inter-object navigation mechanism in the programming language. If relation R exists between classes C1 and C2, class C2 plays the role role. Any user of an instance o of C1 must be able to access the instances of C2 related to o (if relation visibility allows it). To do so, the set of instances of C2 related to o must be obtained using the following primitive: SetOfC2& GetRole().

Figure 13.2 Relation with a 0–1 cardinality.

The example in Figure 13.2 illustrating the `marriage` relation, therefore, enables the `husband`, if he exists, to be accessed for `Smith`, a given instance of `woman`. It corresponds to the following code:

```
if (Smith.Gethusband().Card() !=0)
    the_husband = Smith.Gethusband()[0];
```

Implementing relation access methods (general case)
The way in which the `GetRole()` method is implemented depends on both the storage mode used for `C1` and `C2`, and any programming constraints. In all cases, the links between `C1` and `C2` must be handled.

In C++, pointers are commonly used to define links, but other more specific cases may exist. For example, if the instances of the `man` and `woman` classes are stored in a database, the `Gethusband()` and `Getwife()` methods send queries to the database instead of consulting 'list of pointers' attributes (`SetOfMan` or `SetOfWoman`).

A class relation relation defines a semantic link between two classes. The way in which this relation is accessed (implemented) is not specified in the model; that is the programmer's job. The purpose of defining the `GetRole()` method is to define a single relation access interface for class users, regardless of how the relation is implemented. The same interface can thus be used to access attributes or relations and invoke methods.

Figure 13.3 Relation between a source and its binary file.

In Figure 13.3, the compilation relation can be implemented using naming conventions: a C++ source is called 'source_name.C++' and the resulting binary file is called 'source_name.o'. To determine which binary file is linked with a source, the list of files is simply consulted to determine which file has a '.o' suffix and a prefix equal to the 'source_name'. The `Getcompilation_result()` method enables this file to be accessed.

13.2.3 Adding coding information to the class relation model

Directives

Directives are used to annotate a model and prepare it for implementation. They enable the *H* language to be used on a model so that it can be implemented in a specific way. C++ specific keywords, such as `friend`, `inline`, `virtual` and `volatile`, can be used to annotate a model. Consequently, the class relation model remains independent of the programming languages, even though the annotations have adapted it to them.

Hypergenericity rules are defined to include implementation-related directives. Directives, such as `@persistent` which indicates that a class is persistent, `@window` which indicates that a class corresponds to a displayable window, and `@transmute(Class2)` which indicates that a class can be transmuted into another, are used by the programmer to guide how each modelled item is implemented.

Directives are determined by the virtual machine (programming language, librairies, and so on) and preliminary design (implementation principles), and are used during coding.

Code segments

The programmer does not necessarily have to model the whole application or its behaviour. For example, if a sequence of library primitive calls is required, the programmer may decide to code them directly in a final programming language. For this reason, text annotations can be included to assign source language code to a given modelling item. This is typically the case for method bodies or object flow sub-processes which are coded directly in the implementation language. The following example illustrates how a method is implemented in C++:

```
method (P1 : in C1) ...
processing
   text : C++
   int i;
   for (;;)
     {
     if (i++ > a + b) ...
   end text
```

Programming example

The following programming example corresponds to the `elevator` class constructor in the class relation syntax:

```
create (assigned_number : in integer)
description
text : detailed_design
     The main constructor actions are to initialize values for
the created instance and define the values for all relations, the
minimum cardinality of which is not null. In this example, the
instance of elevator must create all its instances (C++ 'new'
instruction). The 'delete' method must of course perform the exact
opposite.
end text
pre
   text : analysis
        The assigned_number must be between 0 and 4 inclusive.
   end text
   text : C++
```

```
          ==> assigned_number > 0
          ==> assigned_number < 4
       end text
 processing
       text C++
          elevator_number = assigned_number;

          for (int i = 0; i< 7; i++)
                floor_button [i] = new button (i);
          access_door = new door;
          alarm_button = new button ("alarm");
          stop_button = new button ("stop");
          floor_detector = new detector (floor_detection,
                              elevator_number);
          overload_detector = new detector (overload,
                                 elevator_number);
          position_display_unit = new display_unit;
       end text
 end method create
```

End of the coding phase

The coding phase is completed when executable code has been generated and executed. To reach this stage, all the required information must be added using directives or freeform sections, *H* rules must be applied to the model and the resulting application must be compiled.

13.3 Unit tests

Testing can determine the presence of bugs, never their absence (E.W. Dijkstra)

13.3.1 Checking class validity

Test procedures

It must be assumed that an untested class does not operate correctly. There is confusion between the testing and the debugging phases. The purpose of testing is to prove that an element is correct, whereas the purpose of debugging is to detect and correct any errors in that element. Debugging is an element of the coding phase.

Exhaustive testing is not humanly possible owing to the great number of possible combinations that require testing. Testing does not enable the project team to prove that the software is reliable. The only result that can be expected is a high level of confidence that the tested element operates correctly. Testing is divided into several stages:

- *Test definition*: the test objective, individual tests and the expected results are defined. This activity normally takes place before the corresponding software item is developed, that is, during analysis (validation test), preliminary design (integration test) or detailed design (unit test).
- *Test development*: once the tests have been defined and the software elements developed, specific programs or environments are often built to execute tests.

- *Test execution*: this activity corresponds to the actual running of the tests to check that they produce the expected results and that no bug is detected. Invariant, pre- and post-condition checks ensure consistency (bug-free), but the test results must still be analysed.

Class validity

It is accepted that an element is considered to be valid if it meets all aspects of its specification. If, however, the specification does not exist or is too vague, it is not possible to state formally whether the corresponding software is operational or not. If the program stops unexpectedly during processing, an unprofessional programmer may state that the software is operating correctly as the specification did not state that it should not stop suddenly.

In a more formal definition, software is declared correct in class relation terms if each instance systematically complies with the class invariant and all methods called in valid conditions (that is when pre-conditions are respected) comply with their post-conditions once processing has been completed.

Pre- and post-conditions must therefore be checked during testing, the purpose being to detect errors as soon as they occur. If these checks are not conducted, some errors may be detected much later in the processing or, worse, may not be detected at all. Pre- and post-conditions and invariants do not remove the need for tests as their primary aim is more to ensure that the software complies with the model. Consequently, post-conditions must be defined as precisely as possible, as they specify what results should be obtained when the methods are invoked.

The more precisely the invariants, pre- and post-conditions are defined, the less important test verifications become.

13.3.2 Defining tests

Principle

In an object-oriented application, unit tests are conducted at class level. A class is tested by applying one or more *test sequences,* comprising one or more *test sets,* to a set of *test instances*. Each test set defines specific messages to be transmitted and the expected results. A test set is therefore created for each method; they are then grouped together at the class level to determine unit tests.

The test technique used must have the following characteristics:

- The test code must not modify the actual code for the tested class,
- The test code must be able to call the *private* or *protected* sections of the tested class, so that it can test the whole class,
- The unit test must be applicable to all classes, even abstract classes, which do not in fact have any instances.

A test strategy must first be set up (extreme case tests, 'black box' tests, 'white box' tests, and so on) to help choose the values and test situations.

Formalizing unit tests

Unit test definitions are based on a simple formal representation annotating the class to be tested (in the same manner as coding). Here again, the `text` and `end text` keywords are used to add unit test information to the model. The next example contains a simplified unit test formal representation.

Defining test sets

Test sets are defined for each method, using a list of headers to indicate the name of the test set, its description (for documentation purposes only), its input values and its expected results.

```
method (P1 : in integer, P2 : out boolean, P3 : inout string)
    text : test:set1
        Title : Test for minimum and maximum input values
        Input : P1 := -10000; P3 := "Example"
        Output : P2 = FALSE AND P3 = ""
        Input : P1 := 100000; P3 := ""
        Output : P2 = FALSE AND P3 = ""
    end text
    text : test:set2
        Title : Nominal operations test
        Input : P1 := 100; P3 := "Example 1"
        Output : P2 = TRUE AND P3 = "Example 2"
    end text
```

The parameter *passing mode* is used to determine which values must be supplied in input and which must be checked as output. The above example is simple as non-elementary classes do not need to be handled as call parameters.

In more complex cases, the instances created at tested class level (sequence definition) can be handled by name for each test set. Finally, the **Instance** keyword indicates the current instance, that is, the one on which the test set is being executed.

Defining test sequences

The purpose of *test sequences* is to determine the order in which test sets are applied to the instances of the class to be tested, depending on the execution context. To set up a test sequence, an initial test execution context must be established (class instances used, any initialization tasks, declaration of a set of instances for the class to be tested). The test sequences are then declared.

```
class Example ...
    text : test:main -- Sequence initialization
        I1 := create:set1;
        I2 := create:set2;
        seq1;
        seq2;
    end text
    text : test:seq1
```

```
        Instance := I1;
        method:;
        method2:;
end text
text: test:seq2
        Instance := I2
        method:set1
        Instance :=I1
        method:set2
end text
```

Two unit test sequences (`seq1` and `seq2`) are defined. They concern instances `I1` and `I2` and implement test sets on a constructor (via the created instances) and the `method2()` and `method()` methods. In the first sequence, all method test sets are activated (the test set name has not been specified), whereas the second sequence executes `set1` and `set2` on specific instances for the `method()` method.

13.3.3 Implementing unit tests

A specific test class must be created (Figure 13.4) so that the tested code is not modified and abstract classes can be tested. `TestC`, inheriting from the class to be tested, must be created for each class `C` to undergo unit tests. This enables:

- Abstract classes to be tested by working on instances of `TestC` which are not abstract,
- Privileged access to be obtained for all methods in the class to be tested (which is the case for all languages, except C++ where a `friend TestC` declaration can be used),
- Test code to be written without affecting the code for the class to be tested.

Each test sequence and set have a specific method which generates the calls and controls required by the test definition. *Hypergenericity* is used to create this test class automatically from the test specification supplied. Its advantages are twofold. Firstly, programmers can concentrate on test specification rather than on actual test implementation and updating if the tested class is modified. Secondly, test management can be centralized for the whole development team.

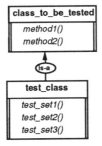

Figure 13.4 A specific test class is created.

Finally, *test logs* can be generated automatically to inform the programmers of the test description, date, input values and results.

Throughout the unit test phase, it should be remembered that dynamic invariant and pre- and post-condition checks provide an additional level of testing.

14 Comparing models (OMT)

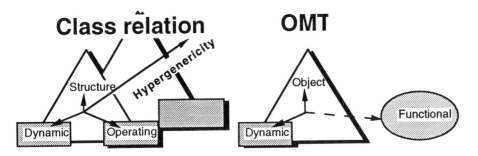

14.1 Overview

14.1.1 Object-oriented models

Since 1988, many models and methods have been developed (there are now more than thirty). Examples are:

- Objectory by Ivar Jacobson (Jacobson et al., 1992).
- OOA (object oriented analysis) by Schlear and Mellor (Schlear and Mellor, 1988).
- OOA (object oriented analysis) (Coad, 1990) and OOD (object oriented design) (Coad, 1991) by P. Coad.
- OMT (object modelling technique) by J. Rumbaught and associates (Rumbaugh et al, 1991).
- Class relation, as early as 1990 (Desfray, 1989; 1990; 1992).
- The Grady Booch approach (Booch, 1991).
- The James Martin approach (Martin and Odell, 1992).

All these approaches implement the *relation* concept on an object-oriented model, but each has specific characteristics.

14.1.2 Comparison with OMT

The *class relation* and *OMT* models are both based on the object model and the entity-relationship model. They can therefore be compared (which is not possible with some other models). Moreover, OMT is one of the most frequently used models at the present time. This is why it has been selected for the comparison.

The OMT model was created by a General Electric research team and was discussed in a book published in 1991 (OMT, 1991). This book was used as the basis for the comparison, although the model has undergone several changes since.

(A new edition of the book has been announced, but was not available to the author at the time of writing this book.)

The purpose of this comparison is to focus on the similarities and differences between the two models, moving from one to the other to explain their respective philosophies and, wherever possible, why the differences exist.

14.2 Need to upgrade existing models

The models presented up so far were a preliminary answer to modelling requirements. They continue, however, to evolve and all the models presented below have inherent limitations and/or disadvantages.

Completeness

Modelling requirements cover all the following aspects (see Table 14.1 for more information): a precise description of system concepts, how these concepts are used, a general representation of the system and software architecture, a description of system dynamics and how the system is structured, the ability to describe the rules to be respected within the system and encapsulation management. Unfortunately, these models do not cover every aspect in sufficient detail to be useful. The class relation model contains three sub-models (*structure*, *operating* and *dynamic models*) and is a complete solution.

Table 14.1 Modelling requirements.

Requirement	*Model Concerned*
Accurate description of system *concepts*	*Structure*: class, relation, invariant, and so on
Description of *how* the concepts are used	*Operating*: pre- and post-conditions, control automaton
General representation of the *system*	*Structure*: schema, domains, domain diagrams, flow diagrams
Representation of the software *architecture*	*Structure*: schema, domains, domain diagrams, flow diagrams
Description of system *dynamics*	*Dynamic*: events, trigger automata, object flow
Description of the *rules controlling the system*	*Structure*: invariant *Operating*: pre- and post-conditions
Encapsulation management	*Structure*: visibility for attributes, methods, relations, classes, schemas
System *structuring*	*Structure*: domains and schemas

Consistency

The modelling techniques available must provide strict overall consistency, while remaining closely linked with the object model. The structure model is the central point for all three class relation sub-models, which apply systematic connection and transformation rules. This ensures, for example, that the class relation model is not ambiguous in managing the link between the functional and object models.

Orthogonality

The class relation approach considers a model to be a *super modelling language* used to formalize a problem. This language must be rigorously and consistently defined and underpinned by a guiding theory. As a counter-example, the addition of new concepts, which are either redundant or specific to one programming language, can have an adverse impact on the clarity of some models.

Modelling controls

A model must be supported by controls and evidence. Some models integrate features which cannot be controlled and for which no rules have been established to explain how they should be used. For example, *automaton* models are frequently created, but rules for use with inheritance have yet to be established (state or transition definition rules).

In the computing field, two types of controls exist: static controls (performed on the model) and dynamic controls (conducted when the software is being executed to ensure that it behaves in compliance with the model). Both types of controls can be provided by a class relation model.

Modelling precision

To obtain maximum modelling precision, specific rules must be established to define system invariants and how the system is to be used. The *invariant, pre-* and *post-condition* concepts, frequently included in other models but rarely defined in detail, are required to implement such a feature.

Iterative fine-tuning from analysis through coding (seamlessness)

The class relation approach is used to work on the same model from analysis through to coding. To do so, it provides the necessary descriptive features, implementation specification techniques (*directives*, *named texts*) or an opening on to final coding. It defines where coding information must be inserted, outlines the general software structure and specifies the appropriate encapsulation principles.

Coverage of upward software development phases

The *unit test, integration* and *validation* phases have rarely been discussed in any model presented to date. They are, however, crucially important if high quality results are to be obtained and the project is to succeed. These phases have been defined here and are supported with the appropriate modelling features.

Formal implementation principle descriptions

Experience of application development projects and expertise in programming techniques are key factors contributing to the success of software design and implementation. *Hypergenericity* is used to define a thesaurus for this expertise and experience so that implementation rules can be applied systematically to each new application. This formal representation based on the *H* language enables design work to be transformed into systematically applied rules. It systemizes software design tasks, eliminates duplicate development activities and automates software development as far as possible.

296 Comparing models (OMT)

Provision of a method

A set of model usage rules is supplied to guarantee consistency and some properties of the model. The key techniques required to create and justify class definitions are provided together with the means to promote class reuseability.

Contribution of a methodology

The use of a model throughout each lifecycle phase is described, the common theme being how to systemize and automate a significant percentage of the development activities.

14.3 Class relation/OMT comparison

14.3.1 Basis for the two models

The class relation and OMT models are both based on the object model and make use of expertise acquired on other known computing models, such as:

- Entity-relationship,
- Finite state automata, extended by Harel (1988),
- Data flow.

The class relation model also finds inspiration in the following models:

- Abstract machines,
- Formal models (invariants, pre- and post-conditions).

Both adopt a *modeling* approach, that is, the ability to represent problems in an abstract way, so as to obtain maximum coverage of modelling capacities and the requirements of each lifecycle phase.

OMT is based on the SA/SD approach which is a partially functional approach, whereas class relation rebuilds a complete model on object model foundations, extracting the key features from the above-mentioned computer models.

14.3.2 Object model (class relation, OMT)

Basic model

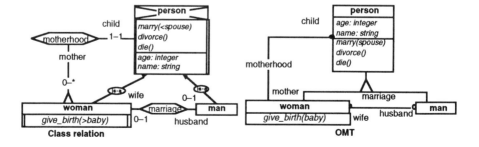

Figure 14.1 Class relation and OMT models of a nineteenth century human society.

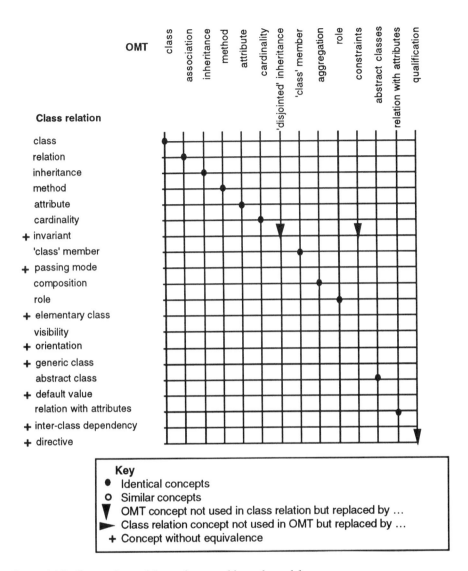

Figure 14.2 Comparison of the notions used in each model.

The object model (also called the *structure model* in the class relation approach) is used to present application concepts, together with their properties and existing interlinks (Figure 14.1). It is based on the fundamental object model (classes, methods, attributes and inheritance) and is enriched by the *relation* concept taken from the entity-relationship model. Both OMT and class relation use this model as a key to all others.

The *class*, *attribute*, *method*, *relation* and *inheritance* concepts are exactly the same (Figure 14.2). Class relation includes the *invariant* concept to express all rules and constraints that have not been specified graphically, whereas OMT has special graphic notations to represent some constraints (exclusive inheritance, inter-relation constraints, and so on). Invariant rules are not presented graphically, but are used to express all types of constraints.

OMT does not include a formal mechanism for representing method definitions; they are expressed in the programming language used. On the other hand, class relation provides a formal method definition, both for analysis and implementation purposes (Figure 14.3). This enables it to be independent of the programming language and remain on a higher plane (for example, the parameter *passing mode* is not expressed in C++).

```
--class relation syntax
example (p1 : in C1, p2 : inout C2, p3 : out C3) return C4;
```

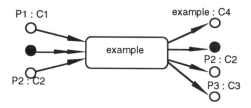

Figure 14.3 External representation of a class relation method.

Class relation introduces the *visibility* concept which is crucial to software *design* and guarantees good *encapsulation* management. OMT simply uses textual annotations (such as {private} for an attribute), which is a disadvantage during design and implementation.

Class relation includes the relation *orientation* concept to specify that one concept is based on another and also enables the programmer to indicate on a more physical level that an object provides a means of accessing another object via a relation. Orientation makes a diagram easier to read by guiding the direction in which it is read.

The notations for relations are different: cardinalities have been inverted. Class relation provides a single notation for roles and cardinalities, whereas OMT provides several, which has an adverse impact on the consistency of graphic presentations. These differences are minor and may change, but it does seem necessary to have:

- The simplest notation possible (such as a rectangle for classes),
- One single notation (which does not allow several things to be expressed in different ways, as in the case of OMT cardinalities or for OMT 'association classes'),
- The most expressive notation possible.

OMT provides some specific features (such as 'qualifiers') which are not fundamental and can therefore be expressed via class relation directives. As far as the basic models are concerned, they are very similar. The class relation model does, however, place great emphasis on the fundamental notions of invariant, visibility and relation orientation. It remains close to the entity-relationship model and has a strong set-based approach.

14.3.3 Structuring

Structuring is a weak point in the OMT model. The OMT model contains the *module* and *sheet* concepts, which are relatively vague and informal (OMT, 1991):

As much as possible, you should use consistent class and association names across modules.

The module name is usually listed at the top of each sheet. There are no other special notations for modules.

A sheet is a single printed page.

A sheet is just a notational convenience, not a logical construct.

On the other hand, Class relation applies very specific structuring concepts based on *domains* and *schemas* (Figure 14.4). It provides diagrams to explain the links between the various structuring units (see the example in Figure 3.4) and enables systems or even architectures to be modelled. Communication between several units is represented in *flow diagrams* (see the example in Figure 3.5) to provide the highest possible view of how the system operates.

Moreover, class *encapsulation* can be managed within schemas and classes can be grouped together for development, test, integration or even reusability purposes.

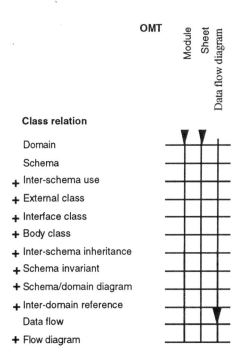

Figure 14.4 Table comparing structuring concepts.

14.3.4 Operating model (class relation)

The operating model is used to express how the methods in each class are used, and also represents the lifecycle for objects within the application. A method and the service it provides cannot simply be specified in terms of its signature (parameters). The *usage conditions* affecting class attributes, method parameters and allowed method call sequences must be defined. It is based on the concepts of *pre-conditions* (rules that must be respected before a method is invoked), *post-conditions* (conditions obtained once the method has been executed) and *control automata* (transitions possible for each method in a class, as illustrated in Figure 3.8). These concepts can also be found in formal languages and in the Eiffel language (Meyer, 1988). The *control automaton* concept is specific to class relation. This model, which is essential when checking application consistency and validity, is used to specify in simple, abstract terms how the services in a class are used and what results are expected.

This model is not part of the OMT approach.

14.3.5 OMT functional model

The OMT functional model is simply a reissue of the *data flow* model to which a few annotations, symbolizing object production for example, have been added (Figure 14.5). It represents major system functions, the data exchanged and the sequence. It reuses the SA/SD approach and starts modelling from a functional point of view.

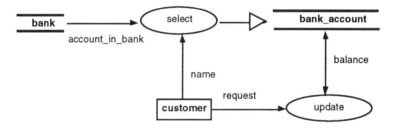

Figure 14.5 Example of an OMT data flow model.

At this stage, class relation and OMT diverge significantly. There is no actual *functional* model in the class relation approach, as the functional/object relationship has not been clearly established. As a result, the switch between the OMT functional model and the object model is relatively vague from a semantic point of view (OMT, 1991):

Often, there is a direct correspondence [author's comment: methods/processes] at each level of nesting [author's comment: the 'nesting' notion has a specific meaning for the data flow model but not for the object model].

Sometimes one process corresponds to several operations [author's comment: operation = method] *and sometimes one operation corresponds to several processes.*

Class relation uses *flow diagrams* on a higher level than in a data flow model. A domain is not a process and no sequences are expressed; it simply shows the data exchanged. It is based on the structure model (domains and schemas), which establishes a direct link with the object model, thus guaranteeing complete consistency and traceability between all models.

Two major problems are inherent in a functional model owing to the link with the object model and its relationship with software structuring. The advantage of this model lies, however, in the fact that it provides a 'bridge' across to the object model for many users of data flow models.

14.3.6 Dynamic model (OMT, class relation)

Events (OMT, class relation)

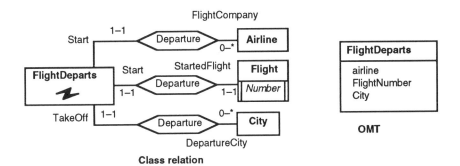

Figure 14.6 Definition of class relation and OMT events.

The definition of events in OMT and class relation is relatively similar. However, class relation does not consider events as representing every kind of information transmition between objects: the event mechanism is complementary to the message passing mechanism, owing to its asynchronous feature and the absence of knowledge of the receiver.

An event is the instantaneous reception of a signal, together with the associated information. [class relation]

In the class relation model, events are fully-fledged classes, whereas the OMT model presents them as being separate entities (which nevertheless have attributes and inheritance links):

The event hierarchy is independent of the class hierarchy. (OMT, 1991)

Figure 14.6 clearly illustrates the advantages of connecting the event notion with other classes. Although the send and receive mechanism is 'orthogonal' to the object model, the definition is closely linked to the other application concepts. The fact that events have methods (class relation) guarantees the power of the object model handling features.

Moreover, class relation provides annotations to define which class can send or receive an event (Figure 14.7). This enables the programmer to specify possible exchanges and the appropriate exhaustivity controls clearly. Finally, the way in which an event is sent is more precise in the class relation model:

302 Comparing models (OMT)

An event can be sent to an object, a class of objects (its current instances) or all application objects (broadcast). [class relation]
An event is a one way transmission from one object to another. An event can be directed at a set of objects or a single object. (OMT, 1991)

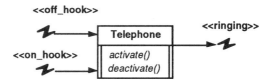

Figure 14.7 Declaring an event send or receive class (class relation).

Automata (OMT, class relation)

Class relation includes *control automata* (operating model), which define the allowed transitions for each method in a class. As a result, control automata provide rules to stipulate how class methods can be used, depending on their current state, and enable the appropriate checks to be performed.

Trigger automata enable object dynamics to be modelled. They must conform with the rules laid down by the control automata.

A trigger automaton defines the transitions that are systematically activated when a given state is obtained, an event occurs or a condition is met. [class relation]

OMT includes the corresponding *state diagrams* concept (Figure 14.8):

A state diagram relates event and states, [...] It specifies the state sequence caused by an event sequence. (OMT, 1991)

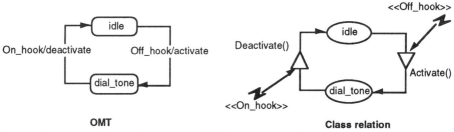

Figure 14.8 Examples of class relation/OMT dynamic models.

In the class relation model, transitions in a *trigger automata* always refer to class methods, whereas OMT *state diagrams* introduce the *activity* and *action* concepts, which are not explicitly linked with class methods. An *activity* is an operation which takes a certain amount of time and is associated with a state in a State Diagram, whereas an *action* is an instantaneous operation associated with an event.

Transitions can often be implemented as operations on objects. The operation name corresponds [author's comment: should correspond] *to the event name.* (OMT, 1991)

Considering, for example, that an event can trigger different operations depending on the state and that, conversely, an operation can be triggered by several events, it is difficult to see how the second OMT rule can be systematically applied.

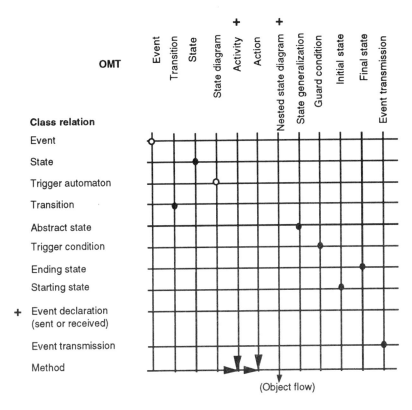

Figure 14.9 Comparing dynamic model concepts (except object flow).

Given its strict definition and link with control automata, class relation provides *mathematically proven* rules to specify trigger (and control) automata by inheritance. These rules can be controlled automatically. This is not possible, however, with the OMT model. Furthermore, problems exist when handling inheritance for classes with a *state diagram*:

Although refinement of inherited state diagrams is possible, usually the state diagram of a subclass should be an independent, orthogonal, concurrent addition to the state diagram inherited from a superclass [...]. (OMT, 1991)

This is a way of getting around the problem by advising against specifying inherited state diagrams. Unfortunately, they are frequently necessary (given the very nature of the object model).

Both the OMT and class relation models can decompose a state (Harel mechanism). On the other hand, OMT enables an *activity* to be decomposed into a 'lower-level state diagram'. This has no significance in class relation (as the activity concept is not used). In the class relation model, method processing is described in the object flow model (see Figure 14.9).

The object flow model (class relation)

The object flow model is derived from the data flow model, in that it describes method processing. *Processes* are either methods or parts of a method. Data flows always reference objects. Control structures (decision, loop), and new mechanisms (exclusion) enabling further information to be provided on processing (if required) can be added to this model.

OMT has extended the automaton model to express processing with a maximal amount of precision. Class relation limits automaton models to the description of 'reactive object' method invocation logic, but on the other hand it does provide a more precise way of describing method processing in object flow diagrams.

Only part of the application dynamics can be modelled in a finite state model (*reactive objects*, such as a *telephone*). It is not recommended that all types of objects be represented systematically in this type of model. On the other hand, *object flow* models can be created for any application, as they are a useful addition to the trigger automaton model.

Scenarios (OMT– class relation)

Both OMT and class relation include the *scenario* concept (Figure 14.10). Both diagrams have the same purpose (to provide processing sequence examples for typical application procedures). On the other hand, the class relation has a richer means of expression.

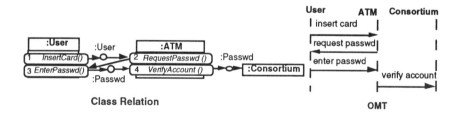

Figure 14.10 Example of class relation and OMT scenarios.

OMT scenarios, taken from the 'use case' approach of Jacobson (1992), present event sequencing examples applicable to several types of objects, whereas class relation scenarios present sequencing examples for message transmissions, events and data flows between each object, class, schema or domain. They are directly linked to the object model and describe data exchanges. They also contain OMT object diagrams. When combined with schemas and domains and the use of flows or events, they provide great potential.

14.3.7 Links with implementation (class relation)

More and more frequently, an object-oriented approach is being used from analysis through to coding, based on *successive refinements* of the same model. This approach ensures development continuity and guarantees improved productivity and development quality. The model must, however, be capable of supporting such features and it must integrate the means to add specific information through to coding, irrespective of the final programming language.

Class relation provides the means to move from analysis through to *final validation* in this manner, as it covers all phases (analysis, preliminary and detail design, coding, unit testing, integration and validation).

One of the main features of the model is the ability to add annotations in order to target a specific implementation, a given language (C++, Smalltalk, Eiffel, SQL, and so on), or to specify code which need not be defined at model level (specific language-related processing, difficulties inherent in the modelling language, and so on).

The *Hypergenericity* concept presented in Chapter 12 also provides a means of automating this refinement process, using the *H* language.

Directives

Directives are used to annotate the model and adapt the 'pure' class relation model to specific requirements (for example, '@virtual' for C++, '@Qualifier(Name)' to express an OMT qualifier, '@Persistent' to define a persistent class, '@transmutable', and so on).

Coding information

Specific areas are reserved to enable the programmer to add the required coding information to the model, regardless of the language selected (C++, SQL, Eiffel, and so on). This technique can be compared with the use of the 'asm' directive in some C languages to provide additional information in Assembler when the language is unsuitable for a given type of processing.

The named text technique, used extensively in the class relation syntax, also enables several languages to be targeted within the same model:

```
example (P1 : in C1, P2 : out C2)
    pre
        text : C++ …
        end text
        text : Ada …
        end text
    processing
        text : C++ …
        end text
        text : Ada …
        end text
```

Language-specific *H* rules then process the corresponding text areas.

14.3.8 Hypergenericity

Hypergenericity is a new development paradigm which will revolutionize the way software is developed and considerably increase the power of modelling and object-oriented programming. It was discovered by the Softeam Research and Development Department and presented in November 1993 at the 'Software Engineering and Application Exhibition' in Paris. This mechanism is not linked specifically with the class relation model, but requires that the underlying model be as complete, consistent and precise as this model.

14.4 Conclusion

14.4.1 Points in common

Generally speaking, both models use the same fundamental models. The object models are almost exactly the same; the dynamic models can be compared.

It should also be noted that the 1994 class relation model has been compared with the 1991 OMT model. To the author's knowledge, the changes made to OMT in 1994 concentrate primarily on the methodology.

14.4.2 Differences in the philosophies

OMT combined the SA/SD approach with the object-oriented approach to cover already known modelling domains and quickly meet the modelling requirements of programmers who are developing applications within the object-oriented paradigm.

Class relation founded its model on the fundamental object model (class, inheritance, attributes, methods) and introduced new notions more closely related with this model. Its philosophy is to build a comprehensive, accurate model and provide high-level modelling capabilities with extensive consistency control and automatic implementation deduction features.

OMT introduces a different set of terminology, over and above the method or message object notions (event, operation, activity, action and process), by considering that a method is close to implementation. This perspective is not the same as the class relation approach, which applies the object model and thus its terminology throughout the lifecycle. OMT terminology can be confusing and developers may find it difficult to handle equivalences.

14.4.3 Key OMT points

The mixed functional (data flow) and object-oriented approach is not coherent. The switch from one model to another gives rise to some problems. The dynamic model is closer to the object model, but the bridges are not systematically and carefully constructed.

OMT suffers from an almost total lack of structuring devices which makes it difficult to control large-scale projects. OMT is relatively imprecise in its description, which has a negative impact on the refinement facilities used during the lifecycle phases, in terms of consistency controls and automatic implementation deduction. To conclude, OMT is an interesting model, in that it contains the basics for object-oriented modelling, but it is still incomplete owing to certain inconsistencies and the lack of precision and comprehensiveness.

14.4.4 Class relation strong points

Class relation provides assistance during the entire lifecycle. Over and above the traditional *class* and *method* notions, it provides specific assistance in the form of the *schema*, *domain*, *Object Flow* and *scenario* concepts which are very useful from many perspectives (during *integration* for example). The invariant, pre- and post-condition and control automaton notions provide a unique contribution towards consistency and control. Finally, the concepts used to fine-tune a model (visibility, directives, named text) are essential if the whole lifecycle is to be covered.

Structuring is another strong point of the model, in that it enables several viewpoints to be defined for the same application (functional, architecture, development structure, integration, and so on) and provides synthesis mechanisms which were lacking in the basic object model.

The multi-view aspect (several consistent graphic representations of the same element) is essential as it enables the programmer to focus on several aspects of the application (analysis, design, real-time problems, and so on).

The class relation model is centred on the object model. More importantly, it is heavily based on the *method* notion which is a powerful structuring mechanism. All concepts and mechanisms used to cover modelling requirements are closely connected with the central object model. This provides great simplicity and consistency even when modelling large-scale applications.

Class relation defines a fully-fledged *modelling language*, which is both complete in its definition and open; parameters can be defined for each usage context or implementation situation. This aspect means that developers are constantly supported, in that they are able to transform a model into an operational result (documentation, code, and so on). It therefore reflects the will to generate fully-fledged *model compilers*, which go beyond just inputing graphic models, to provide consistency controls and maximum automatic generation. Finally, this approach allows programming language masking, so that programmers can concentrate on expressing what must be developed, rather than how it should be done.

Appendix I
Class relation model syntax

The following syntax is a simplified version of the full model syntax. Its main purpose is to add information to the graphic model by specifying documentary text, code or pre- and post-condition or invariant rules. There is no syntax correspondence for some parts of the model, such as data flows, the object flow model and scenarios, as it would be of little interest.

The *H* language is considered to be like any other programming language and its syntax, which is an extension of the class relation syntax, is not presented here.

I.1 Backus-Naur form

A simple variation of the Backus-Naur form (BNF) is used to describe the syntax. The following notation conventions have been adopted:

- The *keywords* are in bold (**class**).
- The *syntax categories*, developed individually after the '::=' symbol, are referenced by name in italics (*MemberDeclaration*).
- The *end names*, with no specific character attributes, correspond to modeling names (ClassName).
- The *optional parts* are placed in square brackets ([*DirectiveList*]).
- *Elements repeated* zero or more times are placed in curly brackets ({*NamedText*}).
- Choices are separated by vertical bars (<MethodName | **create** | **delete**>).
- *Special characters* in the syntax are placed in single quotes (';').

I.2 Syntax review

```
ClassRelationUnit ::= DomainDefinition | SchemaDefinition | ClassDefinition

DomainDefinition ::= domain [DirectiveList] [project] DomainName
    refers [DirectiveList] UnitName {',' [DirectiveList] UnitName} ';'
    {NamedText}

SchemaDefinition ::= schema [abstract] [library] [DirectiveList] SchemaName
    [is-a SchemaName {',' SchemaName}]
    [use SchemaName {',' SchemaName}]
    [interface ClassName {',' ClassName} ';']
    [body ClassName {',' ClassName} ';']
```

```
      {NamedText}
      [invariant {NamedText}]
      [context {ContextDeclaration}]
      end schema SchemaName

ClassDefinition ::=
      class [abstract | elementary] [event | main] [library] [DirectiveList]
       ClassName
      [is-a [DirectiveList] ClassName {',' [DirectiveList] ClassName}]
      [<interface | body> [DirectiveList] SchemaName]
      [receives [DirectiveList] ClassName {',' [DirectiveList] ClassName} ';'
      [sends [DirectiveList] ClassName {',' [DirectiveList] ClassName} ';']
      {NamedText}
      [invariant {NamedText}]
      [public [DirectiveList] {MemberDeclaration}]
      [protected [DirectiveList] {MemberDeclaration}]
      [private [DirectiveList] {MemberDeclaration}]
      {AutomatonDeclaration}
      [context ContextDeclaration]
      body ClassName
      [DirectiveList]
      [MethodImplementation]
      end class ClassName

UnitName ::= ClassName | SchemaName | DomainName

ContextDeclaration ::=
      {ConstantDeclaration}
      {EnumerateDeclaration}
      {InstanceDeclaration}

MemberDeclaration ::= [method {MethodDeclaration}]
      [relation {RelationDeclaration}]
      [attribute {AttributeDeclaration}]

AutomatonDeclaration ::= [redefines] automaton [DirectiveList] AutomatonName
      [state StateDeclaration]
      control {ControlTransition}
      {NamedText}
      trigger {TriggerTransition}
      {NamedText}
      end state

MethodDeclaration ::= <[class | abstract] [DirectiveList]
      <MethodName [':' [in | inout]]|create|delete> '('ParametersDeclaration
      [return <ClassName | Directive>] ';'>
      | <redefines [DirectiveList] <MethodName | create | delete> ';'>
      {NamedText}
```

```
RelationDeclaration ::= [class | abstract] [DirectiveList]
      <<comp | RelationName> ':' [oriented] Cardinality [as RoleName]
      with ClassName Cardinality [as RoleName]>
      | <redefines [DirectiveList] <comp | RelationName> with ClassName>
      [attribute {AttributeDeclaration}] ';'
      {NamedText}

AttributeDeclaration ::= <[class] [DirectiveList] AttributeName
      ':' [set of] ClassName [':=' Value] ';'>
      | <redefines [DirectiveList] AttributeName ';'>
      {NamedText}

MethodImplementation ::= [DirectiveList] <MethodName | create | delete>
      [':' [in | inout]] '('ParameterImplementation')'
      [return <[set of] ClassName | Directive>]
      [use ClassName {, ClassName}]
      {NamedText}
      [pre {NamedText}]
      [processing {NamedText}]
      [post {NamedText}]
      [exception {NamedText}]
      end method MethodName return ValueOrExpression ';'

ParametersDeclaration ::= [ParameterDeclaration {',' ParameterDeclaration}]

Cardinality ::= < <UnsignedInteger | ConstantName> '-'
      <UnsignedInteger | ConstantName | *> > | all

StateDeclaration ::= CompleteStateName {',' CompleteStateName}

ControlTransition ::= [Condition] CompleteStateName '==>'
      [Condition] CompleteStateName MethodName ';'

TriggerTransition ::= [DirectiveList]
      [Condition] [triggers ClassName {, ClassName}] CompleteStateName '==>'
      [triggers ClassName {, ClassName}] CompleteStateName MethodName ';'

EnumerateDeclaration ::=
      enumerate EnumerateName '(' LiteralName {',' LiteralName} ')'

ConstantDeclaration ::=
      const ConstantName ':' ClassName ':=' ValueOrExpression ';'

InstanceDeclaration ::=
      instance InstanceName ':' ClassName ':=' ValueOrExpression ';'

ParameterImplementation ::= ParameterDeclaration [':=' Value
      {',' ParameterDeclaration [':=' Value}
```

312 Class relation model syntax

```
ParameterDeclaration ::= ParameterName ':'
     [DirectiveList] PassingMode [set of] ClassName

Condition ::= '/@' Boolean Expression '@/'

PassingMode ::= in | out | inout

CompleteStateName ::= StateName {':'StateName}

DirectiveList ::= Directive {, Directive}
Directive ::= <['@'DirectiveName ['(' NameList ')']]> | <[/@ FreeText @/]>

NamedText ::= text [':' TextName] FreeText end text
```

Appendix II
Class relation graphic model review

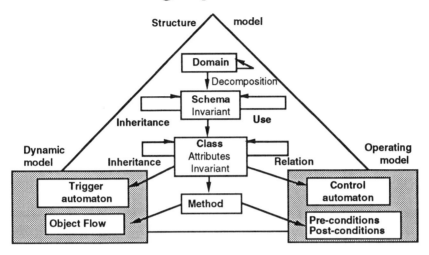

II.1 Structure model

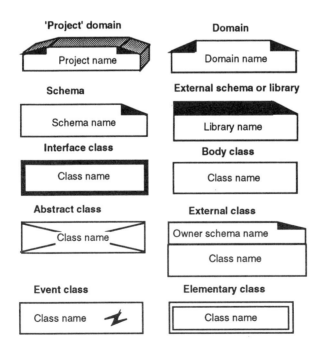

Figure II.1 Class relation units (domain, schema, class).

314 Class relation graphic model review

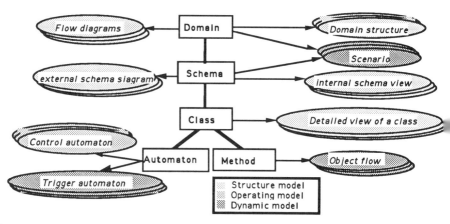

Figure II.2 Different diagrams associated to class relation units.

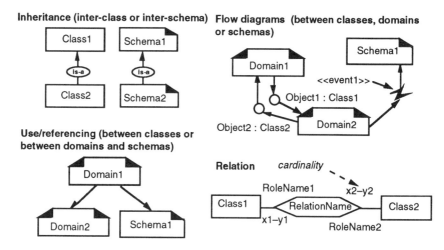

Figure II.3 Links between units (use dependency, relation, inheritance, reference).

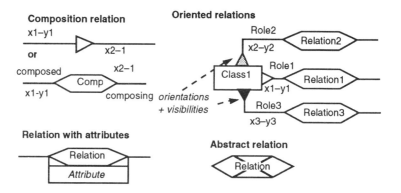

Figure II.4 Properties of relations.

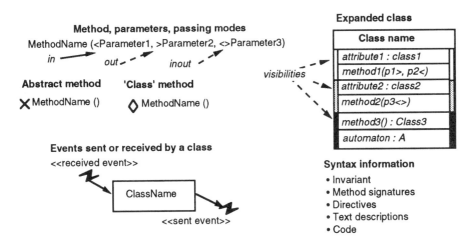

Figure II.5 Detailed class properties (attribute, method, visibility, automaton, invariant, events).

II.2 Operating model

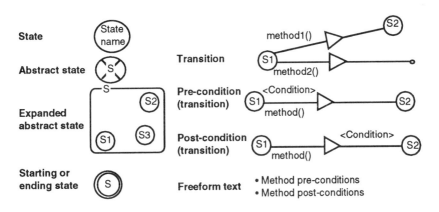

Figure II.6 Operating model elements (states, transitions, pre- and post-conditions.

II.3 Dynamic model

II.3.1 Trigger automaton

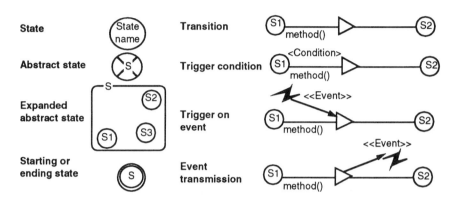

Figure II.7 Trigger automaton elements.

II.3.2 Scenario

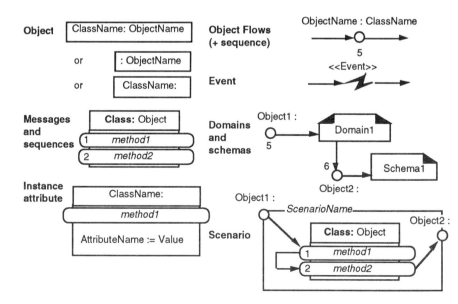

Figure II.8 Scenario elements.

Class relation graphic model review 317

I.3.3 Object flow

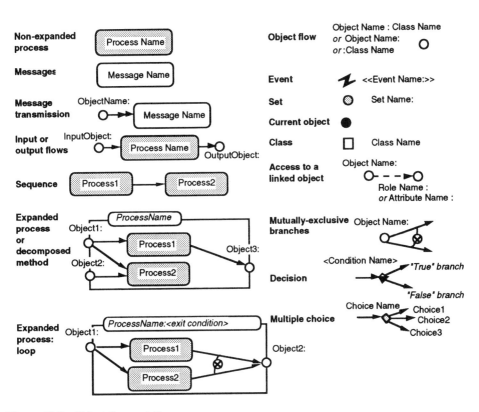

Figure II.9 Object flow notations.

Appendix III Glossary

Abstract class *Class* representing an abstract concept which cannot have a specific *instance*.

Abstract state *State* which is decomposed into *sub-states*, and which represents any of those *sub-states*.

Analysis *Phase* in the software *lifecycle*, the aim of which is to determine the development framework and define the functions to be performed by the system.

Application Software to be developed.

Architecture System structure based on the *virtual machine* and defining processing distribution, data storage and inter-process communication facilities.

Attribute Elementary property of a *class*.

Automaton Representation of all *states* and *transitions* between these *states*. (See also *Control automaton* and *Trigger automaton*.)

Body class *Class* which cannot be accessed by any other *class* that does not belong to its *schema*.

Cardinality For a *relation*, interval for a number of *instances* in the related *class*, linked with any *instance* in the source *class*.

Class Computer representation of the *concept* notion. (See also *Abstract class*, Body class, *Elementary class*, *External class* and *Interface class*.)

Class body Part of the *class* that defines its implementation and which is masked from the user classes.

Class interface Part of a *class* definition that is visible to other *classes* and *objects*.

Clause Expression of a rule that must be systematically applied and used to specify *invariants*, *pre-conditions* and *post-conditions*.

Code Series of programming language instructions used by the *virtual machine*.

Coding Activity in the *development* phase, during which a *model* is translated into code.

Composition Particular type of *relation*, defining a strong dependency between the composing *instance* and the composed *instance* (aggregation).

Concept Means of representing human knowledge.

Conceptual domain Mechanism enabling *concepts* to be structured; it corresponds to the definition and application context for a *concept*.

Conceptual use Dependency via *relations* or *inheritance* links.

Contextual use Dependency on *method parameter classes*.

Control automaton Definition of the allowed transitions for the methods within a class; it defines the class instance lifecycle by specifying their use protocol.

Data flow Information exchanged by two modelling items. A *data flow* is identified by its name and position. It represents the state of an object during processing.

DBMS Database management system. See also *ODBMS* and *RDBMS*.

Detailed design Preparation of the *coding* activity, during which the *preliminary design* is specified in greater detail.

Development *Phase* in the software *lifecycle* during which a *model* is implemented.

Dictionary Directory containing all the terminology used to describe an application. It indicates the equivalences between the modelling items and the corresponding definitions.

Directive Annotation made to a modelling item in order to give it a special meaning. For example `@persistent` is used to model class persistency, `@inline` is used to define method inline substitution (Ada, C++) and `@virtual` is used to define a C++ virtual method. A directive is frequently used to include special implementation specifications for the required programming language or *virtual machine*.

Domain See *Conceptual domain* and *Structuring domain*.

Dynamic model Class relation sub-model used to define how the application operates.

Elementary class *Class*, the *objects* of which are considered to be 'non-decomposable', not identified by the application and not handled on an individual basis.

Elementary validation set Model for a specific execution case corresponding to a user requirement (*method*).

Encapsulation Masking of items, access to which is restricted to a few privileged items. For example, a *private class* is encapsulated in its *schema*, or *objects* encapsulate their associated values and processing.

Event Occurrence of a signal at a given moment in time and the information associated with that signal. An *event* is an *object*. It is used by various software modules to inter-communicate.

Exception Abnormal situation processed by a software package.

External class *Class* referenced in the current *schema* and belonging to another *schema*.

Flow diagram Diagram representing the *flow of data* between several application items (*classes, schemas* and *domains*).

Functional dependency Semantic link between several properties, used to determine the value of a particular property.

Genericity Ability to define programming models and to construct real programs from these models by applying *genericity parameters*.

GUI Graphic user interface.

Hypergenericity Mechanism whereby a model is modified by applying transformation rules. The *H* language describes these rules. Hypergenericity is used to specify modelling automatically. Design or implementation modelling can then be performed automatically from the specifications.

Identifier Minimum sub-set of properties for a *class* characterizing each of its *instances*.

Implementation Construction of a system in compliance with the modelling.

Inheritance Generalization or specialization link between two *classes*, used to define a *class* as if it were a special case of another *class*.

Instance Element created from a *class*. Synonym for *object*.

Instantiation (Object) Action whereby an *object* is created as an instance of a *class*. (Genericity) Action whereby an instantiated *schema* or *class* is created from a *generic schema* or *class*.

Integration *Phase* in the software *lifecycle*, during which the software components resulting from the *development* phase are assembled into one component.

Integration test Test used to check that several software parts work together correctly (*classes, schemas* and *domains*).

Interface class (*Schema*) *Class* that can be accessed from the *schemas* using its *schema*. (Specification) *Classes* initially defined in the specifications by applying the "user" approach.

Invariant Property that must always be true for the item concerned (*class invariant* and *schema invariant*).

Lifecycle See *object lifecycle* and *software lifecycle*.

Member Any property assigned to a given *class*: *relation, attribute, method* or *automaton*.

Message Invokation of an *object*. The *object* interprets the *message* and activates one of the *methods* in its *class* with the corresponding format.

Metamodel *Model* of the *model* itself.

Method (Model use) Rules and the way in which a *model* is used to represent a problem. (Class) Service provided by a *class* to specify the *messages* that can be processed by the *instances*.

Methodology Use of a *model* and methods throughout the application *lifecycle*.

MIt 'Modelling Item'. Representation of any element in the *model* and the most elementary object in the *H* language.

Model Set of notations and associated rules for use. A *model* represents a collection of problems or phenomena. (See also *Dynamic model, Operating model* and *Structure model*.)

Modelling Description of a given problem or phenomenon using a *model*.

Object Independent, active element representing a *class*. (Synonym for *instance*.)

Object flow *Data flow* diagram specific to the object model and describing how each *class method* is processed.

Object lifecycle Series of *states* through which an *object* progresses during its existence, and *transitions* used to change from one *state* to another. (See also *Control automaton*.)

ODBMS Object database management system.

Operating model Class relation sub-model used to define how the classes are used and to specify the object lifecycle.

Operational use Use of a *class* to process a *method*.

Orientation For a *relation*, privileged way in which it is read; it indicates that a *class* is based on another *class*.

Parameter Information received or returned by a *method*.

Passing mode Additional information associated with a *method* or *method parameter*, and indicating whether the information transmitted by the current *instance* in the *method* or the *parameter* is in input, output or input/output mode.

Phase Major activity in the software development *lifecycle* (*analysis, design*, etc.).

Polymorphism Ability to consider several elements of varying natures as if they were of the same form. Polymorphism is one of the fundamental characteristics of the object model, as expressed by *inheritance*.

Post-condition Definition of the conditions in which the system must be placed after a *method* has been executed.

Pre-condition Definition of the conditions required for *method* invocation.

Preliminary analysis *Phase* prior to the *analysis* phase, the purpose of which is to determine the framework for the *application*.

Preliminary design Definition of the *virtual machine* for the *application* and the way in which the *analysis* will be implemented in that *virtual machine*.

322 Glossary

Process (Object flow diagram) Processing unit decomposing a *method*. (Procedure) Current processing sequence used to perform a function considered to be of significance to the *system*.

Prototype Typical representation of a *concept*, characterizing a default *instance* in a *class*.

Pseudo-language Initial textual description of the processing to be performed, containing a mixture of programming language instructions and freeform text.

RDBMS Relational database management system.

Relation 'Stable' link between two instances, as specified on class level. It corresponds to the mathematical notion of relationship between two sets.

Representation Synonym for *view*.

Requirement What the *user* expects from the application. By extension, action taken by the *user* via the *application*.

Role Name characterizing the function of one *class* as determined by the *relation*.

Scenario Diagram used to represent a *procedure* and showing a current message exchange sequence between *objects*. (See also *Validation scenario*.)

Schema Computer representation of a *domain* (conceptual), made up of a group of related *classes*. A *schema* is a *class* definition context (as a *class* cannot be used independently of its *schema*).

Software lifecycle Series of *phases* representing the software development process.

State Representation of a *stable* situation for an *object*, as selected from a series of predefined situations. (See also *Abstract state* and *Terminal state*.)

Structure model Class relation sub-model used to define and structure the application concepts.

Structuring domain Structuring mechanism used by the class relation model, whereby a *domain* is broken down into other *domains*, or into *schemas*.

System Series of cooperating processes with a given objective. The *system* is analysed with the aim of computerizing it either partially or completely.

Terminal state *State* which cannot be decomposed.

Test Activity during which the software is checked to ensure that there are no operating anomalies. (See also *Integration test*, *Unit test* and *Validation test*.)

Transition Representation of the way in which an *object* moves from one *state* to another. *Transitions* are triggered by *methods*.

Transmutation Ability of an *instance* to change owner *classes*.

Trigger automaton Definition of the transitions systematically activated when a given state is obtained, an event occurs or a condition exists.

Unit test Test conducted on methods and classes individually.

Use Dependency link between *classes*, *schemas*, and *domains*. (Inter-class) Indication that the user class knows or handles the used class. (See also *Conceptual use*, *Contextual use* and *Operational use*.) (Inter-schema or inter-domain) Indication that one of the components in a user *schema* or *domain* (*class*, *schema* or *domain*) uses one of the components in the used schema or domain. It is usually deduced from an *inter-class use*.

User Notion external to the modelled *application*, but using that *application*. It is at the origin of the *requirements*, and the entry point for the *modelling* approach. A *user* is represented by a *class*.

Validation *Phase* in the software *lifecycle*, the purpose of which is to check that the developed *application* complies with the specifications.

Validation scenario *Scenario* based on *unit validation sets* used to specify *application validation*.

Validation test Test used to check that the software *application* complies with its specifications.

View (Synonym for *representation*) Image representing all or part of a *model*. A *model* can be presented in different ways (*views*), each of which can contain identical or specific items and is used to describe a different aspect of the problem. For example, *domains* can be shown in *domain views*, *flow diagram* views, *internal domain views*, and so on.

Virtual machine Low-level layer on which the software is implemented. It includes the physical machine and all the libraries and utilities used (operating system, database, windowing system, network layers, and so on).

Visibility Definition of access rights to a *class* property or to the *class* itself (public, protected, private).

Appendix IV
References and bibliography

Boehm, B.W. (1981) *Software Engineering Economics*. Englewood Cliffs NJ : Prentice–Hall.
Boehm, B.W. (1988) *A Spiral Model of Software Development and Enhancement*. Computer, May, p 61–72
Booch, G. (1991) *Object Oriented Design with Applications*. Redwood City CA Benjamin Cummings.
Chen, P. (1976) The Entity–Relationship Model : *Toward a Unified View of Data*. ACM trans. on Database Systems, 1 (1), 9–36
Coad, P. (1991 a) *Object Oriented Analysis*, 2nd ed. New York: Yourdon Press Computing Series.
Coad, P. (1991 b) *Object Oriented Design*. New York: Yourdon Press Computing Series
Codd, E.F. (1970) *A Relational Model of Data for Large Shared Data Banks*. ACM , 13 (6)
Cointe, P. (1987) *Meta Classes are First Classes : The Objvlisp Model*. OOPSLA 87
Cox, Brad J. (1986) *Object Oriented Programming : an Evolutionary Approach*. New York: Addison-Wesley
DeMarco, T. (1979) *Structured Analysis and System Specification*. Englewood Cliffs NJ: Prentice-Hall
Desfray, P. (1989) *Defining an Object Oriented Design Model from an Entity–Relationship Model*. Second International Workshop, Software Engineering and its Applications, Toulouse, December
Desfray, P. (1990) *A Method for Object Oriented Programming: The Class–Relationship method* TOOLS'90, Paris, June
Desfray, P. (1991) *Object Oriented Structuring: an Alternative to Hierarchical Models*. Tools'91, Santa Barbara, California
Desfray, P. (1992) *Ingénierie des Objets-Approche Classe-Relation*. Paris: Masson
Desfray, P. (1993) *Hypergenericity: Automating Object Oriented Programming.* Software Engineering and its Applications Sixth International Conference
Elmasri, R.A. ,Weeldreyer J. and Hevner, A. (1985) *The Category Concept : an Extension to the Entity–Relationship Model*. In Data and Knowledge–Engineering, pp. 75–116. Amsterdam: North-Holland
Gane, C. and Sarson, T. (1978) *Structured System Analysis: Tools and Techniques*. Englewood Cliffs NJ: Prentice–Hall
Halbert, D., andO'Brien, P. (1987) *Using Types and Inheritance in Object Oriented Languages*. ECOOP 87, BIGRE no 54
Harel, D. (1988) *On Visual Formalisms. comm.* of the ACM , 31(5)
Robinson, L. (1979) *The HDM handbook*. SRI Project 4828
Hoare, C.A.R. (1985) *Programs and Predicates*. In Mathematical Logic and Programming Language. Englewood cliffs NJ, Prentice–Hall
Jacobson, I., Christerson, M., Jonsson, P. and Övergaard, G. (1992) *Object-Oriented Software Engineering*. ACM Press
Jones, C.B. (1986) *Systematic software development using VDM*. Englewood Cliffs NJ: Prentice–Hall
Martin, J. and Odell, J. (1992) *Object Oriented Analysis and Design*. Englewood Cliffs NJ: Prentice–Hall
Loomis, M.E.S., Shah, A.V. and Rumbaugh, J.E. (1987) *An Object Modeling Technique for Conceptual Design*. ECOOP'87, June
Meyer, B. (1986) *Genericity Versus Inheritance*. OOPSLA 1986 pp. 391–405
Meyer, B. (1988) *Object Oriented Software Construction*. Englewood Cliffs NJ: Prentice–Hall International Series in Computer Science
Minsky, M. and Winston, P. (1975) *A Framework for Representing Knowledge*. In The Psychology of Computervision, New York: McGraw–Hill
Rumbaugh, J., Blaha, M., Premerlani, W., Eddy, F. and Lorensen, W. (1991) *Object Oriented Modeling and Design*. Englewood Cliffs NJ: Prentice Hall

Shlaer, S. and Mellor, S. J. (1988) *Object Oriented System Analysis, Modelling the World in Data.* New York Yourdon Press Computing Series

Shlaer, S. and Mellor, S. J. (1992) *Object Lifecycles, Modeling the World in States.* New York Yourdon Press Computing Series

Stroustrup, B. and Ellis, M. (1990) *The annotated C++ Reference Manual.* New York: Addison-Wesley

Ward, P. (1990) *The Transformation Schema: An Extension of the Data Flow Diagram to Represent Control and Timing.* IEEE Transactions on Software Engineering, February, pp. 198–210

Wasserman, A., Pircher, P. and Muller, R. (1989) *An Object Oriented Structured Design Method for Code Generation.* ACM SIGSOFT 14(1)

Wasserman, A.I., Pircher, P.A. and Muller, R.J. (1989 b) *Concepts of Object Oriented Structured Design.* TOOL'S 89

Ward, P. and Mellor, S. (1986) *Structured Development of Real Time Systems.* New York: Yourdon Press

Yourdon, E. and Constantine, L. (1975) *Structured Design.* New York: Yourdon Press

Index

Abstract
   class 44, 146
   concept 15
   machine 36, 175
   relation 54
   schema 131
   state 88; transforming a terminal state into 94
   types 18
   world 15
Access rights 69
Ada 18, 96, 121, 278, 279
all
   cardinality 57, 149
   keyword 50
Analysis 203, 239
   applying the model to the architecture 206
   detailed *see* Detailed analysis
   example 193
   existing situation 181
   finalizing 180
   iterative technique 178
   model validation 192
   phase 168, 170
   preliminary *see* Preliminary analysis
   purpose 183
Application
   client/server 263–65
   decomposition 122
   multi-tasking 140
   starting 107
Architecture 164
   active elements 205
   applying the analysis model 206
   concept 204
   constraints 232
   defining 204
   diagram 157, 205, 228, 231
   technical study 205
Assign
   H language instruction 250

Asynchronous events 115
Attribute 19, 20, 31, 212, 283, 297
   class 20, 56, 284
   correspondence with methods 57
   default value 47, 284
   definition 47
   encapsulation 255–56
   handling 105
   in a scenario 110
   inheritance 75
   non-decomposable value 152
   public 283
   relation with 52
   specific object values 20
   technical 209
   transforming a relation 60
Automaton
   comparison with OMT 302
   control *see* Control automaton
   diagram 121
   trigger *see* Trigger automaton

Backstepping 170
Base class 20
begin
   keyword 249
Binding
   static and dynamic 280
Body
   class 129
   definition 67
Boehm 172
boolean *see* Predefined elementary class 147

C++ 18, 96, 211, 244, 278, 279, 305
   code deduction 281
   pre-processor 282

328 Index

Cardinality 76
  all 57, 149
  class relation 149
  relation 50
Case study
  database 213–20
  multi-tasking application 221–24
Categorization
  concepts 10
  char *see* Predefined elementary class 147
Chen 36
Chomsky 14
Class 164, 297
  abstract 44, 146
  adapting analysis 209
  and the dynamic model 99
  as a data flow 103
  attribute 20, 56, 284
  base 20
  body 129
  checking validity 288
  concept 41
  control automaton 89
  correspondence with relations 58
  defining for users 188
  defining interface 186
  defining key concepts 42
  definition 19
  dependency 281
  derived 20
  detailed view 32, 120
  determination 164
  dynamic model for interface 189
  elementary *see also* Elementary class 164, 283
  end 164
  event 113
  example interface 201
  external 130
  family of objects 19
  generalizing analysis 208
  generic 226, 244
  gradual determination 143
  H *see* H class
  handling its instances 266
  implemented 240
  initial identification 185
  instance 31
  interface 129, 162, 180, 186, 244, 268
  invariant 31
  justifying definitions 157
  listing services 189
  main 107
  masking derived 163
  members 45, 56
  method 20, 57, 103
  modelled 240
  modelling viewpoint 41
  non-elementary 145
  object 22, 38, 42
  operating model for interface 189
  persistent 244
  preliminary analysis example 195
  printable 243
  processing 22
  programming viewpoint 42
  properties 43
  prototype 47
  prototyping internal 190
  relation 57
  relation cardinality 149
  representation 43
  set of pertinent objects 41
  single-instance 149
  stability 39, 41
  state 89
  structuring 188
  structuring example 198
  technical 207
  transforming a relation 58, 60
  transition 89
  transmutable 244
  usage 33
  user 180
  user and interface in dynamic model 191
  user and interface in operating model 191
  user and interface in structure model 191
  validity 289
  view 38
  visibility 31
class relation

design approach 231–32
strong points 307
structuring 119
Class relation diagram 72
Class relation model 4
  adding coding information 286
  basic structure 29
  carrying through 172
  comparison with OMT 293–307
  components 6, 29
  diagrams 32
  during detailed analysis 190
  formal representation 37
  key premises 36
  role in each phase 176
  syntax 309
  syntax and graphic views 37
Classification
  concepts 10
Client/server application 263–65
Clos 278
CODASYL 215
Code 145
  deduction 281
  segments 287
Code and test lifecycle 170
Code generation
  maximization 281
Code production 126
Coding 174
  adding to class relation model 286
  comparison with OMT 305
  description 277
  ending 288
  impact of hypergenericity 273
  objectives 277
  phase 168, 170
Commit 214
Communication
  by events 115
comp
  keyword 53
Composition relation 52, 61
Computerization
  process 172
Concept
  abstract 15
  categorization 10

classification 10
communication 13
context 13
definition 10
development 10
domain 13
grouping in domains 14
justification 17
ordering 123
prototype 12
real world 15
transformation 19
typical representation 12
Conceptual
  development issues 175
  domain 127
  use 63, 281
Conceptual link 31
Conceptual model 15
  validity 16
Condition
  H language 253
Consistency
  dictionary 188
Constructor 43, 77
Context 13
  managing H language 249
Contextual use 62, 281
Control automaton 33, 36, 90, 300, 302
  abstract state 88
  association with pre- and post-conditions 92
  class 89
  definition 87
  multiple control states 92
  notation 90
  specification 94
  state 88
  sub-state 88
  syntax 93
  transformation by inheritance 93
  transition 88
Control structure 104
  definition 104
  H language 250
  streamlining 23
Controlling
  software development 125

Create
  H language instruction 250
create() 20, 22, 42, 77, 82, 90, 92
Current system
  representation 184

Data
  flow 157
  persistent 215
  sinks 101
  sources 101
  storage 101
  symbolic link 105
Data definition language 214
Data flow 18, 102
  and events 115
  and objects 101
  as a parameter 103
  definition 100
Data flow diagram 100
Data flow model 36, 301
  adaptation to objects 101
  principles 100
Data management language 214
Data models 18
Data sink 101
Data source 101
Data storage units 101
Database 204
  case study 213–20
  hierarchical 215
  network 215
  object-oriented 216
  relational 216
  schema 214
Database schema
  logical and physical 262–63
DBMS 213
DDL 214
Debugging 288
Decomposition
  application 122
  by inheritance 73
  control automaton 93
  mutual use 159
Deduction
  C++ code 281

Default value
  attribute 47, 284
  method 46
Delete
  H language instruction 250
delete() 22, 42, 77, 83, 90, 92
Denormalizing 211
Dependency
  functional 58, 151
  inter-class 61, 165, 281
  inter-domain 137
  inter-schema 137
  mutual 158
  removing mutual 231
  schema property 132
Derived class 20
  masking 163
  visibility 74
Design 158, 162, 239
  class relation approach 231–32
  database case study 213–20
  description 203
  detailed see Detailed design
  example 232–38
  impact of hypergenericity 273
  iterative technique 178
  multi-tasking application case
    study 221–24
  phase 168
  preliminary see Preliminary
    design
Destructor 43, 77
Detailed analysis 174
  class relation model 190
  events 191
  example 197
  purpose 186
  scenarios 190
Detailed design
  impact of hypergenericity 273
  overview 275
  phase 168, 170
  tasks 275
Determination
  classes 164
Development
  conceptual issues 175
  constraints 173
  description 275

framework 183
guidelines 3
impact of hypergenericity 273
incremental 170, 273
logical issues 176
phase 167, 174
physical issues 176
reducing complexity 239
Diagram
   architecture 157, 205, 228, 231
   automaton 121
   class relation 32, 72
   domain 126, 184
   event 113
   flow 5, 32, 77, 141, 157, 185
   functional dependency 151
   inheritance 21, 44
   integration domain 237
   object flow 33, 77, 99, 115, 180
   scenario 109, 116
   schema 126
Dictionary 156, 164
   checking consistency 188
   creation 185
   example 194
   example consistency checks 199
Directive 31, 244, 286, 298
   @* 244
   comparison with OMT 305
   inline 244
   virtual 244
Displayable objects 260–61
DML 214
Domain 5, 32, 33, 119, 173, 195, 205, 222, 299, 301
   concept 13
   concept grouping 14
   conceptual 127
   defining 186
   diagram 126, 184
   external view 32
   hypergenericity 271
   implementation 271
   integration 229
   internal view 32
   links 136
   project 137
   structuring 124, 135, 136
   technical 205

   view 34, 138
Downward phases 168
Dynamic
   binding 280
   typing 265–66
Dynamic model 5, 6, 33, 276
   comparison with OMT 301
   definition 99
   example interface classes 201
   example users 201
   for interface classes 189
   for users 189
   interface and user classes 191
   link with classes and methods 99
   link with structure model 99
   object encapsulation and independency 99
   role 29
   structuring 120

Eiffel 18, 36, 108, 279, 300, 305
Elementary class 5, 145, 164, 283
   characteristics 146
   no identifier 148
   predefined *see* Predefined elementary class
   rules 147
Encapsulation 65, 162, 165, 175
   advantages 68
   attribute 255–56
   real world 65
End
   class 164
   keyword 249
   processes 106
Ending state 92, 93
Entity-relationship model 4, 36, 53, 151
   Extended 4
Enumerate (predefined elementary class) 147
Event 33, 99, 100, 111, 114, 163, 165, 231, 302
   and data flows 115
   and instances 116
   and trigger automata 116
   class 113

communication 115
comparison with OMT 301
criteria 112
definition 112
diagram 113
during detailed analysis 191
effect on inheritance 117
in flow diagrams 141
keyword 113
reception 114, 115
sending from a trigger automaton 117
symbol 103
synchronous or asynchronous 115
transmission 114, 115
when to use 113
Exception programming 96
combined with pre- and post-conditions 97
predefined elementary class 147
combined with use 96
principle 96
Exclusion operator 104
Exhaustivity
checking 180
Extended entity-relationship model 4
Extensibility 23
guaranteeing 86
External
class 130

Factorization 23, 155
Files 204
storing and retrieving objects 256–59
Finalization
model definition 165
Flavors 18, 278
Flow 33
Flow diagram 5, 32, 34, 77, 99, 100, 109, 141, 157, 164, 185, 195, 206, 222, 236, 299, 301
combination with scenarios 142
Functional dependency 58, 151
diagram 151

Functional model
OMT 300
Functional sequencing 175
Fundamental requirements 187
Future system
representation 185

Generalization
property 158
Generation
automatic 3
maximum code 281
Generic class 226, 244
Genericity 181, 224–26, 241
and inheritance 225
applications 226
definition 224
in a model 226
instance 225
parameter 225
Graphic
user interface 233, 239, 269
view 37

H class 246
boolean 246
integer 246
MIt 246
SetOfMIt 246
sets 247
string 246
H language 7, 172, 242, 244–53, 279
assign instruction 250
conditions 253
context management 249
control structures 250
create instruction 250
delete instruction 250
instructions 250
loop 251
messages 270
methods 247–48
operators 250
select instruction 252

Index **333**

variables 248
Harel 36
Heir
  visibility 69
Hierarchical database 215
Hypergenericity 5, 7, 38, 172, 174, 231, 233, 241, 281
  advantages 239
  comparison with OMT 306
  definition 242
  domains 271
  examples 254–70
  impact on lifecycle 273
  implementing 277
  methodology 272
  persistent 254
  principle 242
  role 241
  structuring rules 270
  temporary 253

Identification
  initial classes 185
Identifier
  object 76, 148
Implementation 174, 239
  directives 243
  domain 271
  independent of specifications 68
  inheritance 213
  multiple model 271
  principles   239 *see also* Implementation principles
Implementation directives
  definition 243
Implementation principles
  separation from model 240
Implemented classes 240
Implementer
  visibility 69
Incremental development 170, 273
Independency
  between specifications and implementation 68
  model/phase 174
Inheritance 19, 20, 31, 73, 85, 156, 157, 224, 241, 297

  and genericity 225
  attribute 75
  concept 41
  decomposition 73
  definition 43
  diagram 44
  effect of events 117
  implementation 213
  integration issues 230
  inter-schema 130, 131
  link 130
  methods 75
  properties 75
  relations 76
  removing multiple 211
  repeated 212
  rules 83
  security 85
  transforming a control automaton 93
  virtual 212
  visibility 73
Inheritance diagram 21
Initial class identification 185
inline
  directive 244
Instance 31
  accessing 149
  and events 116
  class attributes 47
  class handling 266
  genericity 225
  handling 145
  sets 148
  single class 149
Instantiation 19, 164, 226
Instruction
integer (predefined elementary class) 147
Integration 126, 158, 226–31
  and inheritance 230
  definition 226
  domain 229
  domain diagram 237
  example 227
  interface classes 231
  levels 228
  phase 168, 170, 174
  plan 228

plan modelling 229
preparing 232, 237
principles 229
test 229, 231
Inter-class
   dependency 61, 165
   use 61
Inter-domain
   dependency 137
   links 136
Interface
   class 129, 180, 244, 268
   class definition 186
   class integration 231
   class to remove mutual use 162
   classes 186
   classes in dynamic model 189, 191
   classes in operating model 189, 191
   classes in structure model 191
   definition 67
   example classes in dynamic model 201
   example classes in operating model 201
   graphic user 269
Internal class
   prototyping 190
Interrupt 204
Inter-schema
   dependency 137
   usage 133
Inter-set relation 49
Invariant 31, 33, 36, 73, 284, 289, 297
   definition 64
   expression 64
   schema 134
   set of properties 64
   validity conditions 86
Invocation operator 250
Invoking a method 78
Iteration 180
Iterative analysis and design technique 178

Keyword
   all 50
   begin 249
   comp 53
   end 249
   event 113
   main 107
   private 70, 71
   protected 70, 71
   public 70, 71
   redefines 73, 75, 95
   return 46
   static 278, 283
   use 63
   virtual 212

Language
   H *see also* H language, 242
   modelling 37, 277
   natural 14
   object-oriented 18
   object-oriented programming 278
   programming 211, 277
Laws
   normal form *see* Normal form laws
Library 205
   schema 135
Lifecycle 90, 167, 168, 169
   adaptations 170
   advantages 170
   backstepping 170
   basic phases 167
   code and test 170
   forms 168
   generalized 173
   impact of hypergenericity 273
   influence on object model 172
   overview 167
   spiral 171
   upward and downward phases 168
   V 168, 169
   waterfall 168, 171
Link
   conceptual 31

inheritance 130
inter-concept 48
inter-domain 136
inter-schema 130
procedural 104
stability between objects 39
symbolic data 105
use 130
Lisp 278
Logical
  database schema 262–63
  development issues 176
Loop
  H language 251
Loops 278

Main
  class 107
  keyword 107
  object 107
Man/machine interface
  example 202
Masking
  derived classes 163
  properties 74
Member
  class 45, 56
  visibility 69
Message 20, 78
  basic control structure 20
  control automaton 90
  H language 270
  parameters 20
  receiver object 46, 110
  sequence in a scenario 110
  transmission 19
Meta-model 244
  and modelling items 245
Method 1, 7, 19, 20, 31, 35, 283, 297
  and processes 102
  and the dynamic model 99
  as a set of services 45
  class 20, 57
  correspondence with attributes 57
  default value 46
  defining 81
  definition 20
  external view 102
  graphic representation 47
  H language 247–48
  inheritance 75
  internal view 102
  invocation 78
  parameters 46, 102
  passing mode 46
  post-condition 83
  pre-condition 82
  send() 113
  start() 108
  syntax 81
  unnamed 248
Methodology 1, 7, 167
Meyer 225
Miller 123
MIt *see* Modelling items
Model 1
  abstract representation 2
  absurd 154
  applying to the architecture 206
  class relation *see* Class relation model
  communication 3
  comparison 293
  conceptual *see* Conceptual model
  correctness rules 156
  data 18
  definition 123
  definition finalization 165
  dynamic *see* Dynamic model
  entity-relationship 4
  extended entity-relationship 4
  fine-tuning mechanism 38
  genericity 226
  independent of phase 174
  limitations 16
  multiple implementations 271
  object *see* Object model
  object-oriented 293
  OMT *see also* OMT model, 293
  operating *see* Operating model
  processing 18
  real world 12

reusing during detailed analysis 188
separating from implementation principles 240
simulation 2
structure *see* Structure model
techniques for valid definition 156
validation 192
views 30
Modelled classes 240
Modelling 3
  correct and valid 154
  example 33, 54, 106, 110
  integration plan 229
  language 37, 277
  multi-view 139
  problem 17
  rules 145
  scenarios 109
  software 188
  system 141
  users 188
Modelling items 244
  and the meta-model 245
  complex 245
  simple 245
Modula 121
Modula2 18
Multi-tasking application
  case study 221–24
  example 140
Multi-valued relation 59
Multi-view modelling 139
Multiple inheritance
  removing 211
Mutual
  dependency 158
  removing dependency 231
  schema usage 133
  use 158

Natural language 14
Network 204
  database 215
Non-elementary class 145
Normal form laws 5
  advantages 151
  denormalizing 211
  first 53, 152
  second 152
  third 153

OBS (organization breakdown structure) 125
Object 19
  abstract 15
  and data flows 101
  categories 10
  class 22, 38, 42
  constructor 77
  control automaton 87
  destructor 77
  displayable 260–61
  identifier 76, 148
  lifecycle 77, 87
  main 107
  message receiver 46
  operational element 19
  preexisting 107
  reactive 111, 114
  real world 15
  stability 39
  state 89
  stimuli 20
  storing and retrieving in files 256–59
  transition 90
Object flow 33, 100
Object flow diagram 77, 99, 102, 115, 180
  level of detail 106
Object flow model 36, 99, 101, 165, 198, 201, 276
  comparison with OMT 304
  components 102
  for users 190
  validation 193
Object model 4
  advantages 23
  comparison with OMT 296
  fundamentals 9
  influence of lifecycle on 172
  languages 18

Object-oriented
  database 216
  languages 18
Objective C 279
Objvlisp 18, 278
OMT 293
  comparison with class relation model 29–307
  functional model 300
  strong points 306
OMT model 7
Operating model 6, 33, 99, 165
  comparison with OMT 300
  definition 81
  example interface classes 201
  for interface classes 189
  interface and user classes 191
  structuring 120
Operational
  requirements 187, 197
  use 62, 277, 281
Operator
  H 250
  invocation 250
  scope 249
Ordering
  concepts 123
  processing 33
Organization breakdown structure (OBS) 125
Orientation
  relation 50, 72

Parameters 248
  data flow 103
  for a method 102
  genericity 225
  message 20
  method 46
Passing mode 46
  inout 46
  method 46
Persistent
  class 244
  data 215
  hypergenericity 254
Petri network model 36

Phase
  analysis 168, 170
  class relation model role 176
  coding 168, 170
  design 168
  detailed design 168, 170
  development 174
  downward 168
  integration 168, 170, 174
  model independency 174
  overview 167
  preliminary design 168, 170
  preparation 168
  roles 174
  software lifecycle 167
  unit test 168, 170
  upward 168
  validation 168, 170, 174
Phases 167
Physical
  database schema 262–63
  development issues 176
Piaget 14
Plan
  integration *see* Integration
Pointer 244
Polymorphism 22
Polyseme 157
Post-condition 31, 33, 36, 75, 90, 284, 289, 300
  applicability 96
  association with control automata 92
  combined with exception mechanism 97
  defining 165, 276
  definition 83
  increased security 85
  reinforced by inheritance 85
  rules 85
Pre-condition 31, 33, 36, 75, 90, 284, 289, 300
  applicability 96
  association with control automata 92
  combined with exception mechanism 97
  defining 165, 276
  definition 82

increased security 85
    reduced by inheritance 83
    rules 84
Predefined elementary class 147
    boolean 147
    char 147
    enumerate 147
    exception 147
    integer 147
    real 147
    state 147
    string 147
Predefined variable 249
Preexisting objects 107
Preliminary analysis 172, 173, 174
    constraint definition 184
    defining domains 186
    defining interface classes 186
    defining scenarios 186
    defining users 186
    example 194
    purpose 184
    requirements definition 184
Preliminary design
    impact of hypergenericity 273
    overview 203
    phase 168, 170
Preparation phase 168
Pre-processor 282
Printable class 243
private
    keyword 70, 71
Problem modelling 17
Procedural link 104
Process 102, 204, 221
    computerization 172
    definition 100
    end 106
Processing
    class 22
    models 18
    ordering 33
    sequence representation 100
Programming
    example 287
    exceptions 96
    languages 211, 277
    object-oriented languages 278
    simplification 24

Project 32
    domain 137
    management 125
    management lifecycle 167
Property
    dependency 132
    generalization 158
    inheritance 43, 75
    masking 74
    schema 131
protected
    keyword 70, 71
Prototype
    class 47
    concept 12
Prototyping 171
    internal classes 190
Pseudo-code 276
Pseudo-language 106, 145
public
    keyword 70, 71
Public attribute 283

Qualifier 298
Quality 182

Reactive object 114
real (predefined elementary class) 147
Real world 154
    encapsulation 65
    model 12
    object 15
Reception
    events 114, 115
redefines
    keyword 73, 75, 95
Redundant relation 212
Relation 31, 35, 285, 293, 297
    abstract 54
    cardinality 50, 149
    class 57
    composition 52, 61
    correspondence with classes 58
    definition 48

H management rules 261–62
handling 105
inheritance 76
inter-set 49
multi-valued 59
orientation 50, 72
redundant 212
role 49
stability 48
transforming into a class 58, 60
transforming into an attribute 60
visibility 71
with attributes 52
Relational database 216
Reliability
   software 67
Repeated inheritance 212
Representation 4
   typical concept 12
Requirements 232, 239
   defining 184, 187
   definition 186
   definition example 197
   example 193
   fundamental 187
   operational 187, 197
Retrieving objects in files 256–59
Return
   keyword 46
   value 46
Reusability 23, 126, 181, 274
   favouring 240
   of modelling 181
Reuse 23
Risk analysis 171
Role
   definition 49
Rollback 215
Root class 108

Scenario 5, 33, 35, 99, 100, 121, 138, 165, 180, 185, 192, 223
   combination with flow diagrams 142
   comparison with OMT 304
   defining 186, 190, 276
   definition example 196
   detailed analysis 190
   development 109
   Diagram 109, 116
   example 202
   message sequence 110
   modelling 109
   processing 108
   processing sequence 109
Schema 32, 34, 119, 190, 205, 207, 231, 299
   abstract 131
   class definition context 131, 133
   database 214
   definition 127
   dependency property 132
   diagram 126
   for structuring purposes 133
   inheritance 130, 131
   interface and body 129
   internal view 32
   invariant 134
   library 135
   link 130
   logical and physical database 262–63
   mutual usage 133
   properties 131
   representation 129
   technical 205
   view 138
Scope operator 249
Seamlessness 295
Select
   H language instruction 252
self
   Smalltalk 79
send( )
   method 113
Server 215
Services 186
   defining for users 188
   definition example 200
   listing class 189
Sets 149, 247
Simula 18, 278
Single-instance class 149
Sink
   data 101
Smalltalk 18, 278

Softeam 5
Software
 development phase 167
 lifecycle *see* Lifecycle
 modelling 188
 reliability 67
 solidity 67
 specifying scenarios 190
Software component
 use and reuse 126
Software development
 controlling 125
Solidity
 software 67
Source
 data 101
Spiral lifecycle 171
SQL 214, 305
Stability 89
 class 39, 41
 definition 39
 inter-object link 39
 object 39
 relation 48
start() method 108
Starting
 an application 107
Starting state 92, 93
State 88
 abstract 88
 ending 92, 93
 multiple control 92
 object 89
 starting 92, 93
 terminal 89
 trigger automaton 111
state (predefined elementary class) 147
State Diagram 302
static
 binding 280
 keyword 278, 283
Storage
 objects in file 256–59
Storage units 101
string (predefined elementary class) 147
Structure model 6, 99, 151, 179
 basic notions 41

fundamentals 31
 interface and user classes 191
 link with dynamic model 99
 scenario 109
 structuring 32, 120
Structuring 119
 classes 188
 comparison with OMT 299
 domain 124, 135, 136
 gradual process 139
 hypergenericity rules 270
 O.B.S. 125
 principle 122
 techniques 121
 with schemas 133
 with the dynamic model 120
 with the operating model 120
 with the structure model 120
Structuring unit
 instruction 121
 instruction block 121
 module 121
 sub-program 121
Sub-state 88, 94
Symbol table
 class relation modelling example 149
Symbolic data link 105
Synchronous events 115
Synonym 157
Syntax
 class relation model 309
 method 81
 trigger automaton 111
 view 31, 37
System
 determining from user requirements 179
 dynamics 99
 functions 183
 modelling 141
 representing the current 184
 representing the future 185

Task 204, 221
Temporary hypergenericity 253
Terminal state 89

transformation into abstract state 94
Test
  defining 289
  impact of hypergenericity 273
  integration 231
  procedure 288
  sequences 290
  sets 290
This
  C++ 79
Thread 204, 221
Transformation
  control automaton 93
  relation to attribute 60
  relation to class 58, 60
  terminal state to abstract state 94
Transition 88
  class 89
  graphic view 111
  object 90
  trigger automaton 111
Transmission
  events 114, 115
Transmutable class 244
Transmutation 267–68
Trigger
  indeterminacy 112
  with single condition 112
Trigger automaton 33, 99, 114, 165, 223, 224, 302
  defining 276
  definition 111
  for events 116
  sending events 117
  state 111
  syntax 111
  transition 111
Typing
  dynamic 265–66

Unit test 31, 158, 174, 231
  description 288
  formalizing 290
  implementing 291
  phase 168, 170
  preparation 277

Unnamed method 248
Upward phases 168
Usage
  links 130
  mutual schema 133
Use
  combined with exception mechanism 96
  conceptual 63, 158, 281
  contextual 62, 158, 281
  decomposition 159
  inter-class 61
  keyword 63
  mutual 158
  operational 62, 158, 277, 281
  removing mutual 159, 162
  types 281
User 164, 173, 186, 232
  classes 180
  classes in dynamic model 191
  classes in operating model 191
  classes in structure model 191
  defining 179
  defining classes and services 188
  definition 178
  definition example 196
  dynamic model 189
  example classes and services 198
  example in dynamic model 201
  graphic interface 269
  modelling 188
  object flow model 190
  preliminary analysis 186
  visibility 69
User requirements
  determining system notions 179
User-oriented analysis and design technique 178

V lifecycle 168, 169
  limitations 171
Validation 231
  elementary sets 192
  model 192
  object flow models 193
  phase 168, 170, 174

preparation 192, 202
Validity
   class 289
   conceptual model 16
Variable
   H language 248
   predefined 249
Version management 127
View 4
   class 32, 38
   detailed class 120
   domain 32, 138
   external method 102
   for each model 30
   graphic 37
   internal method 102
   multiple modelling 139
   schema 32, 138
   syntax 31, 37
Virtual
   directive 244

inheritance 212
keyword 212
Virtual machine 135, 203, 231, 239, 287
   definition 204
Visibility 65, 162, 190, 246
   categories 69
   class 31
   derived class 74
   heir 69
   implementer 69
   inheritance 73
   member 69
   relation 71
   rules 70
   user 69
Vlifecycle 169

Waterfall lifecycle 168, 171

MASSON Éditeur
120, boulevard Saint-Germain
75280 Paris Cedex 06
Dépôt légal : octobre 1994

SNEL S.A.
Rue Saint-Vincent 12 – 4020 Liège
septembre 1994